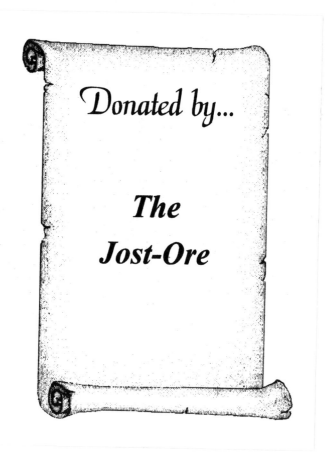

PRISMS

PRISMS

THEODOR W ADORNO

Translated from the German by
SAMUEL and SHIERRY WEBER

The MIT Press
Cambridge, Massachusetts

First MIT Press edition, 1981

Printed and bound in the United States of America

Library of Congress Cataloging in Publication Data

Adorno, Theodor W., 1903–1969.
  Prisms.
  (Studies in contemporary German social thought)
  Translation of Prismen.
  1. Culture. I. Title. II. Series.
HM101.A4513 1981   306   81-15613
ISBN 0-262-01064-X   AACR2

CONTENTS

SERIES FOREWORD

From Hegel and Marx, Dilthey and Weber, to Freud and the Frankfurt School, German social theory enjoyed an undisputed preeminence. After the violent break brought about by National Socialism and World War II, this tradition has recently come to life again, and indeed to such an extent that contemporary German social thought has begun to approach the heights earlier attained. One important element in this renaissance has been the rapid and extensive translation into German of English-language works in the humanities and the social sciences, with the result that social thought in Germany is today markedly influenced by ideas and approaches of Anglo-American origin. Unfortunately, efforts in the other direction, the translation and reception of German works into English, have been sporadic at best. This series is intended to correct that imbalance.

The term *social thought* is here understood very broadly to include not only sociological and political thought as such but also the social-theoretical concerns of history and philosophy, psychology and linguistics, aesthetics and theology. The term *contemporary* is also to be construed broadly: though our attention will be focused primarily on postwar thinkers, we shall also publish works by and on earlier thinkers whose influence on contemporary German social thought is pervasive. The series will begin with translations of works by authors whose names are already widely recognized in English-speaking countries—Adorno, Bloch, Gadamer, Habermas, Marcuse, Ritter—and by authors of similar accomplishment who are not yet so familiar outside of Germany—Blumenberg, Peukert, Schmidt, Theunissen, Tugendhat. Subsequent volumes will also include monographs and collections of essays written in English on German social thought and its concerns.

To understand and appropriate other traditions is to broaden the horizons of one's own. It is our hope that this series, by tapping a neglected store of intellectual riches and making it accessible to the English-speaking public, will expand the frame of reference of our social and political discourse.

Thomas McCarthy

FOREWORD TO THE ENGLISH EDITION

Although the author is delighted that for the first time one of his German books is now to appear in English—in a very meticulous and thoughtful translation—he is none the less fully aware of the difficulties which confront such texts in the English-speaking world. That he is no stranger to Anglo-Saxon norms of thought and presentation has been demonstrated, the author believes, in his English-language writings: his contributions to *The Authoritarian Personality*, his essays on music sociology for the Princeton Radio Research Project, and subsequent studies such as 'How to Look at Television', or 'The Stars Down to Earth'.[1] These norms are essential to him as a control, lest he reject common sense without first having mastered it; it is only by use of its own categories, that common sense can be transcended. This, however, must remain the author's aim as long as he considers matters of fact to be not mere fact, unreflected and thinglike, but rather processes of infinite mediation, never to be taken simply at face-value. He cannot accept the usual mode of thought which is content to register facts and prepare them for subsequent classification. His essential effort is to illuminate the realm of facticity—without which there can be no true knowledge—with reflections of a different type, one which diverges radically from the generally accepted canon of scientific validity.

To justify this procedure it would have been best to restate the considerations now collected in the *Negative Dialektik*.[2] The author has decided against this not merely for considerations of

[1] cf. *The Authoritarian Personality* (New York, 1950; paperback edition, New York, 1964); *Radio Research* (New York, 1941 ff.); 'How to Look at Television', *The Quarterly of Film, Radio and Television* VIII (Spring 1954), p. 214 ff.; 'The Stars Down to Earth', *Jahrbuch für Amerikastudien* 2 (Heidelberg, 1957).
[2] Frankfurt am Main, 1966.

time, but also because one of his primary concerns has been not to accept uncritically the conventional opposition between methodology and material knowledge. In thus presenting a book that consists of individual studies, he hopes to be able to concretize that type of knowledge towards which he is inclined. Even without an explicit epistemology, the essays should be able to speak for themselves. If this is possible, it will be due in no small measure to the quality of the translation as well as to the Introduction by Samuel M. Weber, which the author would wholeheartedly endorse as an accurate presentation of his intentions were he not afraid, in so doing, of seeming immodest.

Finally, the author could wish for nothing better than that the English version of *Prisms* might express something of the gratitude that he cherishes for England and for the United States—the countries which enabled him to survive the era of persecution and to which he has ever since felt himself deeply bound.

T. W. A.
Frankfurt, March 1967

TRANSLATING THE UNTRANSLATABLE

Man lives with things mainly, even exclusively—since sentiment
and action in him depend upon his mental representations—
as they are conveyed to him by language. Through the same
act by which he spins language out of himself he weaves himself into it, and every language draws a circle around the
people to which it belongs, a circle that can only be transcended in so far as one at the same time enters another one.
Wilhelm von Humboldt

Je suis au bout de l'anglais. *James Joyce*

The translation of philosophical prose, of cultural criticism, might at first glance seem to pose few problems, at least by comparison to that of poetry. Literature is said to define itself through the union of form and content, the 'how' taking precedence over the 'what'. A poem should not mean but be. By implication, the being of non-imaginative, non-literary writing is absorbed in its meaning, which is situated beyond language. Here it is the 'what' that counts, the means of presentation being considered incidental. The convenient distinction between literature and non-literature, however, evaporates at the lightest touch of reflection on the history of philosophy. Are Plato's dialogues non-imaginative? Hegel's Master and Servant? Is the form, structure and language of their argument merely a bridge to reach conceptual content on the other side? Is the language of great philosophy merely a means of presentation? Or is it the constitutive medium in which content crystallizes and from which it can no more be detached than the meaning of a poem from its form. Such considerations, however rudimentary and evident, are enough to transport one to the very limits of English and of the conceptual horizons it describes. For if it is true that philosophy in its greatest productions is no less imaginative, no less literary than literature, then what is literature? It is not that a definition is lacking—no phenomenon as complex and vital as literature is susceptible of univocal determination—but rather that there is no name in English for that which as 'literature' is too broadly described, as 'poetry' too narrowly. Efforts at circumscribing the difficulty with notions such as 'imaginative' writing or 'fiction' are no more satisfactory. Is the *Symposium*, the *Phenomenology of Mind* not fictitious? Non-imaginative? The circumscribed phenomenon, nameless in English, has a name in German: *Dichtung*. The essays collected in *Prisms* are not *Dichtung*. They *are* literature, if by literature is meant language in which imagination, fiction and form are moments which constitute the 'content', a content which in principle can be distinguished from that of *Dichtung*, if at all, through its less mediate relation to truth. Like *Dichtung*, the specificity of Adorno's thought

11

is inseparable from its articulation. If conceptual concreteness may be measured by the density with which thought and articulation permeate each other, then Adorno's style can be characterized by the constant striving to be concrete. It is, however, a concreteness which has no place within the intellectual horizons of English. In English what is concrete is what is immediate, tangible, visible. Whatever the historical causes of this empirical orientation may have been, contemporary English does not tolerate the notion that what is nearest at hand may in fact be most abstract, while that which is invisible, intangible, accessible only to the mind may in fact be more real than reality itself. 'Aren't there enough words for you in English?' Joyce was once asked: 'Yes,' he replied, 'there are enough, but they aren't the right ones.'[1] Words such as *Dichtung, Geist, Sache*, all of which may easily be attacked as imprecise and unclear, nevertheless designate a dimension of intellectual experience which has its concreteness in the dynamic nature of thought; they designate moments, stages of the mind on its way to truth. The fact that English demands empirical concreteness from the outset produces the confusion of literature with *Dichtung*, of mind with *Geist*, declares illegitimate the determinate indeterminacy of *Sache*—subject-matter, thing, item—as the object not yet illuminated by reason. Yet it is not merely that English forces one to distinguish between 'words' and 'things' and proscribes *Sachen*; the tyranny of empiricism is far more effective in estranging the entire speculative dimension from the realm of ordinary discourse. *Erkenntnis, Begriff, Aufhebung*—all are translatable, if by that is meant finding English words with equivalent 'meanings', by 'cognition', 'concept' and the ridiculous 'sublation'. What is lost, however, is the concreteness which the words have in German as abstractions from the language of everyday activity. *Anschauung, Vorstellung, Aufhebung*, formed, like so many philosophical terms in German, from verbs describing familiar and rudimentary actions, are rendered into an English which deprives them of their effective connotations and thereby of their truth-content, generally by latinizing them;[2] thus, *Erkenntnis*

[1] cf. Richard Ellmann, *James Joyce* (New York: Oxford University Press, 1965), p. 410.
[2] A process which Marx observed at work in the distinction made by seventeenth-century English economists between the Germanic 'worth', and the French 'value' to distinguish immediate use-value from reflected exchange-value. The roots of the process can probably be traced back beyond the Norman invasion to the decline of the early Christian Church in England, precipitated by the invasion of the Danes at the end of the eighth century.

must become cognition, and *erkennen*, a household word, is circumscribed as 'the cognitive act'; 'knowing' and 'knowledge' designate the static fund of facts, information and insights over which the knower disposes, but the simple and crucial notion of coming-to-know, er-kennen, must be reserved for specialists; 'learn' is similarly unsatisfactory, being too heavily burdened with passivity, which, if it does indeed conform to empirical fact, nevertheless deprives English of the name for a cognitive process that would be universal, spontaneous, active. Yet perhaps the most serious obstacle to the development and articulation of dialectical thinking in English is not semantic but syntactic. The criterion of clarity is rigidly enforced by a grammar which taboos long sentences as clumsy and whose ideal remains brevity and simplicity at all costs. Polemical exceptions, from Sterne to Byron, have only reinforced the prevailing maxim that if something is worth saying it can be said directly and to the point. This tendency of English syntax to break thought down into its smallest, self-contained, monadic parts is probably the most formidable barrier to dialectics. The absence of word-genders and inflections make long sentences prohibitively clumsy if not impossible, and thus prevent or discredit the complex hypotactic constructions which are the life-blood of dialectical thinking. Similarly, long paratactic constructions are to be broken down into shorter sentences. If this has helped the English-speaking world to keep its feet on the ground, as it undoubtedly has, it has also hindered it from seeing much beyond, a danger sporadically recognized by English cultural critics at least since Matthew Arnold. At the opposite extreme is German Idealism, which developed the remarkable syntactic flexibility of German into its present form, the grandeur and perils of which can be seen in the prose of Hegel and of Hoelderlin.[3] The structure of the German sentence, above all, the relation between main and subordinate clauses—the latter being in no way as 'subordinate' as its English name and hierarchical grammar would suggest—is a dynamic continuum that is only realized as a meaningful whole with the completion of the *Nebensatz* in its final verb. German sentences have a history; sentences in English tend to be stillborn. This is no less true of substantives which in German can be preceded by long appositional clauses, expressing not a property but a process. The Hegelian use of abstract substantives as subjects—as with *Begriff*, which thus took on a life of its

[3] The first sentence of Hoelderlin's essay, *Über die Verfahrungsweise des poetischen Geistes* (On the Mode of Procedure of the Poetic Spirit), which seeks to articulate the self-estrangement and reproduction of the *Geist* in the world, stands as the most extreme example of this tendency.

own—was only possible because of such tendencies of German grammar, enabling the sentence to embody the dialectical thought just as the paragraph embodies the argument. Adorno is thus able to use an 'either-or' construction in which the second half of the alternative follows two sentences after the first. This gives whole arguments a tautness and coherence otherwise found only in sentences, if at all. All this, in German no less than in English, breaks with generally acceptable usage, with ordinary language. In German this amounts to reawakening a potential which has been largely neglected today but which still slumbers within the recesses of the language. Is it possible, however, to translate this into a language which lacks these qualities, even as potential?

This requires reflection on the notion of translation itself. Where the meaning of the original work is not external to its language, translation can no longer be conceived as the reproduction of meaning in a more or less transformed linguistic setting. With the abstraction of meaning from the particular universe of discourse in which it constituted itself, the meaning is no longer that which it was. Adorno's language, constantly struggling with the communicative aspect of German, wrests its meanings from the latent potential which still inheres in German, in its syntactic flexibility which has remained relatively unimpaired by the semantic impoverishment and which thus provides an Archimedean point from which the critic is able not so much to invoke judgments against language from a fictitious point outside but rather to turn it against itself by means of inner contradictions which, if latent, still survive. If Adorno appears to do violence to ordinary German, it is as shock therapy which legitimizes itself in exposing the violence that language has already inflicted upon itself. This is possible because the tyranny of communicative speech has not yet succeeded in eliminating the traditional 'metaphysical surplus'—in Adorno's words—of German, which in turn becomes ideological once it narcissistically confuses metaphysics with reality. Yet what of English, which lacks a metaphysical surplus to oppose to its communicative element? The answer is that if Adorno is translatable at all, something which can by no means be taken for granted, it is precisely by virtue of his untranslatability. The unresolved tension which shapes an Adorno sentence, aphorism, essay, book, from beginning to end, lives from and bears witness to the impossibility of a harmonious union of form and content, language and meaning, an idea which survives in his work precisely in and through its determinate negation. The abyss which forms between the supposedly concrete use of language, which degrades it to an abstract semiotic system, and its

14

supposedly abstract, mimetic form, as which language once sought to become as concrete as an abstraction is permitted to be, is lit up with a glare which if it is dazzling in German is blinding in English. All satisfaction at the word which by virtue of its context reveals its ambiguity and testifies against itself, at the thought which can unfold itself in a sentence as it cannot in reality, is prohibited from the start in English. The barriers to the articulation of any meaning not restricted to reiterating reality emerge with stunning clarity. The fatal illusion that such barriers can be overcome by the subjective intellect, however brilliant it may be, that their mere articulation is their elimination, is swept away. The untranslatability of Adorno is his most profound and cruel truth. What remains is not the saturated unity of language and meaning but their disjunction, 'allegorical' in the sense given to the word by Walter Benjamin. In the translation which makes literalness its guiding principle, the allegorical core of Adorno's work becomes manifest. If the English-speaking reader is barred from participating in Adorno's most brilliant successes, where he hits the mark and language becomes thought, there may be consolation in the fact that the untranslatability of those successes traces the contours of a failure—the failure of language to say what must be said, its estrangement from itself—whose shadow even the most brilliant success only darkens.

SAMUEL M. WEBER

CULTURAL CRITICISM AND SOCIETY

To anyone in the habit of thinking with his ears, the words 'cultural criticism' (*Kulturkritik*) must have an offensive ring, not merely because, like 'automobile', they are pieced together from Latin and Greek. The words recall a flagrant contradiction. The cultural critic is not happy with civilization, to which alone he owes his discontent. He speaks as if he represented either unadulterated nature or a higher historical stage. Yet he is necessarily of the same essence as that to which he fancies himself superior. The insufficiency of the subject—criticized by Hegel in his apology for the *status quo*— which in its contingency and narrowness passes judgment on the might of the existent, becomes intolerable when the subject itself is mediated down to its innermost make-up by the notion to which it opposes itself as independent and sovereign. But what makes the content of cultural criticism inappropriate is not so much lack of respect for that which is criticized as the dazzled and arrogant recognition which criticism surreptitiously confers on culture. The cultural critic can hardly avoid the imputation that he has the culture which culture lacks. His vanity aids that of culture: even in the accusing gesture, the critic clings to the notion of culture, isolated, unquestioned, dogmatic. He shifts the attack. Where there is despair and measureless misery, he sees only spiritual phenomena, the state of man's consciousness, the decline of norms. By insisting on this, criticism is tempted to forget the unutterable, instead of striving, however impotently, so that man may be spared.

The position of the cultural critic, by virtue of its difference from the prevailing disorder, enables him to go beyond it theoretically, although often enough he merely falls behind. But he incorporates this difference into the very culture industry which he seeks to leave behind and which itself needs the difference in order to fancy itself culture. Characteristic of culture's pretension to distinction, through which it exempts itself from evaluation against the material conditions of life, is that it is insatiable. The exaggerated claims of culture, which in turn inhere in the movement of the mind, remove it ever further from those conditions as the worth of sublimation becomes increasingly suspect when confronted both by a material fulfillment near enough to touch and by the threatening annihilation of uncounted human beings. The cultural critic makes such distinction his privilege and forfeits his legitimation by collaborating with culture as its salaried and honoured nuisance. This, however, affects the substance of criticism. Even the implacable rigour with which criticism speaks the truth of an untrue consciousness remains imprisoned within the orbit of that against which it struggles, fixated on its surface manifestations. To flaunt one's superiority is, at the same time, to feel in on the job. Were one to study the profession of critic in bourgeois society as it progressed towards the rank of cultural critic, one would doubtless stumble on an element of usurpation in its origins, an element of which a writer like Balzac was still aware. Professional critics were first of all 'reporters': they oriented people in the market of intellectual products. In so doing, they occasionally gained insights into the matter at hand, yet remained continually traffic agents, in agreement with the sphere as such if not with its individual products. Of this they bear the mark even after they have discarded the role of agent. That they should have been entrusted with the roles of expert and then of judge was economically inevitable although accidental with respect to their objective qualifications. Their agility, which gained them privileged positions in the general competition—privileged, since the fate of those judged depends largely on their vote—invests their judgments with the semblance of competence. While they adroitly slipped into gaps and won influence with the expansion of the press, they attained that very authority which their profession already presupposed. Their arrogance derives from the fact that, in the forms of competitive society in which all being is merely there *for* something else, the critic himself is also measured only in terms of his marketable success—that is, in terms of his *being for* something else. Knowledge and understanding were not primary, but at most by-products, and the more they are lacking, the more they are replaced by Oneupmanship and conformity. When the critics in their playground—art—no longer understand what they judge and enthusiastically permit themselves to be degraded to propagandists or censors, it is the old dishonesty of trade fulfilling itself in their fate. The prerogatives of information and position permit them to express their opinion as if it were objectivity. But it is solely the objectivity of the ruling mind. They help to weave the veil.

The notion of the free expression of opinion, indeed, that of intellectual freedom itself in bourgeois society, upon which cultural criticism is founded, has its own dialectic. For while the mind extricated itself from a theological-feudal tutelage, it has fallen increasingly under the anonymous sway of the *status quo*. This regimentation, the result of the progressive societalization of all human relations, did not simply confront the mind from without; it immigrated into its immanent consistency. It imposes itself as relentlessly on the autonomous mind as heteronomous orders were formerly imposed on the mind which was bound. Not only does the mind mould itself for the sake of its marketability, and thus reproduce the socially prevalent categories. Rather, it grows to resemble ever more closely the *status quo* even where it subjectively refrains from making a commodity of itself. The network of the whole is drawn ever tighter, modelled after the act of exchange. It leaves the individual consciousness less and less room for evasion, preforms it more and more thoroughly, cuts it off *a priori* as it were from the possibility of differencing itself as all difference degenerates to a nuance in the monotony of supply. At the same time, the semblance of freedom makes reflection upon one's own unfreedom incomparably more difficult than formerly when such reflection stood in contradiction to manifest unfreedom, thus strengthening dependence. Such moments, in conjunction with the social selection of the 'spiritual and intellectual leaders', result in the regression of spirit and intellect. In accordance with the predominant social tendency, the integrity of the mind becomes a fiction. Of its freedom it develops only the negative moment, the heritage of the planless-monadological condition, irresponsibility. Otherwise, however, it clings ever more closely as a mere ornament to the material base which it claims to transcend. The strictures of Karl Kraus against freedom of the press are certainly not to be taken literally. To invoke seriously the censors against hack-writers would be to drive out the devil with Beelzebub. Nevertheless, the brutalization and deceit which flourish under the aegis of freedom of the press are not accidental to the historical march of the mind. Rather, they represent the stigma of that slavery within which the liberation of the mind—a false emancipation—has taken place. This is nowhere more striking than where the mind tears at its bonds: in criticism. When the German fascists defamed the word and replaced it with the inane notion of 'art appreciation', they were led to do so only by the rugged interests of the authoritarian state which still feared the passion of a Marquis Posa in the impertinence of the journalist. But the self-satisfied cultural barbarism which clamoured for the abolition of criticism, the incursion of the wild horde into the preserve of the mind, unawares repaid kind in kind. The bestial fury of the Brownshirt against 'carping critics' arises not merely from his envy of a culture which excludes him and against which he blindly rebels; nor is it merely his resentment of the person who can speak out the negative moment which he himself must repress. Decisive is that the critic's sovereign gesture suggests to his readers an autonomy which he does not have, and arrogates for itself a position of leadership which is incompatible with his own principle of intellectual freedom. This is innervated by his enemies. Their sadism was idiosyncratically attracted by the weakness, cleverly disguised as strength, of those who, in their dictatorial bearing, would have willingly excelled the less clever tyrants who were to succeed them. Except that the fascists succumbed to the same naivete as the critics, the faith in culture as such, which reduced it to pomp and approved spiritual giants. They regarded themselves as physicians of culture and removed the thorn of criticism from it. They thus not only degraded culture to the Official, but in addition, failed to recognize the extent to which culture and criticism, for better or for worse, are intertwined. Culture is only true when implicitly critical, and the mind which forgets this revenges itself in the critics it breeds. Criticism is an indispensable element of culture which is itself contradictory: in all its untruth still as true as culture is untrue. Criticism is not unjust when it dissects—this can be its greatest virtue—but rather when it parries by not parrying.

The complicity of cultural criticism with culture lies not in the mere mentality of the critic. Far more, it is dictated by his relation to that with which he deals. By making culture his object, he objectifies it once more. Its very meaning, however, is the suspension of objectification. Once culture itself has been debased to 'cultural goods', with its hideous philosophical rationalization, 'cultural values', it has already defamed its *raison d'être*. The distillation of such 'values'—the echo of commercial language is by no means accidental—places culture at the will of the market. Even the enthusiasm for foreign cultures includes the excitement over the rarity in which money may be invested. If cultural criticism, even at its best with Valéry, sides with conservativism, it is because of its unconscious adherence to a notion of culture which, during the era of late capitalism, aims at a form of property which is stable and independent of stock-market fluctuations. This idea of culture asserts its distance from the system in order, as it were, to offer universal security in the middle of a universal dynamic. The model of the cultural critic is no less the appraising collector than the art critic. In general, cultural criticism recalls the gesture of bargaining, of the expert questioning the authenticity of a painting or classifying it among the Master's lesser works. One devaluates in order to get more. The cultural critic evaluates and hence is inevitably involved in a sphere stained with 'cultural values', even when he rants against the mortgaging of culture. His contemplative stance towards culture necessarily entails scrutinizing, surveying, balancing, selecting: this piece suits him, that he rejects. Yet his very sovereignty, the claim to a more profound knowledge of the object, the separation of the idea from its object through the independence of the critical judgment threatens to succumb to the thinglike form of the object when cultural criticism appeals to a collection of ideas on display, as it were, and fetishizes isolated categories such as mind, life and the individual.

But the greatest fetish of cultural criticism is the notion of culture as such. For no authentic work of art and no true philosophy, according to their very meaning, has ever exhausted itself in itself alone, in its being-in-itself. They have always stood in relation to the actual life-process of society from which they distinguished themselves. Their very rejection of the guilt of a life which blindly and callously reproduces itself, their insistence on independence and autonomy, on separation from the prevailing realm of purposes, implies, at least as an unconscious element, the promise of a condition in which freedom were realized. This remains an equivocal promise of culture as long as its existence depends on a bewitched reality and, ultimately, on control over the work of others. That European culture in all its breadth—that which reached the consumer and which today is prescribed for whole populations by managers and psychotechnicians—degenerated to mere ideology resulted from a change in its function with regard to material *praxis*: its renunciation of interference. Far from being culture's 'sin', the change was forced upon culture by history. For it is only in the process of withdrawing into itself, only indirectly that is, that bourgeois culture conceives of a purity from the corrupting traces of a totalitarian disorder which embraces all areas of existence. Only in so far as it withdraws from a *praxis* which has degenerated into its opposite, from the ever-changing production of what is always the same, from the service of the customer who himself serves the manipulator—only in so far as it withdraws from Man, can culture be faithful to man. But such concentration on substance which is absolutely one's own, the greatest example of which is to be found in the poetry and theoretical writings of Paul Valéry, contributes at the same time to the impoverishment of that substance. Once the mind is no longer directed at reality, its meaning is changed despite the strictest preservation of meaning. Through its resignation before the facts of life and, even more, through its isolation as one 'field' among others, the mind aids the existing order and takes its place within it. The emasculation of culture has angered philosophers since the time of Rousseau and the 'ink-splattering age' of Schiller's *Robbers*, to Nietzsche and finally, to the preachers of commitment for its own sake. This is the result of culture's becoming self-consciously cultural, which in turn places culture in vigorous and consistent opposition to the growing barbarism of economic hegemony. What appears to be the decline of culture is its coming to pure self-consciousness. Only when neutralized and reified, does Culture allow itself to be idolized. Fetishism gravitates towards mythology. In general, cultural critics become intoxicated with idols drawn from antiquity to the dubious, long-evaporated warmth of the liberalist era, which recalled the origins of culture in its decline. Cultural criticism rejects the progressive integration of all aspects of consciousness within the apparatus of material production. But because it fails to see through the apparatus, it turns towards the past, lured by the promise of immediacy. This is necessitated by its own momentum and not merely by the influence of an order which sees itself obliged to drown out its progress in dehumanization with cries against dehumanization and progress. The isolation of the mind from material production heightens its esteem but also makes it a scapegoat in the general consciousness for that which is perpetrated in practice. Enlightenment as such—not as an instrument of actual domination—is held responsible. Hence, the irrationalism of cultural criticism. Once it has wrenched the mind out of its dialectic with the material conditions of life, it seizes it unequivocally and straightforwardly as the principle of fatality, thus undercutting the mind's own resistance. The cultural critic is barred from the insight that the reification of life results not from too much enlightenment but from too little, and that the mutilation of man which is the result of the present particularistic rationality is the stigma of the total irrationality. The abolition of this irrationality, which would coincide with the abolition of the divorce between mental and physical work, appears as chaos to the blindness of cultural criticism: whoever glorifies order and form as such, must see in the petrified divorce an archetype of the Eternal. That the fatal fragmentation of society might some day end is, for the cultural critic, a fatal destiny. He would rather that everything end than for mankind to put an end to reification. This fear harmonizes with the interests of those interested in the perpetuation of material denial. Whenever cultural criticism complains of 'materialism', it furthers the belief that the sin lies in man's desire for consumer goods, and not in the organization of the whole which

24

withholds these goods from man: for the cultural critic, the sin is satiety, not hunger. Were mankind to possess the wealth of goods, it would shake off the chains of that civilized barbarism which cultural critics ascribe to the advanced state of the human spirit rather than to the retarded state of society. The 'eternal values' of which cultural criticism is so fond reflect the perennial catastrophe. The cultural critic thrives on the mythical obduracy of culture.

Because the existence of cultural criticism, no matter what its content, depends on the economic system, it is involved in the fate of the system. The more completely the life-process, including leisure, is dominated by modern social orders—those in the East, above all—the more all spiritual phenomena bear the mark of the order. Either, they may contribute directly to the perpetuation of the system as entertainment or edification, and are enjoyed as exponents of the system precisely because of their socially preformed character. Familiar, stamped and Approved by Good Housekeeping as it were, they insinuate themselves into a regressive consciousness, present themselves as 'natural', and permit identification with powers whose preponderance leaves no alternative but that of false love. Or, by being different, they become rarities and once again marketable. Throughout the liberalist era, culture fell within the sphere of circulation. Hence, the gradual withering away of this sphere strikes culture to the quick. With the elimination of trade and its irrational loopholes by the calculated distributive apparatus of industry, the commercialization of culture culminates in absurdity. Completely subdued, administered, thoroughly 'cultivated' in a sense, it dies out. Spengler's denunciation: that mind and money go together, proves correct. But because of his sympathy with direct rule, he advocated a structure of existence divested of all economic as well as spiritual mediations. He maliciously threw the mind together with an economic type which was in fact obsolete. What Spengler failed to understand was that no matter to what extent the mind is a product of that type, it implies at the same time the objective possibility of overcoming it. Just as culture sprang up in the marketplace, in the traffic of trade, in communication and negotiation, as something distinct from the immediate struggle for individual self-preservation, just as it was closely tied to trade in the era of mature capitalism, just as its representatives were counted among the class of 'third persons' who supported themselves in life as middlemen, so culture, considered 'socially necessary' according to classical rules, in the sense of reproducing itself economically, is in the end reduced to that as which it began, to mere communication. Its alienation from human affairs terminates in its absolute docility before a humanity which has been enchanted and transformed into clientele by the suppliers. In the name of the consumer, the manipulators suppress everything in culture which enables it to go beyond the total immanence in the existing society and allow only that to remain which serves society's unequivocal purpose. Hence, 'consumer culture' can boast of being not a luxury but rather the simple extension of production. Political slogans, designed for mass manipulation, unanimously stigmatize, as 'luxury', 'snobbism', and 'highbrow', everything cultural which displeases the commissars. Only when the established order has become the measure of all things does its mere reproduction in the realm of consciousness become truth. Cultural criticism points to this and rails against 'superficiality' and 'loss of substance'. But by limiting its attention to the entanglement of culture in commerce, such criticism itself becomes superficial. It follows the pattern of reactionary social critics who pit 'productive' against 'predatory' capital. In fact, all culture shares the guilt of society. It ekes out its existence only by virtue of injustice already perpetrated in the sphere of production, much as does commerce (cf. *Dialektik der Aufklärung*). Consequently, cultural criticism shifts the guilt: such criticism is ideology as long as it remains mere criticism of ideology. Totalitarian regimes of both kinds, seeking to protect the *status quo* from even the last traces of insubordination which they ascribe to culture even at its most servile, can conclusively convict culture and its introspection of servility. They suppress the mind, in itself already grown intolerable, and so feel themselves to be purifiers and revolutionaries. The ideological function of cultural criticism bridles its very truth which lies in its opposition to ideology. The struggle against deceit works to the advantage of naked terror. 'When I hear the word "culture", I reach for my gun,' said the spokesman of Hitler's Imperial Chamber of Culture.

Cultural criticism is, however, only able to reproach culture so penetratingly for prostituting itself, for violating in its decline the pure autonomy of the mind, because culture originates in the radical separation of mental and physical work. It is from this separation, the original sin as it were, that culture draws its strength. When culture simply denies the separation and feigns harmonious union, it falls back behind its own notion. Only the mind which, in the delusion of being absolute, removes itself entirely from the merely existent, truly defines the existent in its negativity. As long as even the least part of the mind remains engaged in the reproduction of life, it is its sworn bondsman. The anti-philistinism of Athens was both the most arrogant contempt of the man who need not soil his hands for the man from whose work he lives, and the preservation of an image of existence beyond the constraint which underlies all work. In projecting its own uneasy conscience on to its victims as their 'baseness', such an attitude also accuses that which they endure: the subjugation of men to the prevailing form in which their lives are reproduced. All 'pure culture' has always been a source of discomfort to the spokesmen of power. Plato and Aristotle knew why they would not permit the notion to arise. Instead, in questions concerning the evaluation of art, they advocated a pragmatism which contrasts curiously with the *pathos* of the two great metaphysicians. Modern bourgeois cultural criticism has, of course, been too prudent to follow them openly in this respect. But such criticism secretly finds a source of comfort in the divorce between 'high' and 'popular' culture, art and entertainment, knowledge and non-committal *Weltanschauung*. Its anti-philistinism exceeds that of the Athenian upper class to the extent that the proletariat is more dangerous than the slaves. The modern notion of a pure, autonomous culture indicates that the antagonism has become irreconcilable. This is the result both of an uncompromising opposition to being-for-something else, and of an ideology which in its hybris enthrones itself as being-in-itself.

Cultural criticism shares the blindness of its object. It is incapable of allowing the recognition of its frailty to arise, a frailty set in the division of mental and physical work. No society which contradicts its very notion—that of mankind—can have full consciousness of itself. A display of subjective ideology is not required to obstruct this consciousness, although in times of historical upheaval it tends to contribute to the objective blindness. Rather, the fact that every form of repression, depending on the level of technology, has been necessary for the survival of society, and that society as it is, despite all absurdity, does indeed reproduce its life under the existing conditions, objectively produces the semblance of society's legitimation. As the epitome of the self-consciousness of an antagonistic society, culture can no more divest itself of this semblance than can cultural criticism, which measures culture against culture's own ideal. The semblance has become total in a phase in which irrationality and objective falsity hide behind rationality and objective necessity. Nevertheless, by virtue of their real force, the antagonisms reassert themselves in the realm of consciousness. Just because culture affirms the validity of the principle of harmony within an antagonistic society, albeit in order to glorify that society, it cannot avoid confronting society with its own notion of harmony and thereby stumbling on discord. The ideology which affirms life is forced into opposition to life by the immanent drive of the ideal. The mind which sees that reality does not resemble it in every respect but is instead subject to an unconscious and fatal dynamic, is impelled even against its will beyond apologetics. The fact that theory becomes real force when it moves men is founded in the objectivity of the mind itself which, through the fulfilment of its ideological function must lose faith in ideology. Prompted by the incompatibility of ideology and existence, the mind, in displaying its blindness also displays its effort to free itself of ideology. Disenchanted, the mind perceives naked existence in its nakedness and delivers it up to criticism. The mind either damns the material base, in accordance with the ever-questionable criterion of its 'pure principle', or it becomes aware of its own questionable position, by virtue of its incompatibility with the base. As a result of the social dynamic, culture becomes cultural criticism, which preserves the notion of culture while demolishing its present manifestations as mere commodities and means of brutalization. Such critical consciousness remains subservient to culture in so far as its concern with culture distracts from the true horrors. From this arises the ambivalent attitude of social theory towards cultural criticism. The procedure of cultural criticism is itself the object of permanent criticism, both in its general presuppositions—its immanence in the existing society—and in its concrete judgments. For the subservience of cultural criticism is revealed in its specific content, and only in this may it be grasped conclusively. At the same time, a dialectical theory which does not wish to succumb to 'Economism', the sentiment which holds that the transformation of the world is exhausted in the increase of production, must absorb cultural criticism, the truth of which consists in bringing untruth to consciousness of itself. A dialectical theory which is uninterested in culture as a mere epiphenomenon, aids pseudo-culture to run rampant and collaborates in the reproduction of the evil. Cultural traditionalism and the terror of the new Russian despots are in basic agreement. Both affirm culture as a whole, sight-unseen, while at the same time proscribing all forms of consciousness which are not made-to-order. They are thus no less ideological than is criticism when it calls a disembodied culture before its tribunal, or holds the alleged negativity of culture responsible for real catastrophes. To accept culture as a whole is to deprive it of the ferment which is its very truth—negation. The joyous appropriation of culture harmonizes with a climate of military music and paintings of battle-scenes. What distinguishes dialectical from cultural criticism is that it heightens cultural criticism until the notion of culture is itself negated, fulfilled and surmounted in one.

Immanent criticism of culture, it may be argued, overlooks what is decisive: the role of ideology in social conflicts. To suppose, if only methodologically, anything like an independent logic of culture is to collaborate in the hypostasis of culture, the ideological *proton pseudos*. The substance of culture, according to this argument, resides not in culture alone but in its relation to something external, to the material life-process. Culture, as Marx observed of juridical and political systems, cannot be fully 'understood either in terms of itself . . . or in terms of the so-called universal development of the mind'. To ignore this, the argument concludes, is to make ideology the basic matter and thus to establish it firmly. And in fact, having taken a dialectical turn, cultural criticism must not hypostasize the criteria of culture. Criticism retains its mobility in regard to culture by recognizing the latter's position within the whole. Without such freedom, without consciousness transcending the immanence of culture, immanent criticism itself would be inconceivable: the spontaneous movement of the object can be followed only by someone who is not entirely engulfed by it. But the traditional demand of the ideology-critique is itself subject to a historical dynamic. The critique was conceived against idealism, the philosophical form which reflects the fetishization of culture. Today, however, the definition of consciousness in terms of being has become a means of dispensing with all consciousness which does not conform to existence. The objectivity of truth, without which the dialectic is inconceivable, is tacitly replaced by vulgar positivism and pragmatism—ultimately, that is, by bourgeois subjectivism. During the bourgeois era, the prevailing theory was the ideology and the opposing *praxis* was in direct contradiction. Today, theory hardly exists any longer and the ideology drones, as it were, from the gears of an irresistible *praxis*. No notion dares to be conceived any more which does not cheerfully include, in all camps, explicit instructions as to who its beneficiaries are—exactly what the polemics once sought to expose. But the unideological thought is that which does not permit itself to be reduced to 'operational terms' and instead strives solely to help the things themselves to that articulation from which they are otherwise cut off by the prevailing language. Since the moment arrived when every advanced economic and political council agreed that what was important was to change the world and that to interpret it was *allotria*, it has become difficult simply to invoke the *Theses* against Feuerbach. Dialectics also includes the relation between action and contemplation. In an epoch in which bourgeois social science has, in Scheler's words, 'plundered' the Marxian notion of ideology and diluted it to universal relativism, the danger involved in overlooking the function of ideologies has become less than that of judging intellectual phenomena in a subsumptive, uninformed and administrative manner and assimilating them into the prevailing constellations of power which the intellect ought to expose. As with many other elements of dialectical materialism, the notion of ideology has changed from an instrument of knowledge into its strait-jacket. In the name of the dependence of superstructure on base, all use of ideology is controlled instead of criticized. No one is concerned with the objective substance of an ideology as long as it is expedient.

Yet the very function of ideologies becomes increasingly abstract. The suspicion held by earlier cultural critics is confirmed: in a world which denies the mass of human beings the authentic experience of intellectual phenomena by making genuine education a privilege and by shackling consciousness, the specific ideological content of these phenomena is less important than the fact that there should be anything at all to fill the vacuum of the expropriated consciousness and to distract from the open secret. Within the context of its social effect, the particular ideological doctrine which a film imparts to its audience is presumably far less important than the interest of the homeward bound movie-goer in the names and marital affairs of the stars. Vulgar notions such as 'amusement' and 'diversion' are more appropriate than pretentious explanations which designate one writer as a representative of the lower-middle class, another of the upper-middle. Culture has become ideological not only as the quintessence of subjectively devised manifestations of the objective mind, but even more as the sphere of private life. The illusory importance and autonomy of private life conceals the fact that private life drags on only as an appendage of the social process. Life transforms itself into the ideology of reification—a death mask. Hence, the task of criticism must be not so much to search for the particular interest-groups to which cultural phenomena are to be assigned, but rather to decipher the general social tendencies which are expressed in these phenomena and through which the most powerful interests realize themselves. Cultural criticism must become social physiognomy. The more the whole divests itself of all spontaneous elements, is socially mediated and filtered, is 'consciousness', the more it becomes 'culture'. In addition to being the means of subsistence, the material process of production finally unveils itself as that which it always was, from its origins in the exchange-relationship as the false consciousness which the two contracting parties have of each other: ideology. Inversely, however, consciousness becomes at the same time increasingly a mere transitional moment in the functioning of the whole. Today, ideology means society as appearance. Although mediated by the totality behind which stands the rule of partiality, ideology is not simply reducible to a partial interest. It is, as it were, equally near the centre in all its pieces.

The alternatives—either calling culture as a whole into question from outside under the general notion of ideology, or confronting it with the norms which it itself has crystallized—cannot be accepted by critical theory. To insist on the choice between immanence and transcendence is to revert to the traditional logic criticized in Hegel's polemic against Kant. As Hegel argued, every method which sets limits and restricts itself to the limits of its object thereby goes beyond them. The position transcending culture is in a certain sense presupposed by dialectics as the consciousness which does succumb in advance to the fetishization of the intellectual sphere. Dialectics means intransigence towards all reification. The transcendent method, which aims at totality, seems more radical than the immanent method, which presupposes the questionable whole. The transcendent critic assumes an as it were Archimedean position above culture and the blindness of society, from which consciousness can bring the totality, no matter how massive, into flux. The attack on the whole draws strength from the fact that the semblance of unity and wholeness in the world grows with the advance of reification; that is, with division. But the summary dismissal of ideology which in the Soviet sphere has already become a pretext for cynical terror, taking the form of a ban on 'objectivism', pays that wholeness too high an honour. Such an attitude buys up culture *en bloc* from society, regardless of the use to which it is put. If ideology is defined as socially necessary appearance, then the ideology today is society itself in so far as its integral power and inevitability, its overwhelming existence-in-itself, surrogates the meaning which that existence has exterminated. The choice of a standpoint outside the sway of existing society is as fictitious as only the construction of abstract utopias can be. Hence, the transcendent criticism of culture, much like bourgeois cultural criticism, sees itself obliged to fall back upon the idea of 'naturalness', which itself forms a central element of bourgeois ideology. The transcendent attack on culture regularly speaks the language of false escape, that of the 'nature boy'. It despises the mind and its works, contending that they are, after all, only man-made and serve only to cover up 'natural' life. Because of this alleged worthlessness, the phenomena allow themselves to be manipulated and degraded for purposes of domination. This explains the inadequacy of most socialist contributions to cultural criticism: they lack the experience of that with which they deal. In wishing to wipe away the whole as if with a sponge, they develop an affinity to barbarism. Their sympathies are inevitably with the more primitive, more undifferentiated, no matter how much it may contradict the level of intellectual productive forces. The blanket rejection of culture becomes a pretext for promoting what is crudest, 'healthiest', even repressive; above all, the perennial conflict between individual and society, both drawn in like manner, which is obstinately resolved in favour of society according to the criteria of the administrators who have appropriated it. From there it is only a step to the official reinstatement of culture. Against this struggles the immanent procedure as the more essentially dialectical. It takes seriously the principle that it is not ideology in itself which is untrue but rather its pretension to correspond to reality. Immanent criticism of intellectual and artistic phenomena seeks to grasp, through the analysis of their form and meaning, the contradiction between their objective idea and that pretension. It names what the consistency or inconsistency of the work itself expresses of the structure of the existent. Such criticism does not stop at a general recognition of the servitude of the objective mind, but seeks rather to transform this knowledge into a heightened perception of the thing itself. Insight into the negativity of culture is binding only when it reveals the truth or untruth of a perception, the consequence or lameness of a thought, the coherence or incoherence of a structure, the substantiality or emptiness of a figure of speech. Where it finds inadequacies it does not ascribe them hastily to the individual and his psychology, which are merely the façade of the failure, but instead seeks to derive them from the irreconcilability of the object's moments. It pursues the logic of its aporias, the insolubility of the task itself. In such antinomies criticism perceives those of society. A successful work, according to immanent criticism, is not one which resolves objective contradictions in a spurious harmony, but one which expresses the idea of harmony negatively by embodying the contradictions, pure and uncompromised, in its innermost structure. Confronted with this kind of work, the verdict 'mere ideology' loses its meaning. At the same time, however, immanent criticism holds in evidence the fact that the mind has always been under a spell. On its own it is unable to resolve the contradictions under which it labours. Even the most radical reflection of the mind on its own failure is limited by the fact that it remains only reflection, without altering the existence to which its failure bears witness. Hence immanent criticism cannot take comfort in its own idea. It can neither be vain enough to believe that it can liberate the mind directly by immersing itself in it, nor naïve enough to believe that unflinching immersion in the object will inevitably lead to truth by virtue of the logic of things if only the subjective knowledge of the false whole is kept from intruding from the outside, as it were, in the determination of the object. The less the dialectical method can today presuppose the Hegelian identity of subject and object, the more it is obliged to be mindful of the duality of the moments. It must relate the knowledge of society as a totality and of the mind's involvement in it to the claim inherent in the specific content of the object that it be apprehended as such. Dialectics cannot, therefore, permit any insistence on logical neatness to encroach on its right to go from one *genus* to another, to shed light on an object in itself hermetic by casting a glance at society, to present society with the bill which the object does not redeem. Finally, the very opposition between knowledge which penetrates from without and that which bores from within becomes suspect to the dialectical method, which sees in it a symptom of precisely that reification which the dialectic is obliged to accuse. The abstract categorizing and, as it were, administrative thinking of the former corresponds in the latter to the fetishism of an object blind to its genesis, which has become the prerogative of the expert. But if stubbornly immanent contemplation threatens to revert to idealism, to the illusion of the self-sufficient mind in command of both itself and of reality, transcendent contemplation threatens to forget the effort of conceptualization required and content itself instead with the prescribed label, the petrified invective, most often 'petty bourgeois', the ukase dispatched from above. Topological thinking, which knows the place of every phenomenon and the essence of none, is secretly related to the paranoic system of delusions which is cut off from experience of the object. With the aid of mechanically functioning categories, the world is divided into black and white and thus made ready for the very domination against which concepts were once conceived. No theory, not even that which is true, is safe from perversion into delusion once it has renounced a spontaneous relation to the object. Dialectics must guard against this no less than against enthrallment in the cultural object. It can subscribe neither to the cult of the mind nor to hatred of it. The dialectical critic of culture must both participate in culture and not participate. Only then does he do justice to his object and to himself.

The traditional transcendent critique of ideology is obsolete. In principle, the method succumbs to the very reification which is its critical theme. By transferring the notion of causality directly from the realm of physical nature to society, it falls back behind its own object. Nevertheless, the transcendent method can still appeal to the fact that it employs reified notions only in so far as society itself is reified. Through the crudity and severity of the notion of causality, it claims to hold up a mirror to society's own crudity and severity, to its debasement of the mind. But the sinister, integrated society of today no longer tolerates even those relatively independent, distinct moments to which the theory of the causal dependence of superstructure on base once referred. In the open-air prison which the world is becoming, it is no longer so important to know what depends on what, such is the extent to which everything is one. All phenomena rigidify, become insignias of the absolute rule of that which is. There are no more ideologies in the authentic sense of false consciousness, only advertisements for the world through its duplication and the provocative lie which does not seek belief but commands silence. Hence, the question of the causal dependence of culture, a question which seems to embody the voice of that on which culture is thought only to depend, takes on a backwoods ring. Of course, even the immanent method is eventually overtaken by this. It is dragged into the abyss by its object. The materialistic transparency of culture has not made it more honest, only more vulgar. By relinquishing its own particularity, culture has also relinquished the salt of truth, which once consisted in its opposition to other particularities. To call it to account before a responsibility which it denies is only to confirm cultural pomposity. Neutralized and ready-made, traditional culture has become worthless today. Through an irrevocable process its heritage, hypocritically reclaimed by the Russians, has become expendable to the highest degree, superfluous, trash. And the hucksters of mass culture can point to it with a grin, for they treat it as such. The more total society becomes, the greater the reification of the mind and the more paradoxical its effort to escape reification on its own. Even the most extreme consciousness of doom threatens to degenerate into idle chatter. Cultural criticism finds itself faced with the final stage of the dialectic of culture and barbarism. To write poetry after Auschwitz is barbaric. And this corrodes even the knowledge of why it has become impossible to write poetry today. Absolute reification, which presupposed intellectual progress as one of its elements, is now preparing to absorb the mind entirely. Critical intelligence cannot be equal to this challenge as long as it confines itself to self-satisfied contemplation.

34

THE SOCIOLOGY OF KNOWLEDGE AND ITS CONSCIOUSNESS

The sociology of knowledge expounded by Karl Mannheim has begun to take hold in Germany again. For this it can thank its gesture of innocuous skepticism. Like its existentialist counterparts it calls everything into question and criticizes nothing. Intellectuals who feel repelled by 'dogma', real or presumed, find relief in a climate which seems free of bias and assumptions and which offers them in addition something of the pathos of Max Weber's self-conscious and lonely yet undaunted rationality as compensation for their faltering consciousness of their own autonomy. In Mannheim as in his polar opposite, Jaspers, many impulses of Weber's school which were once deeply embedded in the polyhistoric edifice come to light. Most important of these is the tendency to suppress the theory of ideologies in its authentic form. These considerations may justify returning to one of Mannheim's older books, *Man and Society in an Age of Reconstruction*. The work addresses itself to a broader public than does the book on ideology. It cannot be held to each of its formulations. All the greater, however, is the insight it offers into the influence of the sociology of knowledge.

The mentality of the book is 'positivistic'; social phenomena are taken 'as such' and then classified according to general concepts. In the process social antagonisms invariably tend to be glossed over. They survive merely as subtle modifications of a conceptual apparatus whose distilled 'principles' install themselves autocratically and engage in shadow battles: 'The ultimate root of all conflicts in the present age of reconstruction can be seized in a single formula. All down the line tensions arise from the uncontrolled interaction of the "laisser-faire principle" and the new principle of regulation.' As if everything did not depend on who regulates whom. Or, instead of specific groups of people or a specific structure of society, 'the irrational' is made responsible for the difficulties of the age. The growth of antagonisms is elegantly described as 'the disproportionate development of human capacities', as though it were a question of personalities and not of the anonymous machinery which does away with the individual. Right and wrong are glossed over in like

37

manner; the 'average man' is abstracted from them and assigned an ontological 'narrowmindedness' which 'has always been there'. Of his 'experimental self-observation'—the term is borrowed from more exact sciences—Mannheim frankly confesses: 'All these forms of self-observation have the tendency to gloss over and neglect individual differences because they are interested in what is general in man and its variability.' Not, however, in his particular situation and in the real transformations he undergoes. In its neutrality the generalizing order of Mannheim's conceptual world is kindly disposed to the real world; it employs the terminology of social criticism while removing its sting.

The concept of society as such is rendered impotent from the outset by a language which invokes the exceedingly compromised term, 'integration'. Its occurrence is no accident. Mannheim's use of the concept of the social totality serves not so much to emphasize the intricate dependence of men within the totality as to glorify the social process itself as an evening-out of the contradictions in the whole. In this balance, theoretically, the contradictions disappear, although it is precisely they which comprise the life-process of 'society': 'Thus it is not immediately evident that an opinion which prevails in society is the result of a process of selection which integrates many similarly directed expressions of life.' What disappears in this notion of selection is the fact that what keeps the mechanism creaking along is human deprivation under conditions of insane sacrifice and the continual threat of catastrophe. The precarious and irrational self-preservation of society is falsified and turned into an achievement of its immanent justice or 'rationality'.

Where there is integration, elites are never far away. The 'cultural crisis' to which, in Mannheim, terror and horror are readily sublimated becomes for him the 'problem of the formation of elites'. He distills four processes in which this problem is supposed to crystallize: the growing number of elites and the resulting enfeeblement of their influence, the destruction of the exclusiveness of elite groups, the change in the process of selection of elites, and the change in their composition. In the first place, the categories employed in this analysis are highly questionable. The positivist who registers the facts *sine ira et studio* is ready to accept the phrases which conceal the facts. One such phrase is the concept of the elite itself. Its untruthfulness consists in the fact that the privileges of particular groups are presented teleologically as the result of some kind of objective process of selection, whereas in fact no one has selected these elites but themselves. In his use of the concept of the elite Mannheim overlooks social power. He uses the notion 'descriptively', in the manner of formal sociology. This allows him to shed only as much light as he wishes on each particular privileged group. At the same time, however, the concept of the elite is employed in such a way that the present emergency can be deduced from above, from some equally 'neutral' malfunctioning of the elite-mechanism, without regard to the state of political economy. In the process Mannheim comes into open conflict with the facts. When he asserts that in 'mass democratic' societies it has become increasingly easy for anyone to gain entrance into any sphere of social influence and that the elites are thereby deprived of 'their exclusive character, which is necessary for the development of intellectual and psychological impulses', he is contradicted by the most humble prescientific experience. The deficient homogeneity of the elites is a fiction, one related to those of chaos in the world of values and the disintegration of all stable forms of order. Whoever does not fit in is kept out. Even the differences of conviction which reflect those of real interests serve primarily to obscure the underlying unity which prevails in all decisive matters. Nothing contributes more to this obfuscation than talk of 'the cultural crisis', to which Mannheim unhesitatingly adds his voice. It transforms real suffering into spiritual guilt, denounces civilization, and generally works to the advantage of barbarism. Cultural criticism has changed its function. The cultural philistine has long ceased to be the man of progress, the figure with which Nietzsche identified David Friedrich Strauss. Instead, he has learned profundity and pessimism. In their name he denies the humanity which has become incompatible with his present interests, and his venerable impulse to destruction turns against the products of the culture whose decline he sentimentally bemoans. To the sociologist of the cultural crisis this matters little. His heroic *ratio* does not even refrain from turning the trite thesis of the demise of the formative power of European art since the end of the Biedermeyer period against modern art in a manner which is both romantic and reactionary.

Accepted along with elite theory is its specific colouration. Conventional notions are joined by naïve respect for that which they represent. Mannheim designates 'blood, property, and achievement' as the selection principles of the elites. His passion for destroying ideologies does not lead him to consider even once the legitimacy of these principles; he is actually able, during Hitler's lifetime, to speak of a 'genuine blood-principle', which is supposed to have formerly guaranteed 'the purity of aristocratic minority stocks and their traditions'. From this to the new aristocracy of blood and soil it is only a step. Mannheim's general cultural pessimism prevents him from taking that step. As far as he is concerned, there is still too little blood. He dreads a 'mass democracy' in which blood and property would disappear as principles of selection; the all too rapid change of elites would threaten continuity. He is particularly concerned with the fact that things are no longer quite right with the esoteric doctrine of the 'genuine blood-principle'. 'It has become democratic and quite suddenly offers to the great masses of the population the privilege of social ascendancy without any achievement.' Just as the nobility of the past was never any more noble than anyone else, the aristocracy of today has neither an objective nor a subjective interest in really relinquishing the principle of privilege. Elite theory, happy in the invariant, unites different levels of what sociologists today call social differentiation, such as feudalism and capitalism, under the heading 'blood- and property-principle'; with equally good humour it separates what belongs together, property and achievement. Max Weber had shown that the spirit of early capitalism identifies the two, that in a rationally constituted work process the capacity for achievement can be measured in terms of material success. The equation of achievement and material success found its psychological manifestation in a readiness to make success as such a fetish. In Mannheim this tendency appears in sublimated form as a 'status drive'. In bourgeois ideology property and achievement were first separated when it became obvious that 'achievement' as the economic *ratio* of the individual no longer corresponded to 'property' as its potential reward. Only then did the bourgeois truly become a *gentilhomme*. Thus, Mannheim's 'mechanisms of selection' are inventions, arbitrarily chosen co-ordinates distanced from the life-process of actual society.

Conclusions can be drawn from them which bear a fatal resemblance to the lax conceptions of Werner Sombart and Ortega y Gasset. Mannheim speaks of a 'proletarianization of the intelligentsia'. He is correct in calling attention to the fact that the cultural market is flooded; there are, he observes, more culturally qualified (from the standpoint of formal education, that is) people available than there are suitable positions for them. This situation, however, is supposed to lead to a drop in the social value of culture, since it is 'a sociological law that the social value of cultural goods is a function of the social status of those who produce them'. At the same time, he continues, the 'social value' 'of culture necessarily declines because the recruiting of new members of the intelligentsia extends increasingly to lower social strata, especially that of the petty officialdom. Thus the notion of the proletarian is formalized; it appears as a mere structure of consciousness, as with the upper bourgeoisie, which condemns anyone not familiar with the rules as a 'prole'. The genesis of this process is not considered and as a result is falsified. By calling attention to a 'structural' assimilation of consciousness to that of the lowest strata of society, he implicitly shifts the blame to the members of those strata and their alleged emancipation in mass democracy. Yet stultification is caused not by the oppressed but by oppression, and it affects not only the oppressed but, in their essentials, the oppressors as well, a fact to which Mannheim paid little attention. The flooding of intellectual vocations is due to the flooding of economic occupations as such, basically, to technological unemployment. It has nothing to do with Mannheim's democratization of the elites, and the reserve army of intellectuals is the last to influence them. Moreover, the sociological law which makes the so-called status of culture dependent on that of those who produce it is a textbook example of a false generalization. One need only recall the music of the eighteenth century, the cultural relevance of which in the Germany of the time stands beyond all doubt. Musicians, except for the *maestri*, primadonnas, and *castrati* attached to the courts, were held in low esteem; Bach lived as a subordinate church official and the young Haydn as a servant. Musicians attained social status only when their products were no longer suitable for immediate consumption, when the composer set himself against society as his own master—with Beethoven. The reason for Mannheim's false conclusion lies in the psychologism of his method. The individualistic façade of society concealed from him the fact that its essence consists precisely in developing forms which undergo a process of sedimentation and which reduce individuals to mere agents of objective tendencies. Its disillusioned mien notwithstanding, the standpoint of the sociology of knowledge is pre-Hegelian. Its recourse to a group of organizers, in the case of Mannheim's 'law', to the bearers of culture, is based on the somewhat transcendental presupposition of a harmony between society and the individual. The absence of such harmony forms one of the most urgent objects of critical theory, which is a theory of human relations only to the extent that it is also a theory of the inhumanity of those relations.

The distortions of the sociology of knowledge arise from its method, which translates dialectical concepts into classificatory ones. Since in each case what is socially contradictory is absorbed into individual logical classes, social classes as such disappear and the picture of the whole becomes harmonious. When, for instance, in the third section of the book Mannheim distinguishes three levels of consciousness: chance discovery, invention, and planning, he is simply trying to interpret the dialectical scheme of epochs as that of the fluidly changing modes of behaviour of socialized man in general, in which the determinant oppositions disappear: 'It is of course clear that the line which divides inventive thinking, which is rationally striving to realize immediate goals, from planned thinking is not a hard and fast one. No one can say for certain at what degree of foresight and at what point in the widening radius of conscious regulation the transition from inventive to planned thinking takes place.' The notion of an unbroken transition from a liberal to a 'planned' society has its correlative in the conception of that transition as one between distinct modes of 'thinking'. Such a conception awakens the belief that the historical process is guided by an inherently univocal subject embodying the whole of society. The translation of dialectical into classificatory concepts abstracts from the conditions of real social power upon which alone those levels of thought depend. 'The novel contribution of the sociological view of the past and the present is that it sees history as an area open to experimentation in regulatory intervention'—as though the possibility of such intervention always corresponded to the level of insight at the time. Such a levelling off of social struggles into modes of behaviour which can be defined formally and which are made abstract in advance allows uplifting proclamations concerning the future: 'Yet another way remains open—it is that unified planning will come about through understanding, agreement, and compromise, i.e. that the state of mind will triumph in the key-positions of international society which hitherto has been possible only within a given national group, within whose enclaves peace was established by such methods.' Through the idea of compromise the very contradictions which were supposedly resolved through planning are retained; the abstract concept of planning conceals them in advance and is itself a compromise between the laissez-faire principle which is preserved in it and the insight into its insufficiency.

Dialectical concepts cannot be 'translated' into the categories of formal sociology without their truth being impaired. Mannheim flirts with positivism to the extent that he believes himself able to rely on objectively given facts, which, however, in his rather lax manner he describes as 'unarticulated'. These unarticulated facts can then be put through the sociological thought-machine and thus elevated to general concepts. But such classification according to ordering concepts would be an adequate cognitive process only if the facts, which are assumed to be immediately given, could be abstracted from their concrete context as easily as it would appear to the naïve first glance. It is not adequate, however, if social reality has, prior to every theoretical ordering glance, a highly 'articulated' structure upon which the scientific subject and the data of his experience depend. As analysis advances, the initial 'facts' cease to be descriptive, self-contained data, and sociology is all the less at liberty to classify them to suit its needs. That 'facts' must undergo this correction as the theoretical understanding of society proceeds means not so much that new subjective ordering schemes must be devised, as it would seem to naïve experience, as that the data which are presumably given embody more than mere material to be processed conceptually, namely, that they are moulded by the social whole and thus 'structured' in themselves. Idealism can be overcome only when the freedom to conceptualize through abstraction is sacrificed. The thesis of the primacy of being over consciousness includes the methodological imperative to express the dynamic tendencies of reality in the formation and movement of concepts instead of forming and verifying concepts in accordance with the demand that they have pragmatic and expedient features. The sociology of knowledge has closed its eyes to this imperative. Its abstractions are arbitrary as long as they merely harmonize with an experience which proceeds by differentiating and correcting. Mannheim does not allow himself the logical conclusion that the 'unbiased' registration of facts is a fiction. The social scientist's experience does not give him undifferentiated, chaotic material to be organized; rather, the material of his experience is the social order, more emphatically a 'system' than any ever conceived by philosophy. What decides whether his concepts are right or wrong is neither their generality nor, on the other hand, their approximation to 'pure' fact, but rather the adequacy with which they grasp the real laws of movement of society and thereby render stubborn facts transparent. In a co-ordinate-system defined by concepts like integration, elite, and articulation, those determining laws and everything they signify for human life appear to be contingent or accidental, mere sociological 'differentiations'. For this reason, sociology which generalizes and differentiates seems like a mockery of reality. It does not recoil before formulations like 'disregarding the concentration and centralization of capital'. Such abstractions are not 'neutral'. What a theory regards and what it disregards determines its quality. Were 'disregarding' sufficient, one could, for instance, also analyse elites by observing such groups as the vegetarians or the followers of Mazdaznan and then refine this analysis conceptually until its manifest absurdity disappeared. But no corrective could compensate for the fact that the choice of basic

43

categories was false, that the world is not organized according to these categories. All correctives notwithstanding, this falseness would shift the accents so fundamentally that reality would drop out of the concepts; the elites would be 'groups of the Mazdaznan form' which happened to be characterized in addition by the possession of 'social power'. When at one point Mannheim says that 'in the cultural sphere (properly also in the economic) there has never been an absolute liberalism, that alongside of the undirected working of the social forces there has always existed, for instance, regulation in education', he is obviously trying to establish a differentiating corrective to the belief that the principle of laissez-faire, long ago exposed as ideology, ever prevailed in an unrestricted manner. But through the choice of an initial concept which is to be differentiated only afterwards the crucial issue is distorted: the insight that even under liberalism the principle of laissez-faire served only to mask economic control and that accordingly the establishment of 'cultural goods' was essentially determined by their conformity with the ruling social interests. The insight into a basic matter of ideology evaporates into mere finesse; instead of directing itself to the concrete in the first place without hypostasizing indispensable general concepts, the method seeks to conciliate by demonstrating that it remembers the concrete too.

The inadequacies of the method become manifest in its poles, the law and the 'example'. The sociology of knowledge characterizes stubborn facts as mere differentiations and subsumes them under the highest general units; at the same time, it ascribes an intrinsic power over the facts to these arbitrary generalizations, which it calls social 'laws', such as the one relating cultural goods to the social status of those who produce them. The 'laws' are hypostasized. Sometimes they assume a truly extravagant character: 'There is, however, a decisive law which rules us at the present moment. Unplanned spheres regulated by natural selection on the one hand and deliberately organized areas on the other can exist side by side without friction only *as long as the unplanned spheres predominate*' [Mannheim's italics]. Quantified propositions of this form are no more evident than those of Baaderian metaphysics, over which they have the advantage only of a lack of imagination. The falseness of Mannheim's hypostasization of general concepts can be grasped precisely at the point where he interjects the 'principia media' to which he debased the laws of dialectical movement: 'However much we must take the *principia media* and the corresponding concepts ("late capitalism", "structural unemployment", "lower middle-class ideology", etc.) as concrete expressions of a special historical setting, it should nevertheless be borne in mind that what we are doing is differentiating and individualizing abstract and general determinants (general factors). The *principia media* are in a certain sense nothing but temporary groups of general factors so closely intertwined that they operate as a single causal factor. That we are essentially dealing here with general factors in an historical and individual setting is evident from our example. Our first observation implies the general principle of the functioning of a social order with freely contracting legal personalities; the second, the psychological effect of unemployment in general, and the last, the general law that hopes of social advancement tend to affect individuals in a way which obscures their real social position.' It is just as mistaken, Mannheim continues, to believe that conceptions of man in general are valid in themselves as 'to neglect or ignore the general principles of the human psyche within the concrete modes of behaviour of these historical types'. Accordingly, the historical event seems to be determined in part by 'general', in part by 'particular' causes which together form some sort of 'group'. This, however, implies the confusion of levels of abstraction with causes. Mannheim sees the decisive weakness of dialectical thought in its misunderstanding of 'general forces'—as if the commodity forms were not 'general' enough for all the questions with which he deals. 'General forces', however, are not independent in opposition to 'particular' ones, as though a concrete event were 'caused' once by a causal proposition and then again by the specific 'historical situation'. No event is caused by general forces, much less by laws; causality is not the 'cause' of events but rather the highest conceptual generality under which concrete causal factors can be subsumed. The significance of the observation Newton made on the falling apple is not that the general law of causality 'acts' within a complex which includes factors of a lower degree of abstraction. Causality operates only in the particular and not in addition to it. Only to this extent can the falling apple be called 'an example of the law of gravity'; the law of gravity is as much dependent on the falling of this apple as vice-versa. The concrete play of forces can be reduced to schemata of varying levels of generality, but it is not a question of a conjunction of 'general' and 'particular' forces. Mannheim's pluralism, of course, which conceives what is crucial as merely *one* perspective among many, is hardly eager to give up its sums of general and particular factors.

The fact, baptized in advance as a 'unique situation', thereby becomes a mere example of these forces. Dialectical theory, in contrast, can no more accept the concept of the example as valid than could Kant. Examples function as convenient and interchangeable illustrations; hence they are often chosen at a comfortable distance from the true concerns of mankind today, or they are pulled, as it were, out of a hat. But they are quickly forced to pay the consequences. Mannheim writes, for instance: 'An illuminating example of the disturbances which can arise from substantial irrationality may be seen where, for example, the diplomatic staff of a state has carefully thought out a series of actions and has agreed on certain steps, when suddenly one of its members falls prey to a nervous collapse and then acts contrary to the plan, thereby destroying it.' It is useless to portray such private events as 'factors'; not only is the 'radius of action' of the individual diplomat romantically overestimated, but also unless the blunder itself served the course of political developments stronger than the diplomats' considerations it could be corrected in five minutes over the telephone. Or, with the pictorial vividness of a children's book, Mannheim writes: 'As a soldier I must control my impulses and desires to a quite different degree than as a free hunter, whose acts are only periodically purposive and who will only occasionally need to take hold of himself—for instance, at the moment when he has to fire at his prey.' As is generally known, the occupation of hunter has in recent years been replaced by the sport of hunting, but even the sportsman who takes hold of himself only 'at the moment when he has to fire at his prey', apparently in order not to be startled by the crack of his own rifle, will hardly bag much, probably frighten away his prey, and perhaps not even find it. The insignificance of such examples is closely related to the influence the sociology of knowledge has had. Selected for their subjective neutrality and therefore inessential in advance, the examples serve to distract. Sociology originated in the impulse to criticize the principles of the society with which it found itself confronted; the sociology of knowledge settles for reflections on hunters dressed in green and diplomats in black.

The direction in which, in terms of content, the formalism of such conceptualization tends reveals itself when programmatic demands are voiced. An 'optimum' for the thorough organization of society is demanded, but no thought is given to the gap that would have to be breached to attain such an optimum. If things are only put together rationally, everything will fall into place. Mannheim's ideal of a 'desired direction' between 'unconscious conservatism' and 'misdirected utopianism' corresponds to this: 'We can see at the same time, however, the general outline of a possible solution to the present tension, namely a sort of authoritarian democracy making use of planning and creating a stable system from the present conflict of principles.' This is in accordance with the stylistic elevation of the 'crisis' to a 'human problem', in which Mannheim shows himself in agreement with modern German anthropologists, his declaration against them notwithstanding, and with the existentialist philosophers. Two characteristics more than all others, however, reveal the conformism of Mannheim's sociology of knowledge. First, it remains concerned with symptoms. It is thoroughly disposed to overestimate the significance of ideologies as opposed to what they represent. It placidly shares with them precisely that equivocal conception of 'the' irrational to which the critical lever should be applied: 'We must, moreover, realize that the irrational is not always harmful but that, on the contrary, it is among the most valuable powers in man's possession when it acts as a driving force towards rational or objective ends, creates cultural values through sublimation and cultivation, or, as pure élan, heightens the joy of living without breaking up the social order by lack of planning.' There are no further hints as to the nature of this irrational, which is said to produce cultural values through cultivation, although such values are by definition the product of cultivation, or to 'heighten' the joy of living, which is irrational anyway. In any case, however, the equation of the instincts with the irrational is ominous, for the concept is applied in 'value-free' manner both to the libido and to the forms its repression takes. The irrational seems to endow ideologies with substantiality in Mannheim. They receive a paternal reproof but are left intact; what they conceal is never exposed. But the vulgar materialism of prevailing praxis is closely related to this positivistic tendency to accept symptoms uncritically, this perceptible respect for the claims of ideology. The facade remains intact in the glow of amenable observation, and the ultimate wisdom of this sociology is that no impulse could arise within the interior which could seriously threaten to proceed beyond its carefully marked bounds: 'In actual fact the existing body of ideas (and the same applies to vocabulary) never exceeds the horizon and the radius of activity of the society in question.' Whatever 'exceeds' the limits, to be sure, can easily be seen as 'adjustment to the emotional evocation of spiritual values, etc.'. This materialism, akin to that of the family head who considers it utterly impossible for his offspring to have a new thought, since everything has already been thought, and hence recommends that he concentrate on earning a respectable living, this seasoned and arrogant materialism is the reverse image of the idealism in Mannheim's view of history, an idealism to which he also remains true in other respects, especially in his conceptions of 'rationality' and progress, an idealism according to which changes in consciousness are even capable of lifting 'the structural principle of society off its hinges from the inside out, so to speak'.

The real attraction of the sociology of knowledge can be sought only in the fact that those changes in consciousness, as achievements of 'planning reason', are linked directly to the reasoning of today's planners: 'The fact that the complex actions of a functional, thoroughly rationalized society can be thought through only in the heads of a few organizers assures the latter of a key position in society.' The motif which becomes apparent here extends beyond the consciousness of the sociology of knowledge. The objective spirit, as that of those 'few organizers', speaks through it. While the sociology of knowledge dreams of new academic fields to conquer, it unsuspectingly serves those who have not hesitated a moment to abolish those fields. Mannheim's reflections, nourished by liberal common sense, all amount to the same thing in the end—recommending social planning without ever penetrating to the foundations of society. The consequences of the absurdity which has now become obvious and which Mannheim sees only superficially as a 'cultural crisis', are to be mollified from above, that is, by those who control the means of production. This means, however, simply that the liberal, who sees no way out, makes himself the spokesman of a dictatorial arrangement of society even while he imagines he is opposing it. Of course, the sociology of knowledge will reply that the ultimate criterion for judging planning is not power but reason and that reason includes the task of converting the powerful. Nevertheless, since the Platonic philosopher-kings it has been clear what such a conversion involves. The answer to Mannheim's reverence for the intelligentsia as 'free-floating' is to be found not in the reactionary postulate of its 'rootedness in Being' but rather in the reminder that the very intelligentsia that pretends to float freely is fundamentally rooted in the very being that must be changed and which it merely pretends to criticize. For it the rational is the optimal functioning of the system, which postpones the catastrophe without asking whether the system in its totality is not in fact the optimum in irrationality. In totalitarian systems of every kind, planning directed at maintaining the system leads to the barbarous suppression below the surface of the contradictions it inevitably produces. In the name of reason the advocates of planning turn power over to those who already possess it in the name of mystification. The power of reason today is the blind reason of those who currently hold power. But as power moves towards the catastrophe it induces the mind which denies it with moderation to abdicate to it. It still calls itself liberal, to be sure, but for it freedom has already become 'from the sociological point of view nothing but a dispro-portion between the growth of the radius of effective central control on the one hand and the size of the group unit to be influenced on the other'. The sociology of knowledge sets up indoctrination camps for the homeless intelligentsia where it can learn to forget itself.

SPENGLER AFTER THE DECLINE

If the history of philosophy consists less in the solution of its problems than in the fact that they are always being forgotten by the intellectual movements that crystallize around them, Oswald Spengler's doctrine is no exception. It has been forgotten with the rapidity of the catastrophe towards which world history, according to his own theory, was moving. After the initial popular success of *The Decline of the West*, German public opinion very quickly turned against the book. The official philosophers dismissed it as superficial, the certified academic disciplines charged it with incompetence and charlatanism, and in the hustle and bustle of German inflation and stabilization no one wanted anything to do with the thesis of the *Decline*. In the meantime Spengler had published a number of smaller studies whose pretentious tone and glib antitheses left him an easy mark for the prevailing *joie de vivre*.

When the second volume of the *Decline* appeared, in 1922, its reception did not even remotely approach that of the first, even though the thesis of the decline is not concretely developed until the second volume. The laymen who had read Spengler as they had read Nietzsche and Schopenhauer before him had in the meantime become estranged from philosophy; the professional philosophers were soon to flock to Heidegger, whose work was to give their irritation more dignified and refined expression. He exalted death and promised to transform the thought of it into a professional secret for academics; Spengler had simply decreed it without respect to persons. Spengler was left behind, his little book on *Man and Technology* incapable of competing with the smart philosophical anthropologies of the time. Little attention was paid his relations with National Socialism, his dispute with Hitler, and his death. In Germany he was ostracized as a pessimist and reactionary, in the sense given those words by the gentlemen of the time. Abroad, he was considered one of those ideologically responsible for the relapse into barbarism.

Nevertheless, there is good reason to raise the question of the truth and untruth of Spengler's work again. It would be conceding him too much to look to world history, which passed him by on its way to the new order, for the last judgment on the value of his ideas. And there is all the less reason to do so, considering that the course of world history vindicated his immediate prognoses to an extent that would astonish if they were still remembered. Forgotten, Spengler takes his revenge by threatening to be right. His oblivion in the midst of confirmation endows the ominous idea of blind fatality which emerges from his conception with an objective moment. When, at the time, seven German academicians joined forces in the periodical *Logos* to finish off the outsider, their philistine zeal provoked derision. Today their zeal seems less harmless; it testifies to an intellectual impotence comparable to the political impotence of the Weimar Republic faced with Hitler. Spengler found hardly an adversary who was his equal; his oblivion is the product of evasion.

One has only to read Manfred Schroeter's book, *Der Streit um Spengler* [*The Spengler Controversy*], with its complete survey of the critical literature up to 1922, to see how completely the German mind collapsed when confronted with an opponent who seemed to have inherited all the historical force of its own past. Against a man who rebuked them as a sergeant does a raw recruit, German philosophy and science could bring to bear only pedantic punctiliousness in concrete matters, the rhetoric of conformist optimism in its ideas, and, often enough, an involuntary admission of weakness in the form of the assurance that things aren't really all that bad or the sophistical trick of undermining Spengler's relativistic position by exaggerating his own relativism. Behind their pompous haplessness may well have been a secret urge to drop the resistance altogether. But the more the world marches in step with him, the more urgent it is to consider the meaning of the work in which he proclaimed a destiny for mankind which, with the murder of millions, has surpassed his dire prophecy. Spengler's power becomes evident when his theses are confronted with subsequent developments. The sources of this power, which the work possesses despite its manifest empirical and theoretical deficiencies, should be investigated. Finally, while maintaining a fundamental distrust of his thesis, one should ask what considerations could hold their ground against Spengler's arguments while avoiding both the pose of power and the guilty conscience of official optimism.

In demonstrating Spengler's force one should turn first not to his general historical-philosophical concepts of plant-like growth and cultural decay but to his application of this philosophy of history to the phase which he believed to be imminent and which he designated as 'Caesarism', in analogy to the period of the Roman Empire. His most characteristic predictions pertain to questions of mass domination such as propaganda, mass culture, and forms of political manipulation, in particular, certain tendencies inherent in democracy which threaten to turn it into dictatorship. In accordance with Spengler's general view that economic matters do not play a determining role in social reality but are rather the 'expression' of a particular 'state of soul', specifically economic prognoses are of comparatively minor importance. The question of monopolies is not raised, although Spengler is acutely aware of the cultural consequences of the increasing centralization of power. Yet his insight reaches far enough to disclose certain noteworthy economic phenomena, especially concerning the decline of a money economy.

Several lines of thought in the second volume of the *Decline* concern civilization in the era of Caesarism. To begin with, some passages on 'The Physiognomy of the Modern Metropolis'. Of its houses Spengler writes: 'They no longer have anything in common with the houses in which Vesta and Janus, the Lares and Penates resided; rather, they are mere shells, fashioned not by blood but by utility, not by feeling but by the spirit of commercialism. As long as the hearth remains the real, meaningful centre of the family for the pious soul, the last bond to the country has not disappeared. But when that, too, is lost and the mass of tenants and overnight guests in this sea of houses leads a vagrant existence from shelter to shelter, like the hunters and shepherds of primeval times, then the intellectual nomad is fully formed. This city is a world, the world. Only as a whole does it have the meaning of a human habitation. The houses are only the atoms out of which it is assembled.' Werner Sombart developed very similar thoughts in his pamphlet 'Why is there no Socialism in America?'

The image of the latter-day city-dweller as a second nomad deserves special emphasis. It expresses not only anxiety and estrangement but also the dawning ahistorical character of a condition in which men experience themselves solely as objects of opaque processes and, torn between sudden shock and sudden forgetfulness, are no longer capable of a sense of temporal continuity. Spengler, who sees the connection between atomization and the regressive type of man which revealed itself fully only with the onslaught of totalitarianism states: 'Each of these splendid mass cities harbours horrendous poverty, a brutalization of all customs which even now, in the attics and garrets, the cellars and backyards, is breeding a new primitive man.'

In the 'camps' of every variety, where there are no longer even any houses, that regression has become overt. Spengler has little understanding of the conditions of production that have brought about this situation. He sees all the more clearly, however, the frame of mind that grips the masses outside the actual process of production in which they are harnessed, in the phenomena usually grouped under the heading of 'leisure'. 'Intellectual tension knows only one form of recreation, that which is specific to the metropolis, namely, the release of tension in the form of relaxation, "distraction". Genuine play, *joie de vivre*, pleasure, ecstasy are produced by the rhythm of the cosmos, and their essence is no longer understood. But the relief from highly intensive, practical, intellectual work through its opposite, consciously practiced idiocy, the relief of intellectual tension through the physical tension of sports, of physical tension through the sensuous tension of pleasure and the intellectual tension induced by the "excitement" of competition and gambling, the replacement of the pure logic of daily work by consciously savoured mysticism—this recurs in every metropolis in every civilization.'

From this idea Spengler constructed the thesis that 'art itself becomes a sport'. He knew neither jazz nor quiz programmes, but if one were to summarize the most important trends of present-day mass culture, one could hardly find a more pregnant category than that of sports, the hurdling of rhythmic obstacles, the contest, be it between the performers or between the producers and the public. The full force of Spengler's scorn is directed not at the manipulators but at their victims, at those who fall prey to the 'civilizing' industry of an advertising culture. 'The Fellah-type emerges.'

Spengler describes this Fellah-type as the result of the expropriation of human consciousness by the centralized media of public communication. The process is still conceived in terms of the power of money, although he foresees the end of a monetary economy. According to him, the intellect, in the sense of unlimited autonomy, can exist only in connection with the abstract unity of money. However this may be in actuality, his description is entirely correct with respect to the situation under a totalitarian régime which declares ideological war against both money and mind. One could say that Spengler recognized in the press traits which were developed fully only later with the advent of the radio; similarly, the objections he raised to democracy attained their full weight only with the coming of dictatorships. 'Through the newspapers, democracy has utterly excluded the book from the intellectual life of the people. The world of books, with its variety of standpoints which encouraged thought to select and criticize, is now truly possessed only by the few. The people read only one paper, "their" paper, which thrusts its way daily into every house by the millions, spellbinds the mind from early morning on, drives books into oblivion through its format, and on the rare occasions when one book or another does appear, forestalls and nullifies its possible influence by "reviewing" it in advance.'

Spengler sees something of the dual character of enlightenment in the era of universal domination. 'The need for universal education, which was totally lacking in the ancient world, is bound up with the political press. In it is a completely unconscious urge to bring the masses, as the objects of party politics, under the control of the newspapers. To the idealist of early democracy, universal education seemed enlightenment as such, free of ulterior motives, and even today one finds here and there weak minds which become enthusiastic about the idea of freedom of the press, but it is precisely this that smooths the way for the coming Caesars of world-journalism. Those who have learned to read succumb to their power, and the anticipated self-determination of late democracy turns into the radical determination of the people by the powers behind the printed word.'

The things Spengler ascribes to the modest press magnates of the First World War find their mature form in the techniques of manipulated pogroms and 'spontaneous' popular demonstrations. 'Without the reader noticing, the paper—and thus he himself—changes masters'—this remark became literally true in the Third Reich. Spengler calls it 'the style of the twentieth century'. 'Today a democrat of the old type would demand not freedom of but freedom from the press; in the meantime, however, the leaders have turned into parvenus who have to secure their position vis-à-vis the masses.'

Spengler predicted Goebbels: 'No trainer has better control of his animals. Unleash the people as a reading mass, and it storms through the streets, hurls itself at the designated target, makes threats and breaks windows. A gesture to the press, and it quiets down and goes home. The press today is an army with carefully organized weapons, the journalists its officers, the readers its soldiers. But, as in every army, the soldier obeys blindly, and the war aims and operating plans change without his knowledge. The reader neither knows nor is supposed to know the purposes for which he is used and the role he is to play. There is no more appalling caricature of freedom of thought. Formerly no one was allowed to think freely; now it is permitted, but no one is capable of it any

57

more. Now people want to think only what they are supposed to want to think, and this they consider freedom.'

Spengler's specific prognoses are no less astonishing. First, a military prediction, which, incidentally, may have been influenced by certain experiences of the German high command in the First World War, experiences which have since been put into practice: Spengler considers the 'democratic' principle of universal military conscription and the tactics it required obsolete. 'From now on a professional army of voluntary and enthusiastic soldiers will gradually take the place of the standing army, hundreds of thousands will once again serve where there are now millions, but with this change this second century [after the Napoleonic Wars] will truly be one of embattled states. The mere existence of these armies is no substitute for war [as it was, according to Spengler, in the nineteenth century]; they are there for war and they want war. In two generations their will will be stronger than that of all those who want peace. In these wars fought for the heritage of the whole world, the stakes will be continents, India, China, South Africa, Russia, Islam will be called into action, new techniques and tactics will be pitted against each other. The great metropolitan centres of power will dispose at will of the smaller states, their territories and their economies; they will be mere provinces, objects of manipulation, means to ends, their fate without significance for the larger course of things. In a few years we have learned virtually to ignore things which before the war would have petrified the world.'

In the meantime, the mention of Auschwitz already provokes bored resentment. Nobody is concerned with the past any more. In Spengler's scheme the era of embattled states is followed by a world that is ahistorical in a sinister sense: the present economic tendency to create a static situation without crises in the economic sense of the term while eliminating the market and the dynamic of competition coincides with Spengler's prognosis clearly enough. His prediction is fulfilled even more strikingly in the static state of culture, the most advanced efforts of which have been denied understanding and a genuine reception by society since the nineteenth century. This static state compels the incessant and deadly repetition of what has already been accepted, and at the same time standardized art for the masses, with its petrified formulas, excludes history. All specifically modern art can be regarded as an attempt to keep the dynamic of history alive through magic, or to increase the horror at the stasis to shock, to portray the catastrophe in which the ahistorical suddenly begins to look archaic. Spengler's prophecy for the smaller states is beginning to be fulfilled in men themselves, even in the citizens of the largest and most powerful states. Thus history seems to have been extinguished. All events are things that happen to men, not things they bring about themselves. Even the greatest strategic exploits and triumphal processions have a touch of the illusionary; they are not quite real. The word 'phony' catches this. Events are the private affair of the oligarchs and their assassins; they do not arise from the dynamic of society but rather subordinate society to an administration intensified to the point of annihilation.

As objects of political power men surrender their spontaneity: 'With the arrival.of the Age of Empire there are no more political problems. People get along with the situation as it is and with the powers that be. In the age of the embattled states streams of blood reddened the walls of the world-cities in order to transform the great truths of democracy into reality and achieve rights without which life did not seem worth living. Now these rights have been won, but not even punishment can move the grandchildren to make use of them.'

Spengler's prediction of a change in the essence of the political party was radically confirmed in National Socialism—parties became followings. His characterization of the party, presumably inspired by Robert Michels, is of the same clear-sightedness that fascism knew how to use so satanically; the untruth of a humanitarianism that declares itself the measure of the world without being realized is made to justify absolute untruth and inhumanity. Spengler sees the relation of the party structure to bourgeois liberalism. 'The entrance of an aristocratic party into a parliament is just as inherently spurious as that of a proletarian party. Only the bourgeoisie is at home there.' He emphasizes the mechanisms which allow the party system to turn into dictatorship.

Such considerations have been familiar to cyclical philosophies of history since the Stoics. Machiavelli developed the idea that in the long run the decay of democratic institutions would always necessitate dictatorships. But Spengler, who in a certain sense revived at the end of an era the position Machiavelli took at its beginning, shows himself superior to the earlier political philosopher in having experienced the dialectic of history, though he never names it. For him the principle of democracy develops into its opposite through the rule of the party.

'The age of true party rule embraces barely two centuries and for us has been in full decline since the World War. That the voters will act as a group, on the basis of a common impulse, to elect men to manage their affairs, as is naïvely supposed in all constitutions, is possible only at the outset and presupposes the absence of tendencies to organize particular groups. This was so in France in 1789, in Germany in 1848. But to the existence of an assembly is immediately linked the formation of tactical alliances. The cohesion of these groups rests on the will to maintain the dominant position once it has been achieved; they no longer consider themselves in the least the voters' mouthpieces but on the contrary use every means of agitation to make the voters submissive so as to use them for their own purposes. Once a tendency in the people has become organized, it has *ipso facto* become a tool of organization, and it continues relentlessly on its way until the organization in turn becomes the instrument of the leader. The will to power is stronger than any theory. In the beginning the leadership and the apparatus come into being for the sake of the programme; then they are defended by the officials for the sake of power and profit, as is already generally the case today, when thousands of people in all countries make their living through the party and the offices and functions it bestows; finally the programme vanishes from memory and the organization functions for its own sake.'

Spengler refers specifically to Germany, foreseeing the years of minority régimes that helped Hitler to power: 'The German Constitution of 1919, coming into being on the verge of the decline of democracy, most naïvely allows for the dictatorship of party apparatuses, which have captured all rights for themselves and are seriously responsible to no one. The notorious system of proportional representation and the *Reichsliste* insure their maintenance and expansion. In place of the people's rights, which the Constitution of 1848 posited, there are now only the parties' rights, and harmless though this sounds, it implies the Caesarism of the organization. To be sure, in this sense the Constitution of 1919 is the most progressive of the age; it allows the final result to be seen. A few small alterations and it confers unrestricted power upon individuals.'

Spengler's prediction that the power to think will die out culminates in a taboo on thought which he attempts to justify on the basis of the inexorable course of history.

This touches on the Archimedean point of Spengler's scheme. His historical-philosophical assertion that the mind is dying and the anti-intellectual consequences he derives from it apply not only to the 'civilized' phase of history but to man in general as Spengler conceives him. 'Truths exist for the mind; facts, only in relation to life. Historical observation—what I call physiognomic tact—is a matter of blood; it is the gift of judging men extended over the past

60

and the future, an inborn eye for people and situations, for events, for things necessary, things that had to be, and not mere scientific criticism or knowledge of data.'

The decisive factor here is the idea of the gift of 'knowing' men and its coupling with the ideology of blood, which in the meantime has come into its own as the horror Spengler predicted. Behind this notion stands the Machiavellian assumption of an unchangeable human nature which need only be perceived—namely, as the worthless thing it is—to be controlled once and for all, since it must always be the same. Understood in its full implications, to 'know' men is to despise them: 'That's the way they are, and that's that.' The interest which is decisive for this attitude is domination. All of Spengler's categories are determined by this concept. His sympathies are with the rulers, and when speaking of the immense intelligence and iron will of modern industrial leaders, the philosopher of historical disillusionment can gush like one of the pacifists he is always mocking. His entire image of history is measured by the ideal of domination. His affinity for this ideal gives him profound insight whenever it is a question of the possibilities of domination and blinds him with hatred as soon as he is confronted by impulses which go beyond all previous history as the history of domination. In Spengler the tendency of the German Idealists to fetishize broad general concepts in their theories and then impassively sacrifice the existence of the individual human being to them—a tendency Schopenhauer, Kierkegaard, and Marx attacked in Hegel—becomes undisguised joy in actual human sacrifice. Whereas Hegel's philosophy of history speaks with stunned grief of the shambles of history, Spengler sees nothing but facts. Facts can, it is true, arouse regret, if one is so inclined, but they need not cause great concern as long as one is in complicity with historical necessity and one's physiognomics side with the stronger forces. In his fair-minded critique of Spengler in *Essays in Intellectual History*, James Shotwell writes: 'Spengler is interested in the great and tragic drama which he depicts and wastes little idle sympathy upon the victims of the recurring night.'

It is in the sweeping administrative gesture of Spengler's conceptual scheme, which skips over cultures as though they were multicoloured stones and blasts away with Fate, Cosmos, Blood, and Spirit with utter indifference, that the motif of domination expresses itself. Anyone who strips all phenomena down to the formula 'that's all happened before' exercises a tyranny of categories which is only too closely related to the political tyranny about which Spengler is so enthusiastic. He juggles history to make it fit his master-plan just as Hitler shunted minorities from one country to another. In the end everything is taken care of. Nothing is left over and all resistances—which in any case lay only with what had not been grasped —have been liquidated. However inadequate the criticisms of Spengler by the individual sciences may have been, in this respect they have their moment of truth. The fata morgana of the historical large-scale economy, the *Grossraumwirtschaft*, can be escaped only by the individual entity whose obstinacy sets limits on dictatorial subsumption. If, by virtue of his perspective and the broad range of his categories, Spengler is superior to the individual discipline obsessed with details, he is at the same time inferior to it because of that very range; his breadth is the result of his practice of never honestly following through the dialectic of concept and particular detail but instead making a detour through a schematism which uses the 'fact' ideologically to crush thought and never grants it more than an initial co-ordinating glance. In Spengler's world-historical perspective there is an element of ostentation and pomp which resembles the spirit of the Wilhelminian *Siegesallee* [Victory Avenue]; only when the world is transformed into a *Siegesallee* will it take on the form he desires. The superstitious belief that the greatness of a philosophy lies in its grandiose aspects is a bad heritage of Idealism—as though the quality of a painting depending on the sublimity of its subject-matter. Great themes prove nothing about the greatness of insight. If, as Hegel argues, the whole is what is true, then it is so only if the force of the whole is absorbed into the knowledge of the particular.

There is nothing of this in Spengler. The particular never opens itself to him; it is always accounted for in advance by his comparative survey of cultural morphology. His method proudly calls itself physiognomic. In truth his physiognomic thought is chained to the totalitarian character of his categories. Everything individual, however exotic, becomes a sign of something grandiose, of the civilization, because Spengler's conception of the world is so rigorously governed by his categories that there is no room for anything which does not easily and essentially coincide with them. There is an element of truth in this, in that societies based on domination have in fact always crystallized into closed totalities which allow no freedom for anything individual; totality is their logical form. Spengler's physiognomics have the merit of directing attention towards the 'system' in the individual, even where it assumes a semblance of freedom which conceals the universal dependency. But this merit is counterbalanced by the fact that Spengler's insistence on the universal dependence of individual moments on the whole, in the form of the dependence of a culture's expressive characteristics on its totality, is so abstract in its breadth that it tends to obscure the concrete and sharply differentiated moments of dependency which are decisive in human lives. Hence Spengler plays physiognomics against causality. By omitting all causal connections and presenting the typical passively reacting mass man on the same level as the concentration of power, which is the key category of the system and which produced and reproduces the mass men, Spengler is able to simplify social relations of dependency to ones of fate or to a cultural phase. Thus, metaphysically, he makes the impotent mass man himself responsible for the ignominy the Caesars have inflicted upon him. The physiognomic eye loses itself by classifying phenomena under a few invariant catchwords. Instead of immersing himself in the expressive character of the phenomena, Spengler hastens to unload his joyless accumulated wares with the help of shrill advertising slogans.

Spengler scrutinizes the individual sciences from top to bottom, as though for a clearance sale. If one were to characterize Spengler himself in the terminology of the civilization he denounces and name him in his own style, one would have to compare the *Decline of the West* to a department store where the intellectual agent sells the dried literary scraps he purchased at half-price at the close-out sale of culture. His procedure reveals the embittered resentment of the German middle-class scholar who wants to make capital of his learning at last and invest it in the most promising branch of the economy, which at the time was heavy industry. Spengler's insight into the helplessness of liberal intellectuals in the shadow of rising totalitarian power prompts him to become a turncoat. By denouncing itself the mind makes itself capable of providing anti-ideological ideologies. Spengler's proclamation of the demise of culture conceals wishful thinking. The mind which denies itself and sides with force hopes to be pardoned. Lessing's dictum about the man who was too clever to be clever finds its culminating example in Spengler. The introduction to the *Decline of the West* contains a statement that was to become famous: 'If the influence of this book leads men of the new generation to turn from poetry to technology, from painting to the merchant marine, from epistemology to politics, they are doing what I desire. One could wish nothing better for them.'

One can imagine the people to whom this sentence is obsequiously addressed. Spengler shares their belief that it is high time for young people to come to their senses. They are the same people who were later to advocate *Realpolitik*. Spengler's wrath against paintings, poems, and philosophy reveals a profound fear, the fear that in the 'historyless' stage which he depicts with horrified delight, when all 'political problems' and perhaps even the economy itself will have been done away with, culture, if not disposed of in time, might cease to be the harmless façade Spengler would like to demolish. Culture might then expose contradictions which a regimented economic system had allegedly eliminated. Official fascist culture provoked the laughter and incredulity of those upon whom it was forced, and much of the opposition to fascism took refuge in books, churches, and classical drama, all of which were tolerated because they were classics but which ceased to be classics once they were tolerated. Spengler's verdict strikes indiscriminately at official culture and at its opposite; expressionism and the movies are mentioned in one breath. The undifferentiated character of the verdict harmonizes perfectly with the frame of mind of those who hold power in the totalitarian states, those who despise their own lies hate the truth and cannot rest until there is no one left who dares to dream.

The individual disciplines, especially in the Anglo-Saxon countries, usually see Spengler as a metaphysician who violates reality with his arbitrary conceptual schemes. After the idealists, who feel that Spengler denied that the consciousness of freedom had progressed, the positivists are Spengler's most bitter opponents. There is no doubt that his philosophy does violence to the world, but it is the same violence that it endures daily in reality. History, so full of life that progress was too mechanistic for it, nevertheless seems all the more willing to freeze in accordance with the Spenglerian scheme. Whether a philosophy is metaphysical or positivistic cannot be decided at first glance. Metaphysicians are frequently only more far-sighted or less timid positivists. Is Spengler really the metaphysician he and his enemies consider him? If one remains on a formalistic level and considers the predominance of conceptualization over empirical content, the difficulty or impossibility of verification, and the crudely irrational supporting concepts of his epistemology, he is. If, however, one examines the substance of these concepts, one is always led to the desiderata of positivism, in particular, to the cult of the 'fact'. Spengler never misses an opportunity to defame the truth, whatever it may be, and to glorify that which simply is what it is and nothing else, that which needs only to be registered and accepted. '... But in historical reality there are no ideals; there are only facts. There is no causation, no justice, no equity, no goal; there are only facts. Anyone who does not understand this may write books about politics, but he should not meddle in politics itself.'

Spengler turns an essentially critical insight—that truth has been

64

impotent in all previous history, that the merely existent has tyran-
nized all attempts by consciousness to break out of its sphere of
power—unobtrusively into a justification of the merely existent.
The idea that something which exists, which has power, and which
perpetuates itself could nevertheless be wrong never occurs to him;
or, rather, he convulsively forbids himself and others to think such
thoughts. He is overcome with rage when he hears the voice of
impotence, and yet all he can say against it is that it is powerless
now and forever. Hegel's theory that what is real is rational degenerates to a caricature. Spengler retains Hegel's critique of reformers
and the pathos associated with his notion of a meaningful reality,
but by thinking in categories of naked domination he denies reality
any claim to meaning and rationality, the sole possible basis for
the Hegelian pathos. The reason and unreason of history are the
same for Spengler—pure domination—and facts are that through
which domination manifests itself.

Nietzsche, whose domineering tone Spengler constantly imitates
without ever dissociating himself, as Nietzsche did, from complicity
with the world, observes at one point that Kant used scientific means
to defend the common man's prejudices against science. Something
similar applies to Spengler. He used metaphysical weapons to
defend positivism's belief in facts and its ability to adjust to the
given against the critical opposition of metaphysics. A second
Comte, he made positivism into metaphysics, subordination to the
given into *amor fati*, swimming with the stream into cosmic tact,
meaninglessness into mystery, and the denial of truth into truth
itself. This is the source of his power.

Spengler is one of the theoreticians of extreme reaction whose
critique of liberalism proved itself superior in many respects to
the progressive one. It would be worthwhile to investigate the
reasons for this. It is the differences in the relationship to ideology
which are decisive. To the adherents of dialectical materialism
liberal ideology seemed for the most part a false promise. Their
spokesmen questioned not the ideas of humanity, freedom, and
justice but rather the claim of bourgeois society to have realized
those ideas. Ideologies were appearances for them, but the appearance of truth nevertheless. As a result, if not the existent itself at
least its 'objective tendencies' were endowed with a conciliatory gloss.
Talk of the increase of antagonisms and the admission of a real
possibility of a regression to barbarism were not taken seriously
enough for anyone to recognize ideologies as something worse than
apologetic disguises, as the objective absurdity that aids the society
of liberal competition to turn into a system of direct oppression.

The question, for instance, of how the existing order was to be changed by the very people who had to bear its full brunt was hardly ever raised. Concepts like mass and culture continued to be accepted in their positive sense, without anyone even suspecting the dialectic involved, or the fact that the specific category, mass, is a product of the present phase of society, or the simultaneous transformation of culture into a system of regimentation. No one recognized that ideas in their abstract form do not simply represent regulative truths but are themselves afflicted with the injustice under whose spell they were conceived.

The less interested those on the right were in the truth the ideologies contained, albeit in a false form, the more easily they were able to see through them. The advocates of the strong, for whom freedom, humanity, and justice are nothing but a fraud devised by the weak as protection against the strong (in this belief reactionary German theoreticians generally followed Nietzsche), have no difficulty pointing out the contradiction between ideas which are already ailing and reality. Their critique of ideologies outdoes itself. It replaces insight into a bad reality with insight into the badness of ideas, supposedly verified by the fact that the ideas have not yet been realized. What gives this glib criticism its force is its profound complicity with the powers that be. Spengler and his like are not so much prophets of the course the *Weltgeist* will take as its diligent promoters.

Prognosis as such implies manipulation; human spontaneity is abolished. A theory which sees men and their actions as the decisive factor, which no longer thinks in terms of political 'power relations' but rather would put an end to the play of such forces, makes no prophecies. Spengler says that it is necessary to calculate the unknown in history as far as possible. But it is precisely the unknown in mankind that cannot be calculated. History is not an equation, an analytic judgment. To think of it this way is to exclude from the very outset the possibility of anything qualitatively different. Spengler's prediction for history is reminiscent of the myths of Tantalus and Sisyphus and of the words of the oracle, which always announced evil. He is more soothsayer than prophet. In his gigantic and destructive soothsaying the petty bourgeois celebrates his intellectual triumph.

The morphology of world history serves the same purpose for Spengler as graphology did for Klages. The petty-bourgeois' desire to have his fortune told from handwriting, the past, or cards arises from the same trait which Spengler spitefully attacks in the victimized of every kind: the renunciation of conscious self-determination.

Spengler identifies with power, but the soothsaying aspect of his theory reveals the impotence of identification. He is as sure of his case as is the hangman after the verdict has been pronounced. His historical-philosophical world-formula immortalizes his own impotence no less than that of the others.

Perhaps this characterization of Spengler's mode of thought allows some more fundamental critical considerations. His metaphysics is positivist in its resignation to what is so and not otherwise, in its elimination of the category of potentiality, and in its hatred of all thought that takes the possible seriously in its opposition to the actual. At one decisive point, however, Spengler breaks through this positivism—so much so that some of his theological reviewers felt entitled to claim him as an ally. This is the conception of the moving force of history, of 'souldom', of the enigmatic, thoroughly inward, inexplicable quality which sometimes appears in history in a particular type of man, or, as Spengler sometimes calls it, a 'race'.

Despite his belief in facts and his relativistic skepticism, Spengler introduces a metaphysical principle as the ultimate explanation of the historical dynamic, a principle which, as he often asserted, is closely related to Leibniz's concept of entelechy, which Goethe formulated as '*geprägte Form, die lebend sich entwickelt*' ['moulded form, which living does unfold']. This metaphysics of a collective soul which develops and dies like a plant puts Spengler in the company of vitalist philosophers such as Nietzsche, Simmel, and particularly Bergson, whom he slanders. For Spengler, the tactician, discussion of soul and life is a welcome aid in branding materialism as shallow; in fact, however, he objects to it only because it is not sufficiently positivistic for him and would like the world to be other than it is.

But the metaphysics of 'souldom' has consequences more far-reaching than the merely tactical. One could call it a latent philosophy of identity. With a little exaggeration it could be said that for Spengler the history of the world becomes a history of style; man's historical experiences are as much a product of his inner self as are works of art. The man of facts fails to recognize the role played by scarcity in history. The confrontation of man with nature, which first produces the tendency to dominate nature, which in turn results in the domination of men by other men, is nowhere to be seen in the *Decline of the West*. Spengler does not grasp the degree to which historical fatality, which absorbs all his attention, results from the need to confront and transform nature. He sees history aesthetically. Economics becomes a 'form-world' like art, a sphere which is the pure expression of a soul that is as it is, a sphere which constitutes itself essentially independently of the need to reproduce life.

It is no accident that in matters of economics Spengler remains a helpless dilettante. He speaks of the omnipotence of money in the same tone that a petty-bourgeois agitator would use to rant about the international conspiracy on the stock market. He fails to see that in economics the decisive factor is not the medium of exchange but production. He is so fascinated by the façade of money, which he calls its 'symbolic power', that he mistakes the symbol for the thing itself. Blatantly contradicting all their programmes, he charges that the workers' parties want not to overcome money values but to possess them. For him slave economy, industrial proletariat, and mechanized economy are, as categories, not qualitatively different from the plastic arts, musical polyphony, and infinitesimal calculus. They dissolve into signs of something inward. The connections Spengler establishes between the heterogeneous categories of image and reality often shed surprising light on the unity of historical epochs, but by the same token everything which does not freely and autonomously belong to the realm of human expression tends to disappear in the process. Everything that cannot be reduced to a symbol of human nature, which, despite all his fatalism, Spengler endows with sovereignty, survives only in vague references to cosmic interconnections.

Thus the fatalistic determinism of Spengler's conception of history masquerades as the essence of a realm of freedom. But this is mere appearance. The result is a highly paradoxical constellation: precisely because everything external becomes an image of the internal and because the crucial question no longer involves a real process between subject and object, the world seems to grow organically out of the substance of the soul like a plant from a seed. By reducing history to the essence of the soul, Spengler gives it the appearance of a self-contained entity, yet one which for that very reason is actually deterministic. In his article in the Spengler issue of *Logos*, Karl Joel wrote that 'the whole sickness of this significant book' is 'that it has forgotten man with his productivity and freedom. Despite all internalization, he dehumanizes history and makes it into a sequence of typical natural processes. Although he infuses it with soul, he makes history into something corporeal by aiming at its morphology, its physiognomics, and thus at a comparison of its external configurations, its forms of expression, the particular features of its phenomena.'

It is not 'despite all internalization', however, but precisely because of it that history is dehumanized. Nature, with which men have had to struggle in history, is disdainfully pushed aside by Spengler's philosophy. Thus history becomes transformed into a second nature, as blind, closed, and fateful as any vegetable life. What can be called human freedom constitutes itself solely in man's efforts to break the bondage of nature. If this is ignored, if the world is treated as a pure manifestation of the pure essence of man, freedom becomes lost in the exclusively human character of history. Freedom develops only through the resistance of the existent; if freedom is posited as absolute and souldom is raised to a governing principle, that principle itself falls prey to the merely existent.

The hybris of Spengler's conception of history and his debasement of man are actually one and the same thing. Culture is not, as Spengler asserts, the life of collective souls in the process of unfolding themselves; rather, it arises in men's struggle to acquire the means to reproduce themselves. Culture thus contains an element of resistance to blind necessity—the will to determine oneself on the basis of knowledge. Spengler severs culture from mankind's drive to survive. For him it becomes a game in which the soul is its own playmate. He equates the phantasm of culture, a product of pure inwardness, with the real forces of history, indeed, with natural forces, since all others are excluded along with the reality against which they might be tested.

Thus Spengler's very idealism becomes subservient to his philosophy of power. Culture becomes an immanent part of domination; the process which begins and ends in mere inwardness becomes destiny, and history disintegrates to the timelessness of the aimless rise and fall of cultures, which Spengler blames on the late civilizations and which forms the basis of his own world-plan. The element in culture which resists being trapped in nature is ignored. Pure 'souldom' and pure domination are the same thing, just as Spengler's soul brutally and implacably dominates its bearers. Real history is ideologically transfigured into a history of the soul in order to bring what is antithetical and rebellious in man, consciousness, all the more completely under the sway of blind necessity. Spengler provides a final demonstration of the affinity between absolute idealism—his doctrine of the soul stems from Schelling— and demonic mythology. His propensity for mythological modes of thought can be grasped at certain eccentric points. The regular periodicity of certain events, he writes in a footnote in the second volume, 'is yet another indication that the cosmic surgings· in the form of human life on a small planet are not something self-contained but rather stand in profound harmony with the un-ending movement of the universe. In a small but noteworth book by R. Mewes, *Die Kriegs und Geistesperioden im Völkerleben und Verkündigung des nächsten Weltkrieges* [*Periods of War and of Intellect in the Lives of Peoples and the Annunciation of the Next World War*] (1896), the relationship of periods of war to those of the weather, sun-spots, and certain planetary conjunctions is estab-lished and accordingly a great war is foretold for 1910–1920. But these and innumerable other connections which are accessible to our senses conceal a mystery we have to respect.'

Despite his contempt for civilized mysticism, Spengler comes very close to astrological superstition in such formulations. They are the terminal point in the glorification of the soul.

The return of what is always the same, in which such a doctrine of fate terminates, is, however, nothing but the perpetual repro-duction of man's guilt towards man. The concept of fate, which subjects man to blind domination, reflects the domination exercised by men. Whenever Spengler speaks of fate he means the subjugation of one group of men by another. The metaphysics of the soul assists his positivism by hypostasizing the principle of relentlessly self-perpetuating domination as something eternal and inexorable. In reality the inexorability of fate is defined through domination and injustice, and it is this that is absolved by Spengler's world-order. In his system justice appears as the proscribed antithesis to fate. In one of the most brutal passages in his work, an unintended parody of Nietzsche, Spengler laments 'that the world-feeling for race, the political and thus national sense for facts—"my country, right or wrong"—the decision to be the subject and not the object of histor-ical development (for there is no third possibility), in short, the will to power, should be overcome by a trend whose standard-bearers are often men without any originality but therefore all the more obsessed with logic, at home in a world of truths, ideas, and utopias, men of books who believe that they can replace the real with the logical, the force of facts with abstract justice, fate with reason. It begins with men who are always afraid, who retreat from reality into cloisters, cells, studies, and intellectual communities, who declare that world history is a matter of indifference, and ends, in every civilization, with the apostles of world-peace. Every people produces such—historically speaking—waste products. Physiog-nomically, even their heads constitute a group apart. In the history of the mind they occupy a high place—many illustrious names are numbered among them—but from the standpoint of actual history they are inferior.'

To answer Spengler on his own terms would be to overcome historically the 'standpoint of actual history', which is not history but nature in a bad sense, and to transform what is historically possible into reality, something Spengler deems impossible because it has not yet been done. James Shotwell's critique penetrates uncompromisingly to the crux of the matter: 'Winter followed Autumn in the past because life was repetitive and was passed within limited areas of self-contained economy. Intercourse between societies was more predatory than stimulative because mankind had not yet discovered the means to maintain culture without an unjust dependence upon those who had no share in its material blessings. From the savage raid and slavery down to the industrial problems of today, the recurring civilizations have been largely built upon false economic forces, backed up by equally false moral and religious casuistry. The civilizations that have come and gone have been inherently lacking in equilibrium because they have built upon the injustice of exploitation. There is no reason to suppose that modern civilization must inevitably repeat this cataclysmic rhythm.' This insight can explode Spengler's entire conception of history. If the decline of antiquity were dictated by the autonomous necessity of life and by the expression of its 'soul', then it would indeed assume the aspect of fate, and fatalistic traits could easily be transferred to the contemporary situation. If, however, as Shotwell's observations imply, the decline of antiquity is to be understood in terms of its unproductive system of latifundia and the related slave economy, then fate can be mastered if these and similar forms of domination can be overcome, and Spengler's universal structure reveals itself to be a false analogy drawn from a bad but unique occurrence.

To be sure, this involves more than mere faith in continuous progress and the survival of culture. Spengler stressed the primitive nature of culture so emphatically that all naïve trust in its conciliatory power should have been swept away now once and for all. He demonstrates more strikingly than almost anyone else the way the primitive nature of culture always impels it towards decay and the way culture itself, as form and order, is in complicity with blind domination, which, forever in crisis, is always prone to annihilate itself and its victims. Culture bears the mark of death; to deny this would be to remain impotent before Spengler, who betrayed as many of the secrets of culture as did Hitler those of propaganda.

To escape the charmed circle of Spengler's morphology it is not enough to defame barbarism and rely on the health of culture. Spengler could laugh in the face of such blissful confidence. Rather, it is the barbaric element in culture itself which must be recognized.

71

The only considerations that have a chance of surviving Spengler's verdict are those which challenge the idea of culture as well as the reality of barbarism. Spengler's plantlike cultural soul, the vital 'being-in-form', the unconscious archaic world of symbols whose expressive force intoxicates him—all these signs of a self-glorifying life are actually harbingers of doom whenever they appear in reality. For they all testify to the coercion and sacrifice which culture imposes on man. To rely on them and deny the decline is to become even more firmly caught in its fatal coils. It is also to seek to restore that on which history has already pronounced judgment. For Spengler it is the last judgment. In executing it, however, history restores that which has been rightfully condemned, its rights as something irrevocably past.

Spengler's hunter's eye, which mercilessly scrutinizes the cities of mankind as though they were the wilderness they really are, overlooks one thing—the forces released by decay. *'Wie scheint doch alles werdende so krank'* ['*How sick seems all becoming*']—Georg Trakl's line transcends Spengler's landscape. In a world of brutal and oppressed life, decadence becomes the refuge of a potentially better life by renouncing its allegiance to this one and to its culture, its crudeness, and its sublimity. The powerless, who at Spengler's command are to be thrown aside and annihilated by history, are the negative embodiment within the negativity of this culture of everything which promises, however feebly, to break the dictatorship of culture and put an end to the horror of pre-history. In their protest lies the only hope that fate and power will not have the last word. What can oppose the decline of the west is not a resurrected culture but the utopia that is silently contained in the image of its decline.

VEBLEN'S ATTACK ON CULTURE

Veblen's *Theory of the Leisure Class* became famous for its doctrine of conspicuous consumption, according to which the consumption of goods, from the very early 'predatory' stage of history to the present, has served not so much to satisfy men's true needs or to provide what Veblen chooses to call the 'fullness of life' as to maintain social prestige—status. With respect to aesthetics, the conclusions Veblen derives from his critique of consumption as mere ostentation are very close to those of functionalism, which Adolf Loos formulated at about the same time. Where the practical is concerned they resemble those of technocracy. But although these are the elements in Veblen's sociology which were historically effective, they do not adequately describe the objective impulses of his thought, which are directed against the barbaric character of culture. Again and again, from the first sentence of his work, the expression 'barbarian culture' appears, immobile, like a ritual mask. He uses the term to refer specifically to one phase of history, an unusually broad one to be sure, extending from the archaic hunter and warrior to the feudal lord and the absolute monarch, a phase whose boundary with the capitalist period is purposely left unclear. In innumerable places, however, it is unmistakably his intention to denounce the modern as barbaric precisely where it most emphatically raises the claim to culture. According to Veblen the very features which seem to prove that modernity has escaped the principle of unvarnished necessity and become humane are relics of historical epochs long past. For him emancipation from the realm of utility is nothing but the index of a purposelessness arising from the fact that cultural 'institutions' and anthropological characteristics do not change simultaneously and in harmony with the means of production but rather lag behind them and at times come into open contradiction with them. If one follows the direction of Veblen's thoughts instead of concentrating on his formulations, which waver between the vitriolic and the cautious, one arrives at the conception that those characteristics of culture in which greed, the search for personal advantage, and confinement in mere immediacy appear to have been overcome are nothing but residues of objectively obsolete forms of greed, personal ambition, and bad immediacy. They originate in the need to prove that crude practical considerations have been dispensed with, to prove, in particular, that one can spend one's time on the useless in order to improve one's position in the social hierarchy, increase one's social honour, and, finally, strengthen one's power over others. Culture turns against utility for the sake of a mediated utility. It is marked by the life-lie. In tracking down this lie Veblen displays a persistence not unlike that of his contemporary, Freud, in his investigation of the 'dregs of the world of phenomena'. Under Veblen's gloomy gaze, lawn and walking-stick, umpire and domestic animal become revealing allegories of the barbarism of culture.

It was as much this method as the contents of his teaching that led people to defame Veblen as a crazy and destructive outsider. As a professor in Chicago he even created an academic scandal which ended in his dismissal. At the same time, however, his theories have been assimilated. Today they find wide official recognition, and, like Freud's, his striking terminology has penetrated into journalism. One sees here the objective tendency to disarm a tiresome opponent by giving him a warm reception. Veblen's thought, however, is not completely out of harmony with such a reception; he is less an outsider than he seems at first sight. In pursuing his intellectual genealogy one would need to name three sources. The first and most important is American pragmatism. Veblen belongs to the older, Darwinistically inclined tradition in it. 'The life of man in society,' the central chapter of his main work begins, 'just like the life of other species, is a struggle for existence, and therefore it is a process of selective adaptation. The evolution of social structure has been a process of natural selection of institutions. The progress which has been made and is being made in human institutions and in human character may be set down, broadly, to a natural selection of the fittest habits of thought and to a process of enforced adaptation of individuals to an environment which has progressively changed with the growth of the community and with the changing institutions under which men have lived.' The concept of adaptation or adjustment is central. Man is subjected to life as to the experimental conditions set down by some unknown laboratory director, and he is expected to adjust to the natural and historical conditions imposed upon him in such a way that he has a chance to survive. The truth of thought is judged according to whether or not it serves this adaptation and contributes to the survival of the species. Veblen's critique always begins at points where this adaptation is incomplete. He is well aware of the difficulties the doctrine of adaptation encounters in the social realm; he knows that the conditions to which men must adapt are themselves a product of society, that there is an interaction between the internal and the external, and that adaptation may work to reinforce reified conditions. This insight forces him to refine and modify his doctrine continually, but he rarely reaches the point of questioning the absolute necessity of adjustment itself. Progress is adaptation and nothing else. Veblen stubbornly refuses to see that the inner constitution of this concept and its dignity could be qualitatively different in the case of conscious beings than they are in the blind world of nature. The harmony of this fundamental position with the intellectual climate in which Veblen found himself greatly facilitated the reception of his heresies.

The specific content of his adjustment theory, however, has a second source in an older variety of positivism, the school of St. Simon, Comte, and Spencer. The world to which, according to Veblen, men are supposed to adjust is that of industrial technology With St. Simon and Comte, Veblen proclaims its supremacy. For his progress means, concretely, the adaptation of the forms of consciousness and of 'life', that is, the sphere of economic consumption, to those of industrial technology. The means to this adjustment is science. Veblen conceives of it as the universal application of the principle of causality, in opposition to vestigial animism. Causal thinking is for him the triumph of objective, quantitative relations, patterned after industrial production, over personalistic and anthropomorphic conceptions. Above all, the notion of teleology is strictly excluded. The conception of history as slow and irregular but inherently continuous progress in adjusting to the world and demystifying it corresponds to a classificatory theory of stages not unlike Comte's. In this context Veblen occasionally gives indications that he expects the coming phase to witness the abolition of private property. This points to Marx as his third source. Veblen's attitude towards Marxism is controversial. The object of his critique is not the political economy of bourgeois society seen in terms of its foundations but the uneconomic life of that society. His continual recourse to psychology and 'habits of thought' to explain economic facts is incompatible with the Marxian theory of objective value. Nevertheless, Veblen incorporated as many of the secondary theories of Marxism into his basically pragmatic position as he could. Specific categories like conspicuous waste and reversion also originate there. The notion of a kind of consumption which exists not for its own sake but as a reflection of the social qualities of exchange-objects is related to the Marxian theory of commodity fetishism. The thesis of reversion, the compulsive regression to obsolete forms of consciousness under the pressure of economic conditions, is at least indebted to Marx. In Veblen, as in Dewey, the attempt to grasp the process of human adjustment, which is conceived pragmatically, produces dialectical motifs. His thinking is an amalgam of positivism and historical materialism.

Such a formula, however, offers relatively little insight into the heart of Veblen's theory. What is crucial is the force which drives these motifs together in his theory. Veblen's basic experience may be characterized as that of pseudo-uniqueness. As the mass production and centrally organized distribution of goods which are all basically similar advances, and as the technological and economic framework of life increasingly excludes the individuation of the here and now based on hand-production, the appearance of the here and now, that which cannot be replaced by countless other objects, becomes an imposture. It is as if in claiming to be something special and unique—and this claim must be constantly exaggerated in the interest of sales—each object were mocking a condition in which all men are subjugated to an order whose principle is more of the same. Veblen cannot bear this mockery. Bitterly, he insists that the world present itself in that abstract sameness of its objects which is predetermined by the underlying economic conditions. When Veblen argues for a rational organization of consumption, he is actually demanding nothing less than that mass production, for which the purchaser is from the outset an object of calculation, reveal its true colours in the sphere of consumption. Now that such phrases as 'deliciously different' and 'quaint' have become standard formulas in advertising, Veblen's insight is obvious. He was the first, however, to reach it spontaneously. He recognized the pseudo-individuality of things long before technology had snuffed out real individuality. He saw sham uniqueness in the intrinsic inconsistency of the objects themselves, in the contradiction between their form and their function. At the risk of exaggerating, one could say that the kitsch of the nineteenth century, in the form of ostentation,[1] appeared to him as the image of future tyranny. He saw a side of kitsch which escaped aesthetic critics but which helps explain the shockingly catastrophic expression which so many nineteenth-century buildings and interiors have assumed today—the look of oppression.

[1] Its economic basis should be precisely determined. That kind of presentation might well stem from the necessity to depict oneself as a good risk with a high credit rating. This necessity could reflect the scarcity of capital during periods of expansion.

In Veblen's eyes the ornamentation becomes menacing as it becomes increasingly similar to old models of repression. Nowhere does he indicate this more strikingly than in a discussion of the buildings which house charitable institutions: 'Certain funds, for instance, may have been set apart as a foundation for a foundling asylum or a retreat for invalids. The diversion of expenditure to honorific waste in such cases is not uncommon enough to cause surprises or even to raise a smile. An appreciable share of the funds is spent in the construction of an edifice faced with some aesthetically objectionable but expensive stone, covered with grotesque and incongruous details, and designed, in its battlemented walls and turrets and its massive portals and strategic approaches, to suggest certain barbaric methods of warfare.' Veblen uses this emphasis on the threatening aspects of magnificence and ornamentation to support his philosophy of history. For his belief in progress, the images of aggressive barbarism which he saw in nineteenth-century kitsch, and particularly in the decorative efforts of the years after 1870, represented relics of past epochs or indications of the regression of those who were not producing anything, those exempt from participation in the industrial labour-process. But the things Veblen calls archaic characteristics are at the same time indications of the dawning horror. His sad innervation disavows his optimistic outlook. The form human history took for him anticipated its most terrible phase. The shock he experienced in seeing the fortress-like foundlings' home became an historical force in the Columbus House, the National Socialists' neo-functional torture chamber. Veblen hypostasizes total domination. For him all culture becomes the distorted image of naked horror. His fascination with the impending doom explains and justifies the injustice he does culture. Culture, which today has assumed the character of advertising, was never anything for Veblen but advertising, a display of power, loot, and profit. With splendid misanthropy he ignores everything that goes beyond this. The mote in his eye becomes a means of perceiving the bloody traces of injustice even in images of happiness. In the name of the right to unlimited disposition over human history, the metropolis of the nineteenth century assembled a deceptive collection of pillars from Attic temples, Gothic cathedrals, and the arrogant palaces of Italian city-states. Veblen pays it back; for him the real temples, palaces, and cathedrals are already as false as the imitations. World history is the world's fair. Veblen explains culture in terms of kitsch, not vice-versa. His generalization of a situation in which culture is consumed by advertising has been concisely formulated by Stuart Class: 'People above the line of bare subsistence, in this age and all earlier ages, do not use surplus, which society has given them, primarily for useful purposes.' By 'all earlier ages' is meant everything unlike the business culture of the most recent age—the belief in the real power of ritual practices, the impulse of sexuality and its symbolism (sexuality is not mentioned once in the entire *Theory of the Leisure Class*), the compulsion to artistic expression, all yearning to escape the enslavement to utility. Against his will, the pragmatist, mortal enemy of teleological speculation, proceeds according to the scheme of a satanic teleology. His ingenious intelligence does not shrink from using the crudest rationalism to expose the universal domination of the fetish over the ostensible realm of freedom. Under his attack the concretion which imposes unity on the monotony of that which is nature-bound is perverted to a mass-produced article which falsely claims to be concrete.

Veblen's evil eye is fertile. It strikes phenomena which are overlooked or deemed harmless when one does not linger over them but merely dispenses with them from above as nothing more than the façade of society. One of these phenomena is sports. Veblen bluntly characterized every kind of sport, from children's contest and college gymnastics to the grand athletic pageants which subsequently blossomed in the dictatorships of both varieties, as outbursts of violence, oppression, and the predatory spirit. 'These manifestations of the predatory temperament are all to be classed under the head of exploit. They are partly simple and unreflected expressions of an attitude of emulative ferocity, partly activities deliberately entered upon with a view to gaining repute for prowess. Sports of all kinds are of the same general character.' According to Veblen, the passion for sports is of a regressive nature: 'The ground of an addiction to sports is an archaic spiritual constitution.' But nothing is more modern than this archaism; athletic events were the models for totalitarian mass rallies. As tolerated excesses, they combine cruelty and aggression with an authoritarian moment, the disciplined observance of the rules—legality, as in the pogroms of Nazi Germany and the people's republics. Veblen senses the affinity between the excesses of athletics and the manipulating elite: 'If a person so endowed with a proclivity for exploits is in a position to guide the development of habits in the adolescent members of the community, the influence which he exerts in the direction of conservation and reversion to prowess may be very considerable. This is the significance, for instance, of the fostering care latterly bestowed by many clergymen and other pillars of society upon "boys brigades" and similar pseudo-military organizations.' His insight extends even further. He recognizes sports as pseudo-activity, as the channelling of energies which could otherwise become dangerous, as the endowing of meaningless activity with a specious seriousness and significance. The less one suffers from economic constraint, the more one feels impelled to create the semblance of serious, socially reputable and nevertheless non-profit activity. At the same time, however, sports suits the aggressive and practical predatory spirit. It provides a common denominator for the conflicting desires to act purposefully and to waste time. But it thus becomes fraudulent, make-believe. Veblen's analyses, of course, should be expanded. For sports includes not merely the drive to do violence to others but also the wish to be attacked oneself and suffer. Only Veblen's rationalist psychology prevents him from seeing the masochistic moment in sports. It is this which makes sports not so much a relic of a previous form of society as perhaps an initial adjustment to its menacing new form—as opposed to Veblen's complaint that the 'institutions' have remained behind the industrial spirit, which, of course, he limits to technology. Modern sports, one will perhaps say, seek to restore to the body some of the functions of which the machine has deprived it. But they do so only in order to train men all the more inexorably to serve the machine. Hence sports belong to the realm of unfreedom, no matter where they are organized.

Another complex in Veblen's critique of culture, one which seems less topical, is the so-called woman question. Because the final emancipation of women was so self-evident to socialist programmes, there seems for a long time to have been no need to think through the concrete position of women. Since Shaw the woman question has been regarded as comical in bourgeois literature. Strindberg perverted it to the question of men, just as Hitler shifted the emphasis from the emancipation of the Jews to the emancipation from the Jews. The impossibility of liberating women under the present conditions is attributed not to the conditions but to the advocates of freedom, and the frailty of emancipatory ideals, which brings them close to neurosis, is confused with their realization. The open-minded office girl who is satisfied with the world as long as she can go to the movies with her date has supplanted Nora and Hedda, and if she knew about them she would reproach them in chic phrases for being unrealistic. Her counterpart is the man who makes use of his erotic freedom only to take his partner coldly and joylessly in her obtuse compliance and then show his gratitude by deriding her all the more cynically. Veblen, who has much in common with Ibsen, is perhaps the last thinker of note who does not avoid the woman question. As a late apologist of the feminist movement he has absorbed the experiences of Strindberg. For Veblen woman becomes as a social phenomenon what she is for herself psychologically—a wound. He perceives her patriarchal humiliation. He compares her position, which he includes among the relics from the period of the hunter and the warrior, to that of the servant. Free time and luxury are allotted her only to strengthen the status of the master. This implies two contradictory consequences. Taking some liberties with Veblen's text, one might state them as follows: on the one hand, precisely by virtue of her debased situation as 'slave' and object of ostentation, the woman is in a certain sense exempted from 'practical life'. She is, or at least still was in Veblen's time, less exposed to economic competition than the man. In certain social strata and in certain epochs she was protected from the necessity of developing those qualities which Veblen describes under the general heading of the predatory spirit. By virtue of her distance from the process of production she retains certain traits which characterize the human being who is not yet entirely in the grasp of society. Thus women belonging to the upper social strata seem most ready to turn their backs on their class. Opposed to this, however, is a counter-tendency the most prominent symptom of which Veblen designates as the conservatism of woman. She rarely takes part as subject in historical development. The state of dependence to which she is confined mutilates her. This counterbalances the opportunity offered her by her exclusion from economic competition. Measured against the man's sphere of intellectual interests, even that of those men absorbed in the barbarism of business, most women find themselves in a mental state which Veblen does not hesitate to term imbecilic. Following this line of thought, one might reach the conclusion that women have escaped the sphere of production only to be absorbed all the more entirely by the sphere of consumption, to be captivated by the immediacy of the commodity world no less than men are transfixed by the immediacy of profit. Women mirror the injustice masculine society has inflicted on them—they become increasingly like commodities. Veblen's insight indicates a change in the utopia of emancipation. Hope cannot aim at making the mutilated social character of women identical to the mutilated social character of men; rather, its goal must be a state in which the face of the grieving woman disappears simultaneously with that of the bustling, capable man, a state in which all that survives the disgrace of the difference between the sexes is the happiness that difference makes possible.

Veblen, to be sure, did not draw these consequences. Despite his vague talk about the 'fulness of life', his image of society is based not on the ideal of happiness but on that of work. Happiness enters his field of vision only as the fulfilment of the 'work instinct', his supreme anthropological category. He is a puritan *malgré lui-même*. While he never tires of attacking taboos, his criticism stops at the sacredness of work. His critique has something of the paternal platitude which asserts that culture is not sufficiently proud of its own work but instead takes excessive pride in being excluded from work, in leisure. As its guilty conscience, he confronts society with its own principle of utility and proves to it that according to this principle culture is both a waste and a swindle, so irrational that it raises doubts about the rationality of the whole system. Veblen has something of the bourgeois who takes the admonition to be thrifty with grim seriousness. Thus all of culture becomes for him the meaningless ostentatious display typical of the bankrupt. Through his single-minded persistence in this one theme he un-masks the absurdity of a social process which can survive only by making 'false calculations' at every step and constructing labyrinths of deception and illusion. But Veblen had to pay for his method. He idolizes the sphere of production. His theory implies a distinction like that between predatory and productive capital in bourgeois economics. He distinguishes between two categories of modern economic 'institutions: pecuniary and industrial'. He divides human occupations accordingly, and the modes of behaviour which sup-posedly correspond to these occupations as well: 'So far as men's habits of thought are shaped by the competitive process of acquisi-tion and tenure; so far as their economic functions are comprised within the range of ownership of wealth as conceived in terms of exchange value, and its management and financiering through a permutation of values; so far their experience in economic life favours the survival and accentuation of the predatory temperament and habits of thought.' By failing to grasp the social process as a totality, Veblen arrives at a distinction between productive and non-productive functions. His primary target in making this distinction is the irrational mechanisms of distribution, as is evident in his talk of 'that class of persons and that range of duties in the economic process which have to do with the ownership of enterprises engaged in competitive industry; especially those fundamental lines of eco-nomic management which are classed as financiering operations. To these may be added the greater part of mercantile operations.' Only in the light of this distinction does it become clear what Veblen's objection to the leisure class really is. It is not so much the pressure it exerts on the others as the fact that there is not enough pressure on it to satisfy his puritanical work ethos. He be-grudges it its chance to escape, grotesque though that chance is.

The fact that the economically independent are not yet wholly within the grip of the necessities of life seems archaic to him: 'An archaic habit of mind persists because no effectual economic pressure constrains this class to an adaptation of its habits of thought to the changing situation'—an adaptation, it should be noted, that Veblen constantly advocates. The countermotif, it is true, leisure as the precondition of humanity, is not alien to him. But here an atheoretical, pluralistic scheme of thought prevails. Leisure and waste are granted their rights, but only 'aesthetically'; as economist Veblen will have nothing to do with them. One should not overlook the contempt for the aesthetic implied in such a division. The question of what 'economic' means for Veblen becomes thereby all the more imperative. The problem is not the extent to which Veblen's writings can be included in the discipline of economics but rather the meaning of his own conception of economics. The economic in Veblen remains implicitly defined as the 'profitable'. His talk of economics converges with that of the businessman who rejects an unnecessary expense as uneconomical. The concepts of the useful and the useless presupposed in such thinking are not subjected to analysis. Veblen demonstrates that society functions uneconomically in terms of its own criteria. This is both much and little; much, because he thus glaringly illuminates the unreason of reason, little, because he fails to grasp the interdependence of the useful and the useless. He leaves the question of the useless to heteronomous categories produced by the intellectual division of labour and makes himself a cultural efficiency expert whose vote can be vetoed by his aesthetic colleagues. He fails to see in the opposition of jurisdictions itself an expression of the fetishistic division of labour. While as economist he is all too sovereign in his treatment of culture, cutting it from the budget as waste, he is secretly resigned to its existence outside the budgetary sphere. He fails to see that its legitimacy or illegitimacy can be decided only through insight into society as a totality, not from the departmental perspective of the questioner. Thus a moment of buffoonery is inherent in his critique of culture.

Veblen would like to make a clean slate, to wipe away the rubble of culture and get to the bottom of things. But the search for 'residues' regularly falls prey to blindness. As the reflection of truth, appearances are dialectical; to reject all appearance is to fall completely under its sway, since truth is abandoned with the rubble without which it cannot appear. Veblen, however, refuses to see the impulses behind all that against which his basic experience rebels. In the posthumously published papers of Frank

Wedekind is the remark that kitsch is the Gothic or the Baroque of our age. Veblen did not seriously grapple with the historical necessity of kitsch Wedekind has in mind. To Veblen the phony castle is simply anachronistic. He does not understand the distinctly modern character of regression. The deceptive images of uniqueness in an era of mass production are only vestiges for him, not responses to highly industrialized mechanization which betray something of its essence. The world of these images, which Veblen unmasks as that of conspicuous consumption, is a synthetic, 'imaginary' world. It represents the futile but compulsive attempt to avoid the loss of experience involved in modern modes of production and escape the domination of abstract equivalence through self-made concretion. Men prefer to deceive themselves with illusions of the concrete rather than abandon the hope which clings to it. Commodity fetishes are not merely the projection of opaque human relations onto the world of things. They are also the chimerical deities which originate in the primacy of the exchange process but nevertheless represent something not entirely absorbed in it. Veblen's thinking recoils before this antinomy, which, however, is precisely what makes kitsch a style. Kitsch does not designate simply a misuse of work. The fact that the synthetic images depict regressions to the distant past only testifies to its inaccessibility. The most advanced art has conceived images which bring together the level of technical possibilities and the human demand for the concrete, but they have been ill received by society. Perhaps it is permissible to formulate the relationship between progress—'modernity'—and regression—'archaism'—in the form of a thesis. In a society in which the development and the stifling of energies are inexorable consequences of the same principle, each technical advance signifies at the same time a regression.[2] Veblen's talk of the 'barbarian normal' reveals a suspicion of this. Barbarism is normal because it does not consist in mere rudiments but is steadily

[2] Freud's psychological theory, which makes regression the product of a censorship exercised by the ego—the subject of all 'progress'—contains something of this fact, except that regression cannot be determined solely in terms of 'man' and his psyche, the object of all previous history, but must rather be seen as emanating from the actual social process, from the non-conscious subject whose naturalness comes to light in the fact that for every creation it pays the price of annihilation. The ambiguity of 'sublimation' is the psychological symbol of the ambiguity of social progress, just as the Freudian principle of economy, which designates the constant balancing of credit and debit in the psychological household, denotes not a primary and unalterable anthropological condition but rather the perpetual invariance of everything that has happened up to the present.

reproduced along with and in direct proportion to man's domination of nature. Veblen took this equivalence too lightly. He saw the temporal disparity between the castle and the railway station but did not grasp this disparity as a historical law. The station masks itself as a castle, but the mask is its truth. Only when the technical world of things becomes the direct servant of domination is it capable of throwing aside such masks. Only in the totalitarian terror-states does it appear as what it really is.

In overlooking the compulsive element in modern archaism and thinking it possible to root out synthetic images as mere illusions, Veblen also abdicates before the social *quaestio iuris* of luxury and waste, which as world reformer he would prefer to extirpate like a growth. Luxury has a dual character. Veblen concentrates his spotlight on one side of it: that part of the social product which does not benefit human needs and contribute to human happiness but instead is squandered in order to preserve an obsolete system. The other side of luxury is the use of parts of the social product which serve not the reproduction of expended labour, directly or indirectly, but of man in so far as he is not entirely under the sway of the utility principle. Although Veblen does not explicitly distinguish between these two moments of luxury, it is unquestionably his intention to do away with the first as 'conspicuous consumption' and to save the second in the name of the 'fullness of life'. In the crudeness of this intention, however, lies the weakness of his theory. *Faux frais* and happiness cannot be isolated in luxury today. They comprise the inherently mediated identity of luxury. Although happiness exists only when men have momentarily eluded the process of a pernicious 'societalization', the concrete form of their happiness always contains in itself the general condition of society, the negative.[3] Proust's novel might be interpreted as the attempt to develop this contradiction. Thus erotic happiness relates

[3] Veblen's inability to articulate the dialectic of luxury is most strikingly evident in his conception of the beautiful. He tries to purge the beautiful of pomp and ostentation. He thereby deprives it of every concrete social determination and reverts to a pre-Hegelian standpoint on beauty, a purely formal concept oriented on measurable natural categories. His discussion of beauty is very abstract because there is nothing beautiful in which the immanent moment of injustice can be eliminated. To be consistent, Veblen would have to advocate the abolition of art. His pluralism, which adds to the economic principle of thrift the aesthetic one of non-illusion, arises from this inability to be consistent. In their isolation, however, both moments become absurd. Just as the utter expediency of the beautiful thrusts it into irreconcilable contradiction with its purposelessness, Veblen's conception of the economic comes into contradiction with his idea of a good society.

not to man 'as such' but rather to man as he is determined by society and in his social manifestations. Walter Benjamin once wrote that it is as erotically important to the man for his beloved to appear in his company as for her to give herself to him. Veblen would have joined in the bourgeois jeering at this remark and would have talked about conspicuous consumption. But the happiness that man actually finds cannot be separated from conspicuous consumption. There is no happiness which does not promise to fulfil a socially constituted desire, but there is also none which does not promise something qualitatively different in this fulfilment. Abstract utopian thinking which deludes itself about this, sabotages happiness and plays into the hands of that which it seeks to negate. For, although it strives to purge happiness of the social stigma, it is forced to renounce every concrete claim to happiness and to reduce human beings to a mere function of their own work. Even the commodity fetishist who has succumbed to conspicuous consumption to the point of obsession participates in the truth-content of happiness. Although he denies his own living happiness and replaces it with the prestige of things—Veblen speaks of 'social confirmation'—he reveals against his will the secret that lies hidden in all pomp and ostentation, the fact that no individual happiness is possible which does not virtually imply that of society as a whole. Even malice, the flaunting of status, and the drive to impress, in which the social moment of happiness inexorably manifests itself under the principle of competition, contain the recognition of society, of the whole, as the true subject of happiness. Those features of luxury which Veblen designates as 'invidious', revealing a bad will, do not only reproduce injustice; they also contain, in distorted form, the appeal to justice. Human beings are no worse than the society in which they live—therein lies the corrective to Veblen's misanthropy. But his misanthropy is also a corrective. It defames the bad will even in its most sublime impulses because it remains stubbornly loyal to a good will.

It is deeply ironic, however, that Veblen's loyalty is compelled to take the form which he so vigorously condemns in bourgeois society, that of regression. In his mind, the only hope lies in the prehistory of man. All the happiness which for him is excluded by dreamless realism, by pliant adaptation to the conditions of the industrial world, is reflected in the image of a paradisical golden age. 'The conditions under which men lived in the most primitive stages of associated life that can properly be called human, seem to have been of a peaceful kind; and the character—the temperament and spiritual attitude—of men under these early conditions of environment and institutions seems to have been of a peaceful and un-aggressive, not to say an indolent cast. For the immediate purpose this peaceable cultural stage may be taken to mark the initial phase of social development. So far as concerns the present argument, the dominant spiritual feature of this presumptive initial phase of culture seems to have been an unreflecting, unformulated sense of group solidarity, largely expressing itself in a complacent, but by no means strenuous, sympathy with all facility of human life, and an uneasy revulsion against apprehended inhibition or futility of life.' Veblen interprets the demythologizing and humanity which characterize mankind in the bourgeois era not as indications of increasing self-consciousness but rather as a reversion to this primal state. 'Under the circumstances of the sheltered situation in which the leisure class is placed there seems, therefore, to be something of a reversion to the range of non-invidious impulses that characterize the ante-predatory savage culture. The reversion comprises both the sense of workmanship and the proclivity to indolence and good-fellowship.' Karl Kraus, the critic of linguistic ornament, once wrote 'Origin is the goal'. Similarly, the nostalgia of Veblen, the technocrat, aims at the resurrection of the most ancient; the feminist movement is for him the blind and incoherent effort 'to rehabilitate the women's pre-glacial standing'. Such provocative formulations seem like insults to the positivist's sense of fact. But here one of the most curious conjunctions in Veblen's theory manifests itself, that which joins positivism and the Rousseauistic theory of a primitive ideal state. As a positivist who admits no norm but that of adjustment, Veblen sees himself faced with the question why one should not also adjust to the givens of 'the principles of waste, futility and ferocity', which according to his conception comprise the 'canon of pecuniary decency'. 'But why are apologies needed? If there prevails a body of popular sentiment in favour of sports, why is not the fact a sufficient legitimation? The protracted discipline of prowess to which the race had been subjected under the predatory and quasipeaceable culture has transmitted to the man of today a temperament that finds gratification in these expressions of ferocity and cunning. So, why not accept these sports as legitimate expressions of a normal and wholesome human nature? What other norm is there that is to be lived up to than that given in the aggregate range of propensities that express themselves in the sentiments of this generation, including the hereditary strain of prowess?' Here, with a grin not unlike Ibsen's, Veblen follows his reasoning to the point where it is in danger of capitulating to the world as it is, to normal barbarism. His solution is surprising: 'The ulterior norm to which appeal is taken is the instinct of workmanship, which is an instinct more fundamental, of more ancient prescription, than the propensity to predatory emulation.' This is the key to his theory of the primitive age. The positivist permits himself to conceive of human potentiality only by transforming it into a given, something which actually existed in the past. There can be no justification of a reconciled life without that life being more 'given', more positive, more existent than the hell of existence. Paradise is the positivist's aporia. Veblen invents the instinct of workmanship only incidentally, in order to bring paradise and the industrial age together under a common anthropological denominator. As he would have it, men earned their bread by the sweat of their brow even before the Fall.

It was in theories of this kind, impotent and self-caricaturing props in which the idea of the different tries to make its peace with adjustment to the eternally same, that Veblen most exposed himself. It is easy to deride the positivist who strives to break out of facticity. Veblen's entire work is permeated by the motif of spleen. It is one big joke at the expense of that 'sense of proportion' that the positivistic rules of fair play demand. He is insatiable in seeking elaborate analogies between the customs and institutions of sports and religion, or between the aggressive codes of honour of the gentleman and the criminal. He cannot even refrain from complaining about the economic waste involved in the ceremonial paraphernalia of religious cults. He has an affinity with the reformers of life. Often enough his primitivistic utopia degenerates to the crude belief in the 'natural', and he preaches against so-called follies of fashion like long skirts and corsets, for the most part attributes of the nineteenth century which the progress of the twentieth has swept away without thereby bringing the barbarism of culture to an end. Conspicuous consumption becomes an *idée fixe*. To understand the contradiction between this and the sharp insights of Veblen's social analyses, one must consider the cognitive function of spleen itself. Like the image of a peaceful primeval age, spleen in Veblen—and not only in him—is a haven of potentiality. The observer who is guided by spleen attempts to make the overwhelming negativity of society commensurable with his own experience. He seeks to make tangible the impenetrable and alien character of the whole, but it is precisely this quality which lies beyond the grasp of direct, vital experience. The *idée fixe* replaces the abstract general concept in that it rigidifies and stubbornly preserves specific and limited experience. Spleen expresses the desire to compensate for the lack of authority and evidence inherent in a merely mediated and derived knowledge of what is most immediate—real suffering. But this suffering originates in the oppressive social system as a whole and can therefore be elevated to knowledge only in abstract and mediated form. Spleen rebels against this. It draws up schemes for dialogues with Mr. Knownothing. They fail because social estrangement consists precisely in excluding the objects of knowledge from the sphere of immediate experience. The subject's loss of experience in a world dominated by 'more of the same', the premise of Veblen's entire theory, designates the anthropological side of the process of estrangement which since Hegel has been grasped in objective categories. Spleen is a defence mechanism. Always and everywhere, even as early as Baudelaire, its gesture is accusing. But it denounces society in its immediate manifestations and attributes society's guilt to its phenomena. The commensurability of knowledge and experience is purchased at the cost of the insufficiency of that knowledge. In this respect spleen resembles the petty bourgeois sect which attributes the world's downfall to a conspiracy and at the same time frankly admits the absurdity of that with which it is obsessed. When Veblen saddles a surface phenomenon like barbaric lavishness with total responsibility, the very disproportionality of his thesis becomes an element of its truth. It aims to shock. This expresses the incommensurability of this world and the potential experience of it. Knowledge accompanies itself with sardonic laughter over the fact that its actual object evades it as long as it remains human knowledge; only as inhuman knowledge would it be equal to the inhuman world. The sole avenue of intellectual communication between the objective system and subjective experience is the explosion which tears both apart and momentarily illuminates in its glare the figure they form together. Inasmuch as this kind of criticism pounces on barbarism at the nearest street corner instead of consoling itself in the realm of general concepts, it retains, in contrast to less naïve theory, before which it makes itself ridiculous, a memento of what began to be neglected with the conception of 'scientific socialism' and finally disappeared in what Karl Kraus called 'Moskauderwelsch', Bolshevik jargon. Narrowness is not only the complement to broadness; sometimes it is a wholesome antidote to the all too broad overview. As such, it justifies itself in Veblen. His spleen stems from his disgust with the official optimism of the spirit of progress, whose part he himself takes in so far as he swims with the stream of common sense.

Spleen dictates the particular character of Veblen's critique. It is one of disenchantment, of 'debunking'. Veblen eagerly follows a traditional procedure of the Enlightenment, that of exposing religion as a 'hoax of the clergy'. 'It is felt that the divinity must be of a peculiarly serene and leisurely habit of life. And whenever his local habitation is pictured in poetic imagery, for edification or in appeal to the devout fancy, the devout word-painter, as a matter of course, brings out before his auditors' imagination a throne with a profusion of the insignia of opulence and power, and surrounded by a great number of servitors. In the common run of such presentations of the celestial abodes, the office of this corps of servants is a vicarious leisure, their time and efforts being in great measure taken up with an industrially unproductive rehearsal of the meritorious characteristics and exploits of the divinity.' The manner in which the angels are blamed here for the unproductivity of their labour has something of secularized swearing, but also something of the joke which fizzles. The hardened man does not let himself be bothered by the slips, dreams, and neuroses of society. His humour is like that of the husband who forces his hysterical wife to do housework in order to drive those crazy ideas out of her head. While spleen stubbornly clings to the estranged world of things, making the treachery of objects responsible for the subject's misdeeds, the attitude of debunking is that of the person who does not let himself be taken in by the treachery of objects. He strips them of their ideological masks in order to be able to manipulate them better. His rage is directed against the damned swindle rather than against the bad state of affairs. It is no accident that the debunker's hate turns so readily against all mediating functions; swindle and mediation belong together. But thinking and mediation as well. The hatred of thought has its roots in debunking.[4] True criticism of barbarian culture, however, cannot be content with a barbaric denunciation of culture. It must recognize overt uncultured barbarism as the *telos* of that culture and reject it, but it cannot crudely proclaim the supremacy of barbarism over culture simply because barbarism has ceased to lie. Honesty as the triumph of horror echoes in formula-

[4] Consciously, Veblen is quite free of this hatred. But anti-intellectualism is objectively contained in his struggle against the intermediary functions of society as well as in his denunciation of 'higher learning'. In a debunker like Aldous Huxley it gains the upper hand. His work is largely the self-denunciation of the intellectual as a swindler in the name of an integrity which amounts to the glorification of nature. It is very possible that the narrowness of Veblen's theory can ultimately be explained through his inability to think through the problem of mediation. In his physiognomy the zealotry of the Scandinavian Lutheran, which admits no intermediary between God and inwardness, blindly prepared itself to enter the service of a social order which liquidates the mediations between the commanded production and the coerced consumers. The two attitudes, that of radical Protestantism and that of state capitalism, have anti-intellectualism in common.

tions like that about the industrial unproductivity of the heavenly hosts. Such jokes appeal to conformism. The person who laughs at the image of beatitude is closer to the powers that be than is the image, however distorted by power and glory it may be.

Nevertheless, there is a good and wholesome element in Veblen's insistence on the facts, in his tabooing of all images. In him the resistance to a barbaric life has migrated into the strength to adjust to the merciless necessity of that life. For the pragmatist of his type there is no whole, no identity of thinking and being, not even the notion of such an identity. He repeatedly comes back to the position that 'habits of thought' and the demands of the concrete situation are irreconcilable. 'Institutions are products of the past process, are adapted to past circumstances, and are therefore never in full accord with the requirements of the present. In the nature of the case, this process of selective adaptation can never catch up with the progressively changing situation in which the community finds itself at any given time; for the environment, the situation, the exigencies of life which enforce the adaptation and exercise the selection, change from day to day; and each successive situation of the community in its turn tends to obsolescence as soon as it has been established. When a step in the development has been taken, this step itself constitutes a change of situation which requires a new adaptation; it becomes the point of departure for a new step in the adjustment, and so on interminably.' Irreconcilability prohibits the abstract ideal or makes it appear a childish phrase. Truth can be reduced to the smallest step; what is true is what is nearest, not what is farthest. Against the demand to adopt the interest of the 'whole' as opposed to the particular interest, however it is understood, and thereby to transcend the utilitarian narrowness of truth, the pragmatist can rightly contend that the whole is not definitively given, that only the nearest can be experienced and that therefore the ideal is condemned to be fragmentary and uncertain. Against this argument it is not sufficient to invoke the distinction between the total interest of a good society and the limitations of practical utility. The existing society and the other society do not have two different kinds of truth; rather, truth in the latter is inseparable from the real movement within the existing order and each of its moments. Hence the contrast between dialectics and pragmatism, like every distinction in philosophy, is reduced to a nuance, namely, to the conception of that 'next step'. The pragmatist, however, defines it as adjustment, and this perpetuates the domination of what is always the same. Were dialectics to sanction this, it would renounce itself in renouncing the idea of potentiality. But how is potentiality to be conceived if it is not to be abstract and arbitrary, like the utopias dialectical philosophers proscribed? Conversely, how can the next step assume direction and aim without the subject knowing more than what is already given? If one chose to reformulate Kant's question, one could ask today: *how is anything new possible at all?* In the sharpening of this question resides the seriousness of the pragmatist, comparable to that of the physician whose readiness to help is conceived in terms of the similarity of man and animal. It is the seriousness of death. The dialectician, however, should be the one who is not resigned to this fate. For his position the either-or of discursive logic dissolves. Whereas for the pragmatist the bare facts remain 'opaque items', as which they cannot be comprehended but only classified, the dialectician sees himself confronted with the cognitive task of dissolving those phenomenal residues, the 'atoms', by means of the concept. Nothing, however, is more opaque than adjustment itself, which the imitation of mere existence installs as the criterion of truth. The pragmatist insists on the historical index of all truth, and his own idea of adjustment has such an index. It is what Freud called 'ananke'—scarcity. The next step is one of adjustment only as long as scarcity and poverty prevail in the world. Adjustment is the mode of behaviour which corresponds to the situation of 'too little'. Pragmatism is narrow and limited because it hypostasizes this situation as eternal. This is the significance of its concepts of nature and life. What it wants for man is 'identification with the life-process', a mode of behaviour that perpetuates the process by which living beings exist in nature as long as nature does not provide them with sufficient means of subsistence. Veblen's outbursts against the 'sheltered', whose privileged position allows them to a certain extent to avoid adjusting to a changed situation, amounts to a glorification of the Darwinian struggle for existence. It is nothing less than the hypostasis of scarcity, which in its social form has now been made obviously obsolete by the very technological development to which, according to Veblen's doctrine, human beings are supposed to adjust. Thus the pragmatist falls prey to dialectics. The only adequate response to the present technical situation, which holds out the promise of wealth and abundance to men, is to organize it according to the needs of a humanity which no longer needs violence because it is its own master. In one of the finest passages of his work, Veblen recognizes the connection between poverty and the persistence of the bad situation: 'The abjectly poor, and all those persons whose energies are entirely absorbed by the struggle for daily sustenance, are conservative because they cannot afford the effort of taking thought for the day after tomorrow; just as the highly prosperous are conservative because they have small occasion to be discontented with the situation as it stands today.' But the pragmatist, himself regressive, clings to the standpoint of those who cannot think beyond tomorrow, beyond the next step, because they do not know what they will live from tomorrow. He represents poverty. This is his truth, because men are still constrained to be poor, and his untruth, because the absurdity of poverty has become manifest. Today, adjustment to what is possible no longer means adjustment; it means making the possible real.

ALDOUS HUXLEY AND UTOPIA

One of the far-reaching effects of the European catastrophe was to create in America a social type which had never before existed there—the intellectual emigré. Those who came to the new world in the nineteenth century were lured by the unlimited possibilities it offered. They emigrated to make their fortunes or at least find enough to make ends meet, something they could not achieve in the overpopulated European countries. The interests of self-preservation were stronger than those of preserving the self, and the rapid economic growth of the United States took place under the aegis of the same principle that drove the emigrant across the ocean. The newcomer strove for successful adjustment; critical attitudes on his part might have compromised the prospects and the claim to legitimacy of his own efforts. Neither their backgrounds nor their position in the social process enabled the new arrivals to avoid being overpowered by the turbulent struggle for the maintenance of life. Any utopian hopes they might have attached to their resettlement took on a different character in the new context of the saga of struggling upwards, the horizon of a still uncharted existence, the prospect of advancing from dish-washer to millionaire. The skepticism of a visitor like De Tocqueville, who a century ago already perceived the element of unfreedom in unrestrained equality, remained the exception; opposition to what in the jargon of German cultural conservatism was called 'Americanism' was to be found in Americans like Poe, Emerson, and Thoreau rather than in the new arrivals. A hundred years later it was no longer individual intellectuals who emigrated but the European intelligentsia as a whole, by no means only the Jews. They sought not to live better but to survive; opportunities were no longer unlimited, and thus the necessity for adjustment which prevailed in the sphere of economic competition extended implacably to them. In place of the wilderness which the pioneer intended to open up spiritually as well as materially and through which he was to accomplish his spiritual regeneration, there has arisen a civilization which absorbs all of life in its

97

system, without allowing the unregimented mind even those loopholes which European laxness left open into the epoch of the great business concerns. It is made unmistakably clear to the intellectual from abroad that he will have to eradicate himself as an autonomous being if he hopes to achieve anything or be accepted as an employee of the super-trust into which life has condensed. The refractory individual who does not capitulate and completely toe the line is abandoned to the shocks which the world of things, concentrated into gigantic blocks, administers to whatever does not make itself into a thing. Impotent in the machinery of the universally developed commodity relation, which has become the supreme standard, the intellectual reacts to the shock with panic.

Huxley's *Brave New World* is a manifestation of this panic, or rather, its rationalization. The novel, a fantasy of the future with a rudimentary plot, endeavours to comprehend the shocks through the principle of the disenchanted world, to heighten this principle to absurdity, and to derive the idea of human dignity from the comprehension of inhumanity. The point of departure seems to be the perception of the universal similarity of everything mass-produced, things as well as human beings. Schopenhauer's metaphor of nature as a manufactured article is taken literally. Teeming herds of twins are prepared in test tubes: a nightmare of endless doubles like that which the most recent phase of capitalism has spawned into everyday life, from regulated smiles, the grace instilled by charm schools, to the standardized consciousness of millions which revolves in the grooves cut by the communications industry. The here and now of spontaneous experience, long corroded, is stripped of its power; men are no longer merely purchasers of the concerns' mass-produced consumption goods but rather appear themselves to be the deindividualized products of the corporations' absolute power. To the panicked eye, observations that resist assimilation petrify into allegories of catastrophe; it sees through the illusion of the harmlessness of everyday life. For it, the model's commercial smile becomes what it is, the contorted grin of the victim. The more than thirty years since the book's appearance have provided more than sufficient verification: small horrors such as the aptitude tests for elevator boys which detect the least intelligent, and visions of terror such as the rational utilization of corpses. If, in accordance with a thesis of Freud's *Group Psychology and Ego Analysis*, panic is the condition in which powerful collective identifications disintegrate and the released instinctual energy is transformed into raw anxiety, then the person seized by panic is capable of innervating the dark basis of the collective identification—the false consciousness of individuals who, without transparent solidarity and blindly subjected to images of power, believe themselves one with the whole whose ubiquity stifles them.

Huxley is free from the foolhardy sobriety which emerges from even the worst situations with a temporizing 'It's not all that bad'. He makes no concessions to the childish belief that the alleged excesses of technical civilization will be ironed out automatically through irresistible progress, and he scorns the consolation upon which exiles so readily seize: the notion that the frightening aspects of American civilization are ephemeral relics of its primitiveness or potent safeguards of its youth. We are not permitted to doubt that American civilization has not only not lagged behind that of Europe but has indeed forged ahead of it, while the Old World diligently emulates the New. Just as the world-state of *Brave New World* knows only artificially maintained differences between the golf courses and experimental stations of Mombasa, London, and the North Pole, Americanism, the butt of parody, has taken over the world. And that world supposedly resembles the utopia whose realization, as the epigraph from Berdyaev indicates, is foreseeable in the light of technology. But, by extension, it becomes hell; Huxley projects observations of the present state of civilization along the lines of its own teleology to the point where its monstrous nature becomes immediately evident. The emphasis is placed not so much on objective technological and institutional elements as on what becomes of human beings when they no longer know need. The economic and political sphere as such recedes in importance. It is stipulated only that there is a thoroughly rationalized class system on a planetary scale and totally planned state capitalism, that total domination goes along with total collectivization, and that a money economy and the profit motive persist.

'Community, Identity, and Stability' replaces the motto of the French Revolution. Community defines a collectivity in which each individual is unconditionally subordinated to the functioning of the whole (the question of the point of this whole is no longer permitted or even possible in the New World). Identity means the elimination of individual differences, standardization even down to biological constitution; stability, the end of all social dynamics. The artfully balanced situation is an extrapolation from certain indications of a reduction in the economic 'play of forces' in late capitalism—the perversion of the millenium. The panacea that guarantees social stasis is 'conditioning'. The expression is a product of biology and behaviouristic psychology, in which it signifies the evocation of particular reflexes or modes of behaviour through arbitrary

99

transformations in the environment, through control of the conditions; and it has made its way into colloquial American English as the designation for any kind of scientific control over the conditions of life, as in 'air-conditioning'. In *Brave New World* conditioning means the complete preformation of human beings through social intervention, from artificial breeding and technological direction of the conscious and unconscious mind in the earliest stages of life to 'death conditioning', a training that purges children of the horror of death by parading the dying before their eyes while they are being fed candy, which they then forever after associate with death. The ultimate effect of conditioning, which is in fact adjustment come into its own, is a degree of introjection and integration of social pressure and coercion far beyond that of the Protestant ethic; men resign themselves to loving what they have to do, without even being aware that they are resigned. Thus, their happiness is firmly established subjectively and order is maintained. Conceptions of a merely external influence of society upon individuals, through agencies like psychology or the family, are recognized to be obsolete. What today has already happened to the family is inflicted upon it once again in *Brave New World*, from above. As children of society in the literal sense, men no longer exist in dialectical opposition to society but rather are identical with it in their substance. Compliant exponents of the collective totality in which all antitheses have been absorbed, they are 'socially conditioned' in a non-metaphorical sense, not merely adjusted secondarily to the dominant system through 'development'.

The system of class relationships is made eternal and biological: directors of breeding assign each person to a caste designated by a Greek letter while he is still an embryo. Through an ingenious method of cell division, the common people are recruited from identical twins, whose physical and intellectual growth is stunted through an artificial addition of alcohol to the blood. That is, the reproduction of stupidity, which previously took place unconsciously under the dictates of material necessity, must be taken in hand by triumphant mass civilization now that scarcity could be eliminated. The rational fixation of irrational class relations indicates their superfluity. Today class lines have already lost their 'natural' character, an illusion created during the undirected history of mankind, so that classes can be perpetuated only through arbitrary selection and co-option, only through administrative differentiations in the distribution of the social product. By depriving lower-caste embryos and infants of oxygen in the Hatching and Conditioning Centres of *Brave New World*, the directors create an artificial slum atmosphere. In the midst of unlimited possibility they organize degradation and regression. Such regression, however, devised and automatically induced by the totalitarian system, is truly total. Huxley, who knows his way around, points out the signs of mutilation in the upper class as well: 'Even alphas have been conditioned.' Even the minds of those who credit themselves with being individuals are caught up in standardization by virtue of their identification with the 'in-group'. They automatically produce the judgments to which they have been conditioned, rather like the member of the present upper middle class who babbles that the real problem is not material circumstances but a religious regeneration or who insists that he cannot understand modern art. Non-comprehension becomes a virtue. Two lovers from the upper caste fly over the Channel in stormy weather, and the man wishes to delay the flight so as to escape from the crowds and be alone with his beloved for a longer time, closer to her and more himself. In response to her reluctance, he asks whether she understands his wish. ' "I don't understand anything," she said with decision, determined to preserve her incomprehension intact.' Huxley's observation does more than just point up the *rancune* that the statement of the most modest truth provokes in persons who can no longer allow such statements lest their equilibrium be disturbed. It diagnoses a powerful new taboo. The more the existing society, through its overwhelming power and hermetic structure, becomes its own ideological justification in the minds of the disillusioned, the more it brands as sinners all those whose thoughts blaspheme against the notion that what is, is right—just because it exists. They live in airplanes but heed the command, tacit like all genuine taboos, 'Thou shalt not fly'. The gods of the earth punish those who raise themselves above the earth. Avowedly anti-mythological, the pact with the existing order restores mythic power. Huxley demonstrates this in the speech of his characters. The idiocy of mandatory small talk, conversation as chatter, is discretely pursued to the extreme. The phenomenon has long since ceased to be a mere consequence of conventions intended to prevent conversation from becoming narrow shop talk or unabashed presumption. Rather, the degeneration of talk is due to objective tendencies. The virtual transformation of the world into commodities, the predetermination by the machinery of society of everything that is thought or done, renders speaking illusory; under the curse of perpetual sameness it disintegrates into a series of analytic judgments. The ladies of *Brave New World*—and in this case extrapolation is hardly required—converse only as consumers. In principle, their conversation concerns nothing but what is in any case to be found in the catalogues of the ubiquitous industries, information about available commodities. Objectively superfluous, it is the empty shell of dialogue, the intention of which was once to find out what was hitherto unknown. Stripped of this idea, dialogue is ripe for extinction. People completely collectivized and incessantly communicating might as well abandon all communication at once and acknowledge themselves to be the mute monads they have been surreptitiously since the beginnings of bourgeois society. They are swallowed up in archaic childlike dependency.

They are cut off both from the mind, which Huxley rather flatly equates with the products of traditional culture, exemplified by Shakespeare, and from nature as landscape, an image of creation unviolated by society. The opposition of mind and nature was the theme of bourgeois philosophy at its peak. In *Brave New World* they unite against a civilization which lays hands on everything and tolerates nothing which is not made in its own image. The union of mind and nature, conceived by idealist speculation as the supreme reconciliation, now becomes the absolute opposition to absolute reification. Mind, the spontaneous and autonomous synthesis achieved by consciousness, is possible only to the extent to which it is confronted by a sphere outside its grasp, something not categorically predetermined—'nature'. And nature is possible only to the extent to which mind knows itself as the opposite of reification, which it transcends instead of enthroning it as nature. Both are vanishing: Huxley is well acquainted with the latest-model average citizen who contemplates a bay as a tourist attraction while seated in his car listening to radio commercials. Not unrelated is hatred of things past. The mind itself seems a thing of the past, a ridiculous addition to the glorified facts, to the given, whatever it may be, and what is no longer around becomes bric-à-brac and rubbish. 'History is bunk,' an expression attributed to Ford, relegates to the junkpile everything not in line with the most recent methods of industrial production, including, ultimately, all continuity of life. Such reduction cripples men. Their inability to perceive or think anything unlike themselves, the inescapable self-sufficiency of their lives, the law of pure subjective functionalism—all result in pure desubjectivization. Purged of all myths, the scientifically manufactured subject-objects of the anti-*Weltgeist* are infantile. In line with mass culture, the half-involuntary, half-organized regressions of today finally turn into compulsory ordinances governing leisure time, the 'proper standard of infantile decorum', Hell's laughter at the Christian dictum, 'If you do not become as little children. . . .' The blame rests with the substitution of means for all ends. The cult of the instrument, cut off from every objective aim (in *Brave New World*, the implicit religion of today—the auto—becomes literal with Ford for Lord and the sign of the Model T for that of the cross), and the fetishistic love of gadgetry, both unmistakable lunatic traits ingrained in precisely those people who pride themselves on being practical and realistic, are elevated to the norm of life. But that substitution is also in force in areas of the *Brave New World* where freedom seems to have won out. Huxley has recognized the contradiction that in a society where sexual taboos have lost their intrinsic force and have either retreated before the permissibility of the prohibited or come to be enforced by external compulsion, pleasure itself degenerates to the misery of 'fun' and to an occasion for the narcissistic satisfaction of having 'had' this or that person. Through the institutionalization of promiscuity, sex becomes a matter of indifference, and even escape from society is relocated within its borders. Physiological release is desirable, as part of hygiene; accompanying feelings are dispensed with as a waste of energy without social utility. On no account is one to be moved. The original bourgeois *ataraxia* now extends to all reactions. In infecting eros it turns directly against what was once the highest good, subjective eudaemonia, for the sake of which purgation of the passions was originally demanded. In attacking ecstasy it strikes at all human relations, at every attempt to go beyond a monadological existence. Huxley recognizes the complementary relationship of collectivization and atomization.

His portrayal of organized orgiastics, however, has an undertone which casts doubt upon his satirical thesis. In its proclamation of the bourgeois nature of what claims to be unbourgeois, the thesis itself becomes ensnared in bourgeois habits. Huxley waxes indignant at the sobriety of his characters but is inwardly an enemy of intoxication, and not only that from narcotics, which he earlier condemned, thus endorsing the prevailing attitude. Like that of many emancipated Englishmen, his consciousness is preformed by the very Puritanism he abjures. He fails to distinguish between the liberation of sexuality and its debasement. In his earlier novels libertinism already appears, as it were, as a localized thrill without an aura—not unlike the way men in so-called 'masculine' cultures habitually speak of women and love with a gesture in which pride at having won the sovereignty that enables them to discuss such matters is inevitably mixed with contempt. In Huxley everything occurs on a more sublimated level than in the Lawrence of the four-letter words, but everything is also more thoroughly repressed. His anger at false happiness sacrifices the idea of true happiness as well. Long before he acknowledged Buddhist sympathies, his irony displayed, especially in the self-denunciation of the intellectual, something of the sectarianism of the raging penitent, a quality to which his writing is usually immune. The flight from the world leads to the nudist colony, which destroys sexuality by overexposure. Despite the pains Huxley takes to depict the pre-mass-civilization world of the Savage (who is brought to the Brave New World as a relic of humanity), as being distorted, repellent, and insane in its own way, reactionary elements find their way into his portrayal. Freud is included among the anathematized figures of modernity, and at one point he is equated with Ford. He is made a mere efficiency expert of the inner life. With all too genial scorn he is credited with having been the first to discover 'the appalling dangers of family life'. But this is in fact what he did, and historical justice is on his side. The critique of the family as the agent of oppression, a theme familiar to the English opposition since Samuel Butler, emerged just at the time when the family had lost its economic basis and, with it, its last legitimate right to determine human development, becoming a neutralized monstrosity of the sort Huxley so incisively exposes in the sphere of official religion. Huxley ascribes to the world of the future the encouragement of infantile sexuality, in complete misunderstanding, incidentally, of Freud, who all too orthodoxly adhered to instinctual renunciation as a pedagogical aim. But Huxley himself sides with those who are less concerned with the dehumanization of the industrial age than with the decline of its morals. Whether happiness is dependent upon the existence of prohibitions to be broken is an endless dialectical question, but the novel's mentality distorts the question into an affirmative answer, into an excuse for the perpetuation of obsolete taboos—as if the happiness produced by the transgression of taboos could ever legitimate the taboo, which exists not for the sake of happiness but for its frustration. It is true that the regularly occurring communal orgies of the novel and the prescribed short-term change of partners are logical consequences of the jaded official sexual routine that turns pleasure to fun and denies it by granting it. But precisely in the impossibility of looking pleasure in the eye, of making use of reflection in abandoning one's whole self to pleasure, the ancient prohibition for which Huxley prematurely mourns continues in force. Were its power to be broken, were pleasure to be freed of the institutional reins which bind it even in the 'orgy-porgy', Brave New World and its fatal rigidity would dissolve. Its highest moral principle, supposedly, is that everyone belongs to everyone, an absolute interchangeability that extinguishes man as an individual being, liquidates as mythology his claim to exist for his own sake, and defines him as existing merely for the sake of others and thus, in Huxley's mind, as worthless. In the foreword he wrote after the war for the American edition, Huxley claimed, as the ancestor of this principle, de Sade's statement that the rights of man include the absolute sexual disposition of all over all. In this, Huxley sees the foolishness of consequent reasoning consummated. But he fails to see that the heretical maxim is incompatible with his world-state of the future. All dictators have proscribed libertinage, and Himmler's much cited SS-studs were its piously patriotic opposite. Domination may be defined as the disposition of one over others but not as the complete disposition of all over all, which cannot be reconciled with a totalitarian order. This is even more true of work relations than of sexual anarchy. A man who existed only for the sake of others, an absolute ζῶον Πολιτικον, would, to be sure, have lost his individual self, but he would also have escaped the cycle of self-preservation which maintains the Brave New World as well as the old one. Pure fungibility would destroy the core of domination and promise freedom. The weakness of Huxley's entire conception is that it makes all its concepts relentlessly dynamic but nevertheless arms them against the tendency to turn into their own opposites.

The *scène à faire* of the novel is the erotic collision of the two 'worlds': the attempt of the heroine, Lenina, a well-groomed and polished American career woman, to seduce the Savage, who loves her, in a way consonant with the mores of the conscientiously promiscuous. Her opponent belongs to the type of shy, aesthetic youth, tied to his mother and inhibited, who prefers to enjoy his feeling through contemplation rather than expression and who finds satisfaction in the lyrical transfiguration of the beloved. This type, incidentally, is bred at Oxford and Cambridge no less than are Epsilons in test tubes, and it belongs to the sentimental standbys of the modern English novel. The conflict arises from the fact that John feels the pretty girl's matter-of-fact abandonment to be a debasement of his sublime passion for her and runs away. The effectiveness of the scene works against its thesis. Lenina's artificial charm and cellophane shamelessness produce by no means the unerotic effect Huxley intended, but rather a highly seductive one, to which even the infuriated cultural savage succumbs at the end of the novel. Were Lenina the imago of Brave New World, it would lose its horror. Each of her gestures, it is true, is socially preformed, part of a conventional ritual. But because she is at one with convention down to her very core, the tension between the conventional and the natural dissolves, and with it the violence in which the injustice of convention consists; psychologically, poor conventionality is always the mark of unsuccessful identification. The concept of convention does not survive its opposite. Through total social mediation, from the outside, as it were, a new immediacy, a new humanity, would arise. American civilization shows no lack of tendencies in this direction. But Huxley construes humanity and reification as rigid opposites, in accordance with the tradition of the novel, which has as its object the conflict of human beings with rigidified conditions. Huxley cannot understand the humane promise of civilization because he forgets that humanity includes reification as well as its opposite, not merely as the condition from which liberation is possible but also positively, as the form in which, however brittle and inadequate it may be, subjective impulses are realized, but only by being objectified. All the categories examined by the novel, family, parents, the individual and his property, are already products of reification. Huxley curses the future with it, without realizing that the past whose blessing he invokes is of the same nature. Thus he unwittingly becomes the spokesman of that nostalgia whose affinity to mass culture his physiognomic eye so acutely perceives in the test-tube song: 'Bottle of mine, it's you I've always wanted! Bottle of mine, why was I ever decanted?. . . There ain't no Bottle in all the world Like that dear little Bottle of mine.'

The Savage's outburst against his beloved, then, is not so much the protest of pure human nature against the cold impudence of fashion, as was perhaps intended; rather, poetic justice turns it into the aggression of the neurotic who, as the Freud whom Huxley treats rather shabbily could easily have told him, is motivated in his frantic purity by repressed homosexuality. He shouts abuse at the girl like the hypocrite who trembles with rage at things he has to forbid himself. By putting him in the wrong, Huxley distances himself from social criticism. Its actual advocate in the novel is Bernard Marx, an Alpha-Plus who rebels against his own conditioning, a skeptically compassionate caricature of a Jew. Huxley is well aware that Jews are persecuted because they are not completely assimilated and that precisely for this reason their consciousness occasionally reaches beyond the social system. He does not question the authenticity of Bernard's critical insight. But the insight itself is attributed to a sort of organic inferiority, the inevitable inferiority complex. At the same time, following the time-honoured model, Huxley charges the radical Jewish intellectual with vulgar snobbism and, ultimately, with reprehensible moral cowardice. Ever since Ibsen's invention of Gregers Werle and Stockmann, actually since Hegel's philosophy of history, bourgeois cultural politics, claiming to survey and speak for the whole, has sought to unmask anyone who seeks to change things as both the genuine child and the perverse product of the whole which he opposes, and has insisted that the truth is always on the side of the whole, be it against him or present in him. As novelist, Huxley proclaims his solidarity with this tradition; as prophet of civilization, he detests the totality. It is true that Gregers Werle destroys those he seeks to save, and no one is free from the vanity of Bernard Marx who, in raising himself above the general stupidity, thereby imagines himself untainted by it. But the view which evaluates phenomena externally, in a detached, free, superior way, deeming itself above the limitations of negation and the arbitration of the dialectic, is for this very reason neither one of truth nor one of justice. A just reflection should not delight in the inadequacy of things which are better in order to compromise them before things which are worse, but should draw from inadequacy additional strength for indignation. The forces of negativity are underestimated in order to render them impotent. But it befits this position that what is set up as positive and absolute against the dialectic is no less powerless. When, in his crucial conversation with the World Controller Mond, the Savage declares, 'What you need is something with tears for a change,' his deliberately insolent exaltation of suffering is not merely a characteristic of the obdurate individualist. It evokes Christian metaphysics, which promises future salvation solely by virtue of suffering. But, despite all appearances to the contrary, the novel is informed by an enlightened consciousness in which Christian metaphysics no longer dares to assert itself. Hence the cult of suffering becomes an absurd end in itself. It is a mannerism of an aestheticism whose ties to the powers of darkness cannot be unknown to Huxley; Nietzsche's 'Live dangerously', which the Savage proclaims to the resigned, hedonistic World Controller, was a perfect slogan for the totalitarian Mussolini, himself a World Controller of a similar sort.

In a discussion of a biological paper which the World Controller has suppressed, the all too positive core of the novel becomes clearly visible. It is 'the sort of idea that might easily de-condition the more unsettled minds among the higher castes—make them lose their faith in happiness as the Sovereign Good and take to believing instead, that the goal was somewhere beyond, somewhere outside the present human sphere; that the purpose of life was not the maintenance of well-being, but some intensification and refinement of consciousness, some enlargement of knowledge'. However pallid and diluted or cleverly prudent the formulation of the ideal may be, it still does not escape contradiction. 'Intensification and refinement of consciousness' or 'enlargement of knowledge' flatly hypostatize the mind in opposition to praxis and the fulfilment of material needs. For mind by its very nature presupposes the life-process of society and especially the division of labour, and all mental and spiritual contents are intentionally related to concrete existence for their 'fulfilment'. Consequently, setting the mind in an unconditional and atemporal opposition to material needs amounts to perpetuating ideologically this form of the division of labour and of society. Nothing intellectual was ever conceived, not even the most escapist dream, whose objective content did not include the transformation of material reality. No emotion, no part of the inner life ever existed that did not ultimately intend something external or degenerate into untruth, mere appearance, without this intention, however sublimated. Even the selfless passion of Romeo and Juliet, which Huxley considers something like a 'value', does not exist autarchically, for its own sake, but becomes spiritual and more than mere histrionics of the soul only in pointing beyond the mind towards physical union. Huxley unwittingly reveals this in portraying their longing, the whole meaning of which is union. 'It was the nightingale and not the lark' is inseparable from the symbolism of sex. To glorify the aubade for the sake of its transcendent quality without hearing in the transcendence itself its inability to rest, its desire to be gratified, would be as meaningless as the physiologically delimited sexuality of *Brave New World*, which destroys any magic which cannot be conserved as an end in itself. The disgrace of the present is not the preponderance of so-called material culture over the spiritual—in this complaint Huxley would find unwelcome allies, the Arch-Community-Songsters of all neutralized denominations and world views. What must be attacked is the socially dictated separation of consciousness from the social realization its essence requires. Precisely the *chorismos* of the spiritual and the material which Huxley's *philosophia perennis* establishes, the substitution of an indeterminable, abstract 'goal somewhere beyond' for 'faith in happiness', strengthens the reified situation Huxley cannot tolerate: the neutralization of a culture cut off from the material process of production. 'If a distinction between material and ideal needs is drawn,' as Max Horkheimer once put it, 'there is no doubt that the fulfilment of material needs must be given priority, for this fulfilment also involves ... social change. It includes, as it were, the just society, which provides all human beings with the best possible living conditions. This is identical with the final elimination of the evil of domination. To emphasize the isolated, ideal demand, however, leads to real nonsense. The right to nostalgia, to transcendental knowledge, to a dangerous life cannot be validated. The struggle against mass culture can consist only in pointing out its connection with the persistence of social injustice. It is ridiculous to reproach chewing gum for diminishing the propensity for metaphysics, but it could probably be shown that Wrigley's profits and his Chicago palace have their roots in the social function of reconciling people to bad conditions and thus diverting them from criticism. It is not that chewing gum undermines metaphysics but that it *is* metaphysics—this is what must be made clear. We criticize mass culture not because it gives men too much or makes their life too secure—that we may leave to Lutheran theology—but rather because it contributes to a condition in which men get too little and what they get is bad, a condition in which whole strata inside and out live in frightful poverty, in which men come to terms with injustice, in which the world is kept in a condition where one must expect on the one hand gigantic catastrophes and on the other clever elites conspiring to bring about a dubious peace.' As a counterweight to the sphere of the satisfaction of needs, Huxley posits another, suspiciously similar to the one the bourgeoisie generally designates as that of the 'higher things'. He proceeds from an invariant, as it were biological concept of need. But in its concrete form every human need is historically mediated. The static quality which needs appear to have assumed today, their fixation upon the reproduction of the eternally unchanging, merely reflects the character of production, which becomes stationary when existing property relations persist despite the elimination of the market and competition. When this static situation comes to an end needs will look completely different. If production is redirected towards the unconditional and unlimited satisfaction of needs, including precisely those produced by the hitherto prevailing system, needs themselves will be decisively altered. The indistinguishability of true and false needs is an essential part of the present phase. In it the reproduction of life and its suppression form a unity which is intelligible as the law of the whole but not in its individual manifestations. One day it will be readily apparent that men do not need the trash provided them by the culture industry or the miserable high-quality goods proffered by the more substantial industries. The thought, for instance, that in addition to food and lodging the cinema is necessary for the reproduction of labour power is 'true' only in a world which prepares men for the reproduction of their labour power and constrains their needs in harmony with the interests of supply and social control. The idea that an emancipated society would crave the poor histrionics of Lametta or the poor soups of Devory is absurd. The better the soups, the more pleasant the renunciation of Lametta. Once scarcity has disappeared, the relationship of need to satisfaction will change. Today the compulsion to produce for needs mediated and petrified by the market is one of the chief means of keeping everyone on the job. Nothing may be thought, written, done, or made that transcends a condition which maintains its power largely through the needs of its victims. It is inconceivable that the compulsion to satisfy needs would remain a fetter in a changed society. The present form of society has in large measure denied satisfaction to the needs inherent in it and has thus been able to keep production in its control by pointing to these very needs. The system is as practical as it is irrational. An order which does away with the irrationality in which commodity production is entangled but also satisfies needs will equally do away with the practical spirit, which is reflected even in the non-utilitarianism of bourgeois *l'art pour l'art*. It would abolish not merely the traditional antagonism between production and consumption but also its most recent unification in state capitalism, and it would converge with the idea that, in the words of Karl Kraus, 'God created man not as consumer or producer but as man'. For something to be useless would no longer be shameful. Adjustment would lose its meaning. For the first time, productivity would have an effect on need in a genuine and not a distorted sense. It would not allay unsatisfied needs with useless things; rather, satisfaction would engender the ability to relate to the world without subordination to the principle of universal utility.

In his critique of false needs Huxley preserves the idea of the objectivity of happiness. The mechanical repetition of the phrase, 'Everybody's happy now,' becomes the most extreme accusation. When men are products of an order based on denial and deception, and that order implants imaginary needs in them, then the happiness which is defined by the satisfaction of such needs is truly bad. It is a mere appendage of the social machinery. In a totally integrated world which does not tolerate sorrow, the command from Romans (xii.15), 'Weep with the weeping,' is more valid than ever, but 'Be joyous with the joyful' has become a gory mockery —the job the order permits the ordered feeds on the perpetuation of misery. Hence the mere rejection of false happiness has a subversive effect. Lenina's reaction when the Savage finds an idiotic film obnoxious, 'Why did he go out of his way to spoil things?' is a typical manifestation of a dense network of deception. 'One shouldn't spoil it for the others' has always been one of the stock maxims of those who spoil it for the others. But at the same time the description of Lenina's irritation provides the basis for a criticism of Huxley's own attitude. He believes that by demonstrating the worthlessness of subjective happiness according to the criteria of traditional culture he has shown that happiness as such is worthless. Its place is to be taken by an ontology distilled from traditional religion and philosophy, according to which happiness and the objective good are irreconcilable. A society which wants nothing but happiness, according to Huxley, moves inexorably into insanity, into mechanized bestiality. But Lenina's overzealous defensiveness betrays insecurity, the suspicion that her kind of happiness is distorted by contradictions, that it is not happiness even by its own definition. No pharisaical recollection of Shakespeare is necessary to become aware of the fatuousness of the feelies and of the 'objective despair' of the audience which participates in it. That the essence of the film lies in merely duplicating and reinforcing what already exists, that it is glaringly superfluous and senseless even in a leisure restricted to infantility, that its duplicative realism is incompatible with its claim to be an aesthetic image—all this can be seen in the film itself, without recourse to dogmatically cited *vérités éternelles*. The holes in the vicious circles which Huxley draws with so much care are due not to inadequacies in his imaginative construction but to the conception of a happiness subjectively consummate but objectively absurd. If his critique of subjective happiness is valid, then his idea of a hypostatized objective happiness removed from the claims of humanity must be ideological. The source of untruth is the separation of subjective and objective, which has been reified to a rigid alternative. Mustapha Mond, the *raisonneur* and devil's advocate of the book, who embodies the most articulate self-consciousness of *Brave New World*, formulates the alternative. To the Savage's protest that man is degraded by total civilization he replies, 'Degrade him from what position? As a happy, hard-working, goods-consuming citizen he's perfect. Of course, if you choose some other standard than ours, then perhaps you might say he was degraded. But you've got to stick to one set of postulates.' In this image of the two sets of postulates, exhibited like finished products between which one must choose, relativism is apparent. The question of truth dissolves into an 'if-then' relation. Similarly, isolated by Huxley, the values of death and interiority fall prey to pragmatization. The Savage reports that he once stood on a cliff with outstretched arms in burning heat in order to feel what it was like to be crucified. Asked for an explanation, he gives the curious answer: 'Because I felt I ought to. If Jesus could stand it, and then, if one has done something wrong... Besides, I was unhappy, that was another reason.' If the Savage can find no other justification for his religious adventure, the choice of suffering, than the fact that he has suffered, he can hardly contradict his interviewer, who argues that it is more reasonable to take *Soma*, the euphoria-producing cure-all drug, to dissolve one's depressions. Irrationally hypostatized, the world of ideas is demoted to the level of mere existence. In this form, it continually demands justification according to merely empirical norms and is prescribed for the sake of precisely that happiness which it is supposed to negate.

The crude alternative of objective meaning and subjective happiness, conceived as mutually exclusive, is the philosophical basis for the reactionary character of the novel. The choice is between the barbarism of happiness and culture as the objectively higher condition that entails unhappiness. 'The progressive domination of nature and society,' Herbert Marcuse argues, 'does away with all transcendence, physical as well as psychical. Culture, the all-embracing title for one side of the opposition, subsists upon lack of fulfilment, longing, faith, pain, hope, in short, on that which does not exist but leaves its mark in reality. That means, however, that culture exists on the basis of unhappiness.' The kernel of the controversy is the hard and fast disjunction that one cannot be had without the other, technology without death conditioning, progress without manipulated infantile regression. However, the honesty of the thought expressed in the disjunction is to be distinguished from the moral constraint of ideology. Today, only conformism could acquiesce in considering objective insanity to be a mere accident of historical development, for retrogression is essential to the consistent development of domination. Theory is not free to choose good-naturedly that which suits it in the course of history and to omit the rest. Attempts to come up with a *Weltanschauung* which takes a 'positive atittude' to technology but advocates that it ought to be given meaning provide shallow comfort and serve merely to reinforce an affirmative work morale which is itself highly questionable. Nevertheless, the pressure that *Brave New World* exerts on everyone and everything is conceptually incompatible with the deathlike stasis that makes it a nightmare. It is no accident that all the major figures in the novel, even Lenina, show signs of subjective derangement. The alternative is false. The perfectly self-contained state which Huxley depicts with such grim satisfaction transcends itself not by virtue of an ineffective melange of desirable and reprehensible elements brought in from the outside, but by virtue of its objective nature. Huxley is aware that historical tendencies realize themselves behind men's backs. For him the essential tendency is the self-estrangement and perfected externalization of the subject, which makes itself into a mere means in the absence of any end whatsoever. But he makes a fetish of the fetishism of commodities. In his eyes the character of commodities becomes ontic and self-subsistent, and he capitulates to this apparition instead of seeing through it as a mere form of consciousness, false consciousness which would dissolve with the elimination of it economic basis. Huxley does not admit that the phantasmagoric inhumanity of *Brave New World* is actually a relation between human beings, a relation of social labour which is not aware of its own nature— that the totally reified man is one who has been blinded to himself. Instead, he pursues in succession various unanalysed surface phenomena, such as 'the conflict between men and machine'. Huxley indicts technology for something which does not, as he believes (and in this he follows the tradition of romantic philistinism), lie in its essential nature, which is the abolition of labour. It is rather a result of the involvement of technology in the social relations of production; this insight, moreover, is implicit throughout the novel. Even the incompatibility of art and mass production today does not originate in technology as such but rather in the need of these irrationally persisting social relations to maintain the claim to individuation (in Benjamin's words, an 'aura') which is only honoured in the breach. Even the process for which Huxley censures technology, the displacement of ends by means to the point where the latter becomes completely independent of the former, does not necessarily eliminate ends. Precisely in art,[1] where consciousness makes use of unconscious channels, blind play with means can posit and unfold ends. The relation of means and ends, of humanity and technology, cannot be regulated through ontological priorities. Huxley's alternative amounts to the proposition that mankind should not extricate itself from the calamity. Humanity is

[1] Schumann writes somewhere that in his youth he devoted his attention to his instrument, the piano—the means, whereas in his maturity his interest was purely in music—the end. But the unquestionable superiority of his early works to his late ones cannot be divorced from the incessantly productive imaginative richness of his use of the piano, which produces the chiaroscuro, the broken harmonic colour, indeed the density of the compositional structure. Artists do not realize 'the idea' merely by themselves; it is far more the result of technological achievements, often of aimless play.

placed before the choice between regression to a mythology questionable even to Huxley and progress towards total unfreedom of consciousness. No room is left for a concept of mankind that would resist absorption into the collective coercion of the system and reduction to the status of contingent individuals. The very construction which simultaneously denounces the totalitarian world-state and glorifies retrospectively the individualism that brought it about becomes itself totalitarian. In that it leaves no escape open, this conception itself implies the thing that horrifies Huxley, the liquidation of everything that is not assimilated. The practical consequence of the bourgeois 'Nothing to be done', which resounds as the novel's echo, is precisely the perfidious 'You must adjust' of the totalitarian Brave New World. The monolithic trend and the linear concept of progress, as handled in the novel, derive from the restricted form in which the productive forces developed in 'pre-history'. The inevitable character of the negative utopia arises from projecting the limitations imposed by the relations of production (the enthronement of the productive apparatus for the sake of profit) as properties of the human and technical productive forces *per se*. In prophesying the entropy of history, Huxley succumbs to an illusion which is necessarily propagated by the society against which he so zealously protests.

Huxley criticizes the positivistic spirit. But because his criticism confines itself to shocks, while remaining immersed in the immediacy of experience and merely registering social illusions as facts, Huxley himself becomes a positivist. Despite his critical tone, he is in basic agreement with descriptively oriented cultural criticism, which, in lamenting the inexorable decline of culture, provides a pretext for the strengthening of domination. In the name of culture, civilization marches into barbarism. Instead of antagonisms, Huxley envisages something like an intrinsically non-self-contradictory total subject of technological reason, and correspondingly, a simplistic total development. Such conceptions belong to the currently fashionable ideas of 'universal history' and 'style of life' which are part of the cultural façade. Although he gives an incisive physiognomy of total unification, he fails to decipher its symptoms as expressions of an antagonistic essence, the pressure of domination, in which the tendency to totalization is inherent. Huxley expresses scorn for the phrase, 'Everybody's happy nowadays'. But the essense of his conception of history, which is better revealed by its form than by the events which make up its content, is profoundly harmonious. His notion of uninterrupted progress is distinguished from the liberalist idea only in emphasis, not through objective insight. Like a Benthamite liberal, Huxley foresees a development to the greatest happiness of the greatest number, but it discomfits him. He condemns *Brave New World* with the same common sense whose prevalence there he mocks. Hence, throughout the novel there emerge unanalysed elements of that worn-out *Weltanschauung* which Huxley deplores. The worthlessness of the ephemeral and the catastrophic nature of history are contrasted to that which never changes—the *philosophia perennis*, the eternal sunshine of the heavenly realm of ideas. Accordingly, exteriority and interiority move into a primitive antithesis: men are the mere objects of all evil, from artificial insemination to galloping senility, while the category of the individual stands forth with unquestioned dignity. Unreflective individualism asserts itself as though the horror which transfixes the novel were not itself the monstrous offspring of individualist society. The spontaneity of the individual human being is eliminated from the historical process while the concept of the individual is detached from history an dincoporated into the *philosophia perennis*. Individuation, which is essentially social, reverts to the immutability of nature. Its implication in the network of guilt was discerned by bourgeois philosophy at its zenith, but this insight has been replaced by the empirical levelling of the individual through psychologism. In the wake of a tradition whose predominance provokes resistance more readily than it invites respect, the individual is immeasurably exalted as an idea while each individual person is convicted of moral bankruptcy by the epigones of disillusioned romanticism. The socially valid recognition of the nullity of the individual turns into an accusation levelled against the overburdened private individual. Huxley's book, like his entire work, blames the hypostatized individual for his fungibility and his existence as a 'character mask' of society rather than as a real self. These facts are attributed to the individual's inauthenticity, hypocrisy, and narrow egoism, in short, to all those traits which are the stock-in-trade of a subtle, descriptive ego psychology. For Huxley, in the authentic bourgeois spirit, the individual is both everything—because once upon a time he was the basis of a system of property rights—and nothing, because, as a mere property owner, he is absolutely replaceable. This is the price which the ideology of individualism must pay for its own untruth. The novel's *fabula docet* is more nihilistic than is acceptable to the humanity which it proclaims.

Here, however, Huxley does not do justice to the very facts on which he puts his positivistic emphasis. *Brave New World* shares with all fully worked-out utopias the character of vanity. Things have developed differently and will continue to do so. It is not the accuracy of imagination which fails. Rather the very attempt to see into the distant future in order to puzzle out the concrete form of the non-existent is beset with the impotence of presumption. The antithetical component of the dialectic cannot be conjured away syllogistically, for example by means of the general concept of enlightenment. Such an approach eliminates the very material which provides the moving force of the dialectic—those elements that are external to the subject and are not already 'spiritual' and transparent. No matter how well equipped technologically and materially, no matter how correct from a scientific point of view the fully drawn utopia may be, the very undertaking is a regression to a philosophy of identity, to idealism. Hence the ironic 'accuracy' for which Huxley's extrapolations strive does his utopia no service. For however surely the unselfconscious concept of total enlightenment may move towards its opposite, irrationality, it is nevertheless impossible to deduce from the concept itself whether this will occur and if so, whether it will stop there. The looming political catastrophe can hardly fail to modify the escape route of technical civilization. *Ape and Essence* is a somewhat hasty attempt to correct a mistake which derives not from insufficient knowledge of atomic physics but from a linear conception of history, a mistake which thus cannot be corrected by the elaboration of additional material. Where the plausibility of *Brave New World's* prognoses was oversimplified, those of Huxley's second book dealing with the future bear the stigma of improbability (as, for instance, the devil cult). These characteristics can scarcely be defended in the midst of a novel which is realistic in style by allusions to philosophical allegory. But the ideological bias of the conception revenges itself in this inevitability of error. There is an unwitting resemblance to the member of the upper middle class who solemnly insists that it is not in his own interest but in that of all mankind that he advocates the continuance of a profit economy. Men are not yet ready for socialism, the argument runs; if they no longer had to work, they wouldn't know what to do with their time. Such platitudes are not only compromised by the usage to which they are put; they are also completely devoid of truth, since they both reify 'men' in general and hypostatize the observer as a disinterested judge. But this coldness is deeply embedded in Huxley's conceptual framework. Full of fictitious concern for the calamity that a realized utopia could inflict on mankind, he refuses to take note of the real and far more urgent calamity that prevents the utopia from being realized. It is idle to bemoan what will become of men when hunger and distress have disappeared from the world. For although Huxley can find nothing more to criticize in this civilization than the boredom of a never-never land which is in principle unattainable anyway, it is by virtue of the logic of this civilization that the world is subject to hunger and distress. All his indignation at the calamitous state of things nothwithstanding, the basis of Huxley's attitude is a conception of a history which takes its time. Time is made responsible for that which men must accomplish. The relation to time is parasitical. The novel shifts guilt for the present to the generations of the future. This reflects the ominous 'It shall not be otherwise' which is the end-product of the basic Protestant amalgamation of introspection and repression. Because mankind, tainted with original sin, is not capable of anything better in this world, the bettering of the world is made a sin. But the novel does not draw its life from the blood of the unborn. Despite many ingenuities of execution, it fails because of a basic weakness—an empty schematism. Because the transformation of men is not subject to calculation and evades the anticipating imagination, it is replaced by a caricature of the men of today, in the ancient and much abused manner of satire. The fiction of the future bows before the omnipotence of the present; that which does not yet exist is made comic through its resemblance to that which already is, like the gods in Offenbach operettas. The image of the most remote is replaced by a vision of that which is closest to hand, seen through inverted binoculars. The formal trick of reporting future events as though they had already happened endows their content with a repulsive complicity. The grotesqueness that the present assumes when confronted with its own projection into the future provokes the same laughs as naturalistic representations with enlarged heads. The pathetic notion of the 'eternally human' resigns itself to the less humane one of the normal man of yesterday, today, and tomorrow. It is not for its contemplative aspect as such, which it shares with all philosophy and representation, that the novel is to be criticized, but for its failure to contemplate a praxis which could explode the infamous continuum. Man's choice is not between individualism and a totalitarian world-state. If the great historical perspective is to be anything more than the *Fata Morgana* of the eye which surveys only to control, it must open on to the question of whether society will come to determine itself or bring about terrestrial catastrophe.

PERENNIAL FASHION—JAZZ

1

For almost fifty years, since 1914 when the contagious enthusiasm for it broke out in America, jazz has maintained its place as a mass phenomenon. Its method, all declarations of propagandistic historians notwithstanding, has remained essentially unchanged; its prehistory dates back to certain songs from the first half of the nineteenth century, such as 'Turkey in the Straw' and 'Old Zip Coon'. Jazz is music which fuses the most rudimentary melodic, harmonic, metric and formal structure with the ostensibly disruptive principle of syncopation, yet without ever really disturbing the crude unity of the basic rhythm, the identically sustained metre, the quarter-note. This is not to say that nothing has happened in jazz. The monochromatic piano has been forced to cede the dominant role it played during the ragtime period to small ensembles, generally winds. The wild antics of the first jazz bands from the South, New Orleans above all, and those from Chicago, have been toned down with the growth of commercialization and of the audience, and continued scholarly efforts to recover some of this original animation, whether called 'swing' or 'bebop', inexorably succumb to commercial requirements and quickly lose their sting. The syncopation principle, which at first had to call attention to itself by exaggeration, has in the meantime become so self-evident that it no longer needs to accentuate the weak beats as was formally required. Anyone still using such accents today is derided as 'corny', as out-of-date as 1927 evening dress. Contrariness has changed into second-degree 'smoothness' and the jazz-form of reaction has become so entrenched that an entire generation of youth hears only syncopations without being aware of the original conflict between it and the basic metre. Yet none of this alters the fact that jazz has in its essence remained static, nor does it explain the resulting enigma that millions of people seem never to tire of its monotonous attraction. Winthrop Sargeant, internationally known today as the art editor of *Life* magazine, is responsible for the best, most reliable and most sensible book on the subject; twenty-five years ago he wrote that jazz was in no way a new musical idiom but rather, 'even in its most complex manifestations a very elementary matter of incessantly repeated formulae'. This kind of unbiased observation seems possible only in America; in Europe, where jazz has not yet become an everyday phenomenon, there is the tendency, especially among those devotees who have adopted it as a *Weltanschauung*, to regard it falsely as a break-through of original, untrammelled nature, as a triumph over the musty museum-culture. However little doubt there can be regarding the African elements in jazz, it is no less certain that everything unruly in it was from the very beginning integrated into a strict scheme, that its rebellious gestures are accompanied by the tendency to blind obeisance, much like the sado-masochistic type described by analytic psychology, the person who chafes against the father-figure while secretly admiring him, who seeks to emulate him and in turn derives enjoyment from the subordination he overtly detests. This propensity accelerates the standardization, commercialization and rigidification of the medium. It is not as though scurrilous businessmen have corrupted the voice of nature by attacking it from without; jazz takes care of this all by itself. The abuse of jazz is not the external calamity in whose name the puristic defenders of 'real' unadulterated jazz furiously protest; such misuse originates in jazz itself. The Negro spirituals, antecedents of the blues, were slave songs and as such combined the lament of unfreedom with its oppressed confirmation. Moreover, it is difficult to isolate the authentic Negro elements in jazz. The white *lumpenproletariat* also participated in its prehistory, during the period preceding its thrust into the spotlight of a society which seemed to be waiting for it and which had long been familiar with its impulses through the cakewalk and tap dancing.

It is precisely this paltry stock of procedures and characteristics, however, the rigorous exclusion of every unregimented impulse, which makes the durability of this 'speciality'—one which accepts change only when forced to, and then generally only to suit the demands of advertising—so difficult to grasp. For the fact remains that jazz has established itself for a short eternity in the midst of a phase which is otherwise anything but static, and that it displays not the slightest inclination to relinquish any portion of its monopoly but instead only the tendency to adapt itself to the ear of the listener, no matter whether highly trained or undifferentiated. Yet for all of that it has not become any less fashionable. For almost fifty years the productions of jazz have remained as ephemeral as seasonal styles. Jazz is a form of manneristic interpretation. As with fashions what is important is show, not the thing itself; instead of jazz itself being composed, 'light' music, the most dismal products of the popular-song industry, is dressed up. Jazz fans, short for fanatics, sense this and therefore prefer to emphasize the music's improvisational features. But these are mere frills. Any precocious American teenager knows that the routine today scarcely leaves any room for improvisation, and that what appears as spontaneity is in fact carefully planned out in advance with machinelike precision. But even where there is real improvisation, in oppositional groups which perhaps even today still indulge in such things out of sheer pleasure, the sole material remains popular songs. Thus, the so-called improvisations are actually reduced to the more or less feeble rehashing of basic formulas in which the schema shines through at every moment. Even the improvisations conform largely to norms and recur constantly. The range of the permissible in jazz is as narrowly circumscribed as in any particular cut of clothes. In view of the wealth of available possibilities for discovering and treating musical material, even in the sphere of entertainment if absolutely necessary, jazz has shown itself to be utterly impoverished. Its use of the existing musical techniques seems to be entirely arbitrary. The ban on changing the basic beat during the course of the music is itself sufficient to constrict composition to the point where what it demands is not aesthetic awareness of style but rather psychological regression. The limitations placed on metre, harmony and form are no less stifling. Considered as a whole, the perennial sameness of jazz consists not in a basic organization of the material within which the imagination can roam freely and without inhibition, as within an articulate language, but rather in the utilization of certain well-defined tricks, formulas and clichés to the exclusion of everything else. It is as though one were to cling convulsively to the 'latest thing' and deny the image of a particular year by refusing to tear off the page of the calendar. Fashion enthrones itself as something lasting and thus sacrifices the dignity of fashion, its transience.

2

In order to understand how an entire sphere can be described by a few simple recipes as though nothing else existed, one must first free oneself of the clichés, 'vitality' and 'rhythm of the time', which are glorified by advertising, by its journalistic appendage and in the end, by the victims themselves. The fact is that what jazz has to offer rhythmically is extremely limited. The most striking traits in jazz were all independently produced, developed and surpassed by serious music since Brahms. And its 'vitality' is difficult to take seriously in the face of an assembly-line procedure that is standardized down to its most minute deviations. The jazz ideologists, especially in Europe, mistakenly regard the sum of psycho-technically calculated and tested effects as the expression of an emotional state, the illusion of which jazz evokes in the listener; this attitude is rather like regarding those film stars, whose regular or sorrowful faces are modelled on portraits of famous persons, as being therefore of the same stature as Lucrezia Borgia or Lady Hamilton if, indeed, the latter were not already their own mannequins. What enthusiastically stunted innocence sees as the jungle is actually factory-made through and through, even when, on special occasions, spontaneity is publicized as a featured attraction. The paradoxical immortality of jazz has its roots in the economy. Competition on the culture market has proved the effectiveness of a number of techniques, including syncopation, semi-vocal, semi-instrumental sounds, gliding, impressionistic harmonies and opulent instrumentation which suggests that 'nothing is too good for us'. These techniques are then sorted out and kaleidoscopically mixed into ever-new combinations without there taking place even the slightest interaction between the total scheme and the no less schematic details. All that remains is the results of the competition, itself not very 'free', and the entire business is then touched up, in particular by the radio. The investments made in 'name bands', whose fame is assured by scientifically engineered propaganda; and even more important, the money used to promote musical bestseller programmes like 'The Hit Parade' by the firms who buy radio advertising time, make every divergence a risk. Standardization, moreover, means the strengthening of the lasting domination of the listening public and of their conditioned reflexes. They are expected to want only that to which they have become accustomed and to become enraged whenever their expectations are disappointed and fulfilment, which they regard as the customer's inalienable right, is denied. And even if there were attempts to introduce anything really different into light music, they would be doomed from the start by virtue of economic concentration.

The insurmountable character of a phenomenon which is inherently contingent and arbitrary reflects something of the arbitrary nature of present social controls. The more totally the culture industry roots out all deviations, thus cutting off the medium from its intrinsic possibilities of development, the more the whole blaring dynamic business approaches a standstill. Just as no piece of jazz can, in a musical sense, be said to have a history, just as all its components can be moved about at will, just as no single measure follows from the logic of the musical progression—so the perennial fashion becomes the likeness of a planned congealed society, not so different from the nightmare vision of Huxley's *Brave New World*. Whether what the ideology here expresses—or exposes—is the tendency of an over-accumulating society to regress to the stage of simple reproduction is for economists to decide. The fear that marked the late writings of a bitterly disappointed Thorstein Veblen, that the play of economic and social forces was coming to rest in a negative, historical state, a kind of higher-potency feudalism, may be highly unlikely, yet it remains the innermost desire of jazz. The image of the technical world possesses an ahistorical aspect that enables it to serve as a mythical mirage of eternity. Planned production seems to purge the life-process of all that is uncontrollable, unpredictable, incalculable in advance and thus to deprive it of what is genuinely new, without which history is hardly conceivable; in addition, the form of the standardized mass-produced article transforms the emporal sequence of objects into more of the same. The fact that a 1950 locomotive looks different from one made in 1950 leaves a paradoxical impression; it is for this reason that the most modern express trains are occasionally decorated with photographs of obsolete models. The surrealists, who have much in common with jazz, have appealed to this level of experience since Apollinaire: 'ici même les automobiles ont l'air d'être anciennes.' Traces o fthis have been unconsciously assimilated by the perennial fashion; jazz, which knows what it is doing when it allies itself with technique, collaborates in the 'technological veil' through its rigorously repetitive though objectless cultic ritual, and fosters the illusion that the twentieth century is ancient Egypt, full of slaves and endless dynasties. This remains illusion, however, for although the symbol of technology may be the uniformly revolving wheel, its intrinsic energies develop to an incalculable extent while remaining saddled by a society which is driven forward by its inner tensions, which persists in its irrationality and which grants men far more history than they wish. Timelessness is projected on technology by a world-order which knows that to change would be to collapse. The pseudo-eternity is belied, however, by the bad contingencies and inferiorities that have established themselves as universal principle. The men of the Thousand Year Reichs of today look like criminals, and the perennial gesture of mass culture is that of the asocial person. The fact that of all the tricks available, syncopation should have been the one to achieve musical dictatorship over the masses recalls the usurpation that characterizes techniques, however rational they may be in themselves, when they are placed at the service of irrational totalitarian control. Mechanisms which in reality are part and parcel of the entire present-day ideology, of the culture industry, are left easily visible in jazz because in the absence of technical knowledge they cannot be as easily identified as, for example, in films. Yet even jazz takes certain precautions. Parallel to standardization is pseudo-individualization. The more strictly the listener is curbed, the less he is permitted to notice it. He is told that jazz is 'consumer art', made specially for him. The particular effects with which jazz fills out its schema, syncopation above all, strive to create the appearance of being the outburst or caricature of untrammelled subjectivity—in effect, that of the listener—or perhaps the most subtle nuance dedicated to the greater glory of the audience. But the method becomes trapped in its own net. For while it must constantly promise its listeners something different, excite their attention and keep itself from becoming run-of-the-mill, it is not allowed to leave the beaten path; it must be always new and always the same. Hence, the deviations are just as standardized as the standards and in effect revoke themselves the instant they appear. Jazz, like everything else in the culture industry, gratifies desires only to frustrate them at the same time. However much jazz-subjects, representing the music listener in general, may play the non-conformist, in truth they are less and less themselves. Individual features which do not conform to the norm are never-theless shaped by it, and become marks of mutilation. Terrified, jazz fans identify with the society they dread for having made them what they are. This gives the jazz ritual its affirmative character, that of being accepted into a community of unfree equals. With this in mind, jazz can appeal directly to the mass of listeners in self-justification with a diabolically good conscience. Standard procedures which prevail unquestioned and which have been perfected over long periods of time produce standard reactions. Well-meaning educators, who believe that a change in programming would be enough to bring the violated and oppressed to desire something better, or at least something different, are much too credulous. Even when they do not greatly transcend the ideological realm of the culture industry, serious changes in programme policy are angrily rejected in reality. The population is so accustomed to the drivel it gets that it cannot renounce it, even when it sees through it halfway. On the contrary, it feels itself impelled to intensify its enthusiasm in order to convince itself that its ignominy is its good fortune. Jazz sets up schemes of social behaviour to which people must in any case conform. Jazz enables them to practise those forms of behaviour, and they love it all the more for making the inescapable easier to bear. Jazz reproduces its own mass-basis, without thereby reducing the guilt of those who produce it. The eternity of fashion is a vicious circle.

3

Jazz fans, as has once again been emphatically shown by David Riesman, can be divided into two clearly distinguishable groups. In the inner circle sit the experts, or those who consider themselves such—for very often the most passionate devotees, those who flaunt the established terminology and differentiate jazz styles with ponderous pretention, are hardly able to give an account, in precise, technical musical concepts, of whatever it is that so moves them. Most of them consider themselves avant-gardistic, thus participating in a confusion that has become ubiquitous today. Among the symptoms of the disintegration of culture and education, not the least is the fact that the distinction between autonomous 'high' and commercial 'light' art, however questionable it may be, is neither critically reflected nor even noticed any more. And now that certain culturally defeatist intellectuals have pitted the latter against the former, the philistine champions of the culture industry can even take pride in the conviction that they are marching in the vanguard of the *Zeitgeist*. The organization of culture into 'levels' such as the first, second and third programmes, patterned after low, middle and highbrow, is reprehensible. But it cannot be overcome simply by the lowbrow sects declaring themselves to be highbrow. The legitimate discontent with culture provides a pretext but not the slightest justification for the glorification of a highly rationalized section of mass production, one which debases and betrays culture without at all transcending it, as the dawn of a new world-sensibility or for confusing it with cubism, Eliot's poetry and Joyce's prose. Regression is not origin, but origin is the ideology of regression. Anyone who allows the growing respectability of mass culture to seduce him into equating a popular song with modern art because of a few false notes squeaked by a clarinet; anyone who mistakes a triad studded with 'dirty notes' for atonality, has already capitulated to barbarism. Art which has degenerated to culture pays the price of being all the more readily confused with its own waste-products as its aberrant influence grows. Education, traditionally the privilege of the few, is paid its due by self-conscious illiteracy which proclaims the stupor of tolerated excess to be the realm of freedom. Rebelling feebly, they are always ready to duck, following the lead of jazz, which integrates stumbling and coming-too-soon into the collective march-step. There is a striking similarity between this type of jazz enthusiast and many of the young disciples of logical positivism, who throw off philosophical culture with the same zeal as jazz fans dispense with the tradition of serious music. Enthusiasm turns into a matter-of-fact attitude in which all feeling becomes attached to technique, hostile to all meaning. They feel themselves secure within a system so well defined that no mistake could possibly slip by, and the repressed yearning for things outside finds expression as intolerant hatred and in an attiude which combines the superior knowledge of the initiate with the pretentiousness of the person without illusions. Bombastic triviality, superficiality seen as apodictic certitude, transfigures the cowardly defence against every form of self-reflection. All these old accustomed modes of reaction have in recent times lost their innocence, set themselves up as philosophy and thus become truly pernicious.

Gathered around the specialists in a field in which there is little to understand besides rules are the vague, inarticulate followers. In general they are intoxicated by the fame of mass culture, a fame which the latter knows how to manipulate; they could just as well get together in clubs for worshipping film stars or for collecting autographs. What is important to them is the sense of belonging as such, identification, without their paying particular attention to its content. As girls, they have trained themselves to faint upon hearing the voice of a 'crooner'. Their applause, cued in by a light-signal, is transmitted directly on the popular radio programmes they are permitted to attend. They call themselves 'jitter-bugs', bugs which carry out reflex movements, performers of their own ecstasy. Merely to be carried away by anything at all, to have something of their own, compensates for their impoverished and barren existence. The gesture of adolescence, which raves for this or that on one day with the ever-present possibility of damning it as idiocy on the next, is now socialized. Of course, Europeans tend to overlook the fact that jazz fans on the Continent in no way equal those in America. The element of excess, of insubordination in jazz, which can still be felt in Europe, is entirely missing today in America. The recollection of anarchic origins which jazz shares with all of today's ready-made mass movements, is fundamentally repressed, however much it may continue to simmer under the surface. Jazz is taken for granted as an institution, housebroken and scrubbed behind the ears. What is common to the jazz enthusiast of all countries, however, is the moment of compliance, in parodistic exaggeration. In this respect their play recalls the brutal seriousness of the masses of followers in totalitarian states, even though the difference between play and seriousness amounts to that between life and death. The advertisement for a particular song played by a big name band was 'follow your leader, XY.' While the leaders in the European dictatorships of both shades raged against the decadence of jazz, the youth of the other countries has long since allowed itself to be electrified, as with marches, by the syncopated dance-steps, with bands which do not by accident stem from military music. The division into shock-troops and inarticulate following has something of the distinction between party élite and rest of the 'people'.

4

The jazz monopoly rests on the exclusiveness of the supply and the economic power behind it. But it would have been broken long ago if the ubiquitous speciality did not contain something universal to which people respond. Jazz must possess a 'mass basis', the technique must link up with a moment in the subjects—one which, of course, in turn points back to the social structure and to typical conflicts between the ego and society. What first comes to mind, in quest for that moment, is the eccentric clown or parallels with the early film comics. Individual weakness is proclaimed and revoked in the same breath, stumbling is confirmed as a kind of higher skill. In the process of integrating the asocial, jazz converges with the equally standardized schemas of the detective novel and its offshoots, which regularly distort or unmask the world so that asociality and crime become the everyday norm, but which at the same time charm away the seductive and ominous challenge through the inevitable triumph of order. Psychoanalytic theory alone can provide an adequate explanation of this phenomenon. The aim of jazz is the mechanical reproduction of a regressive moment, a castration symbolism. 'Give up your masculinity, let yourself be castrated,' the eunuchlike sound of the jazz band both mocks and proclaims, 'and you will be rewarded, accepted into a fraternity which shares the mystery of impotence with you, a mystery revealed at the moment of the iniation rite'.[1] If this

[1] This theory is developed in the essay, 'Jazz', published in 1936 in the *Zeitschrift für Sozialforschung* (p. 252 ff). and elaborated in a review of the books by Sargeant and Hobson in *Studies in Philosophy and Social Science*, 1941, p. 175. ['Jazz' is reprinted in Th. W. Adorno, *Moments Musicaux*, Frankfurt am Main, 1964, pp. 84–115. Translators' note.]

interpretation of jazz—whose sexual implications are better understood by its shocked opponents than by its apologists—appear arbitrary and far-fetched, the fact remains that it can be substantiated in countless details of the music as well as of the song lyrics. In the book, *American Jazz Music*, Wilder Hobson describes an early jazz bandleader Mike Riley, a musical eccentric who must have truly mutilated the instruments. 'The band squirted water and tore clothes, and Riley offered perhaps the greatest of trombone comedy acts, an insane rendition of "Dinah" during which he repeatedly dismembered the horn and reassembled it erratically until the tubing hung down like brass burnishings in a junk shop, with a vaguely harmonic honk still sounding from one or more of the loose ends.' Long before, Virgil Thomson had compared the performances of the famed jazz trumpeter, Louis Armstrong, to those of the great *castrati* of the eighteenth century. The entire sphere is saturated with terminology which distinguishes between 'long' and 'short haired' musicians. The latter are jazz people who earn money and can afford to appear presentable; the others, the caricature of the Slavic pianist, for instance, whose long mane is exemplary, are grouped under the little esteemed stereotype of the artist who is starving and who flaunts the demands of convention. This is the manifest content of the terminology. What the shorn hair represents hardly requires elaboration. In jazz, the Philistines standing over Samson are permanently transfigured.

In truth, the Philistines. The castration symbolism, deeply buried in the practices of jazz and cut off from consciousness through the institutionalization of perennial sameness, is for that very reason probably all the more potent. And sociologically, jazz has the effect of strengthening and extending, down to the very physiology of the subject, the acceptance of a dreamless-realistic world in which all memories of things not wholly integrated have been purged. To comprehend the mass basis of jazz one must take full account of the taboo on artistic expression in America, a taboo which continues unabated despite the official art industry, and which even affects the expressive impulses of children; progressive education, which seeks to stimulate their faculties of expression as an end in itself, is simply a reaction to this. Although the artist is partially tolerated, partially integrated into the sphere of consumption as an 'entertainer', a functionary—like the better-paid waiter subject to the demands of 'service'—the stereotype of the artist remains the introvert, the egocentric idiot, frequently the homosexual. While such traits may be tolerated in professional artists—a scandalous private life may even be expected as part of the entertainment—everyone else makes himself immediately suspicious by any spontaneous artistic impulse not ordered in advance by society. A child who prefers to listen to serious music or practise the piano rather than watch a baseball game or television will have to suffer as a 'sissy' in his class or in the other groups to which he belongs and which embody far more authority than parents or teacher. The expressive impulse is exposed to the same threat of castration that is symbolized and mechanically and ritually subdued in jazz. Nevertheless, the need for expression, which stands in no necessary relation to the objective quality of art, cannot be entirely eliminated, especially during the years of maturation. Teenagers are not entirely stifled by economic life and its psychological correlative, the reality principle. Their aesthetic impulses are not simply extinguished by suppression but are rather diverted. Jazz is the preferred medium of such diversion. To the masses of young people who, year after year, chase the perennial fashion, presumably to forget it after a few years, it offers a compromise between aesthetic sublimation and social adjustment. The 'unrealistic', practically useless, imaginative element is permitted to survive at the price of changing its character; it must tirelessly strive to remake itself in the image of reality, to repeat the latter's commands to itself, to submit to them. Thus it reintegrates itself into the sphere from which it sought to escape. Art is deprived of its aesthetic dimension, and emerges as part of the very adjustment which it in principle contradicts. Viewed from this standpoint, several unusual features of jazz can be more easily understood. The role played by arrangement, for instance, which cannot be adequately explained in terms of a technical division of labour or of the musical illiteracy of the so-called composers. Nothing is permitted to remain what it intrinsically is. Everything must be fixed up, must bear the traces of a preparation which brings it closer to the sphere of the well known, thus rendering it more easily comprehensible. At the same time, this process of preparation indicates to the listener that the music is made for him, yet without idealizing him. And finally, arrangement stamps the music with the official seal of approval, which in turn testifies to the absence of all artistic ambitions to achieve distance from reality, to the readiness of the music to swim with the stream; this is music which does not fancy itself any better than it is.

The primacy of adjustment is no less decisive in determining the specific skills which jazz demands from its musicians, to a certain extent from its listeners as well, and certainly from the dancers who strive to imitate the music. Aesthetic technique, in the sense of the quintessence of means employed to objectify an autonomous

131

subject-matter, is replaced by the ability to cope with obstacles, to be impervious to disruptive factors like syncopations and yet at the same time to execute cleverly the particular action which underlies the abstract rules. The aesthetic act is made into a sport by means of a system of tricks. To master it is also to demonstrate one's practicality. The achievement of the jazz musician and expert adds up to a sequence of successfully surmounted tests. But expression, the true bearer of aesthetic protest, is overtaken by the might against which it protests. Faced by this might it assumes a malicious and miserable tone which barely and momentarily disguises itself as harsh and provocative. The subject which expresses itself expresses precisely this: I am nothing, I am filth, no matter what they do to me, it serves me right. Potentially this subject has already become one of those Russians, accused of a crime, and who, although innocent, collaborates with the prosecutor from the beginning and is incapable of finding a punishment severe enough. If the aesthetic realm originally emerged as an autonomous sphere from the magic taboo which distinguished the sacred from the everyday, seeking to keep the former pure, the profane now takes its revenge on the descendant of magic, on art. Art is permitted to survive only if it renounces the right to be different, and integrates itself into the omnipotent realm of the profane which finally took over the taboo. Nothing may exist which is not like the world as it is. Jazz is the false liquidation of art—instead of utopia becoming reality it disappears from the picture.

BACH DEFENDED AGAINST HIS DEVOTEES

The view of Bach which prevails today in musicological circles corresponds to the role assigned to him by the stagnation and industriousness of a resurrected culture. In him, it is said, there is once again the revelation—in the middle of the Century of Enlightenment—of the time-honoured bounds of tradition, of the spirit of medieval polyphony, of the theologically vaulted cosmos. His music is said to be elevated above the subject and its contingency; in it is expressed not so much the man and his inner life as the order of Being as such, in its most compelling musical form. The structure of this Being, understood to be immutable and inexorable, becomes a surrogate for meaning; that which cannot be other than its appearance is made the justification of itself. This conception of Bach draws all those who, having lost either the ability to believe or the desire for self-determination, go in search of authority, obsessed by the notion of how nice it would be to be secure. The present function of his music resembles the current vogue of ontology, which promises to overcome the individualistic condition through the postulation of an abstract principle which is superior to and independent of human existence and yet which is free of all unequivocally theological content. They enjoy the order of his music because it enables them to subordinate themselves. His work, which originated within the narrow confines of the theological horizon only in order to break through them and to pass into universality, is called back within the boundaries it transcended. Bach is degraded by impotent nostalgia to the very church composer against whose office his music rebelled and which he filled only with great conflict. What sets him apart from the practices of his age, far from being grasped as the contradiction of his substance with them, is made a pretext for glorifying the nimbus of provincial craftsmanship as a classical quality. Reaction, deprived of its political heroes, takes complete possession of the composer whom it long had claimed as one of its own by giving him the ignominious name of the 'Thomas Cantor'. Dilettante high schools monopolize him, and his influence, unlike that even of Schumann and Mendelssohn, no longer results from the musical substance of his music but rather from its style and play, from formula and symmetry, from the mere gesture of recognition. In being placed into the service of proselytizing zeal, the neo-religious Bach is impoverished, reduced and stripped of the specific musical content which was the basis of his prestige. He suffers the very fate which his fervent protectors are least willing to admit: he is changed into a neutralized cultural monument, in which aesthetic success mingles obscurely with a truth that has lost its intrinsic substance. They have made him into a composer for organ festivals in well-preserved Baroque towns, into ideology.

2

The most elementary historical reflection should arouse doubts concerning the historicist image of Bach. A contemporary of the Encyclopedists, he died six years before Mozart's birth and only twenty before that of Beethoven. Even the boldest construction of the 'non-simultaneity' of music could not sustain the thesis that a single ego can conserve what the spirit of the epoch dissolved, as though the truth of a phenomenon were ever simply attributable to its backwardness. Bad individualism and the irrational belief in timelessness converge; isolating the individual from his relation to the historical stage of consciousness, however polemical that relation may be, can only be arbitrary. To argue that, in his ahistorical workshop—which was nevertheless equipped with all the technical discoveries of the epoch—Bach experienced nothing of its *Zeitgeist* except for the Pietism of the texts he used for his sacred works— Pietism being anti-Enlightenment—is to overlook the elementary fact that Pietism, like all forms of restoration, absorbed the forces of the very Enlightenment that it opposed. The subject which hopes to attain grace by becoming absorbed in itself through reflected 'inwardness', has already escaped dogmatic order and is on its own, autonomous in the choice of heteronomy. Bach's participation in his time, however, is drastically demonstrated by central aspects of his music. The contrast between Philipp Emanuel's generation and his father's often blurs the fact that the latter's work embraces the entire sphere of the 'Galant', not alone in stylistic models like the French Suites—in which at times it seems as if the mighty hand has in advance given definite shape to the genre types of the nineteenth century—but also in the large, completely constructed works like the French Overtures, in which the moments of pleasure and organization are, in Bach's manner, no less present than in Viennese Classicism. Yet is there any openminded person who has played the 'Well-Tempered Clavichord'—the very title of which takes the part of the process of rationalization—from beginning to end without being struck again and again by a lyrical element, whose differentiation, individuation, freedom ally it far more closely to *Vierzehnheiligen* than to an image of the Middle Ages which has in any case become highly questionable? One need only recall the F-sharp Major Prelude and Fugue of the first book, a fugue once compared by a composer to Gottfried Keller's short dance-legend, and which is not merely the direct representation of subjective grace but moreover mocks all the rules of the very fugue that Bach himself created, through a musical progression in which the motif of the middle part transmits its impulses to the developments as the work unfolds. Or the double-fugue in g-sharp minor from the second book, which the late Beethoven must have known well, and which is astonishing not so much for its chromaticism, by no means rare in Bach, but rather for its wavering, deliberately vague harmonization, which, given the 6/8-character of the piece, inevitably evokes Chopin's most mature work; as a whole it is music broken down into countless coloured facets, modern precisely in the sense of that nervous sensibility which Historicism would like to exorcise. Anyone who thinks this argument invalid as a 'romantic misunderstanding' must first, for the sake of the thesis, free himself of that spontaneous relation to the musical idiom and its meaning, a relation which was the prerequisite to understanding music from Monteverdi to Schoenberg. To sacrifice the subject in such works, to hear in them nothing but the Order of Being and not the nostalgic echo that the decline of such an order finds in the mind, is to grasp only the *caput mortuum*. The phantasma of Bach's ontology arises through an act of force mechanically performed by Philistines, whose sole desire is to neutralize art since they lack the capacity to comprehend it.

3

All this, it is true, stands in sharp contrast to those features of Bach which even in his own lifetime were regarded as anachronistic. This anachronistic aspect is at least partly responsible for the enigmatic amnesia in which his work was shrouded for eighty years, and thus, with incalculable consequences for the history of Western music, prevented from taking its place in the tradition and being absorbed in all its breadth by Viennese Classicism. Indeed, not only did Bach fulfil the spirit of the *basso continuo*, with its intervallic-harmonic mode of thinking, but within that spirit he was also the polyphonist who created the form of the fugue from its groping beginnings in the seventeenth century; the theory of the fugue stems from Bach no less than that of strict counterpoint from Palestrina, and he remained its sole master. Yet it is this very duality of mind, harmonic and contrapuntal, circumscribing every one of the compositional problems that Bach paradigmatically resolved, which must exclude the image of him as the consummation of the Middle Ages. Were the image valid, he would neither have had that duality of mind, nor have struggled, especially in the speculative late works, with a paradox which would have been unthinkable for the old polyphonic mind, namely, how, in terms of *basso continuo* harmony, music could justify its progression as meaningful and at the same time organize itself polyphonically, through the simultaneity of independent voices. The expressiveness alone of many of the seemingly archaic pieces should arouse scepticism. The affirmative tone of the E-flat major fugue from the second book of the *Well-Tempered Clavichord* is not the immediate certainty of a sacral community articulated in music and secure in its revealed truth; such affirmation and emphasis are utterly alien to the Dutch. Rather, in its substance—certainly not in its subjective consciousness—it is reflection on the happiness of musical security, the like of which is possessed only by the emancipated subject, for only it can conceive music as the emphatic promise of objective salvation. This kind of fugue presupposes the dualism. It says how beautiful it would be to bring back its message of happiness from the circumscribed cosmos to mankind. To the irritation of today's religious neophytes, it is romantic, although, of course, its vision is far more exalted than that which the later romantic style could allow itself. It does not mirror the solitary subject as the guarantee of meaning, but rather aims at its abolition and transcendence in an objective, comprehensive absolute. But this absolute is evoked, asserted, postulated precisely because and only inasmuch as it is not present in physical experience; Bach's power is that of such evocation. He was no archaic master craftsman but rather a genius of meditation. It is only rising barbarism that limits works of art to what meets the eye, blind to the difference between essence and appearance in them; such a confusion of the being of Bach's music with its intention wipes out the very metaphysics which it is supposed to protect. Since such barbarism blurs not merely the essence, but with it the obvious as well, it overlooks the fact that the particular polyphonic techniques used by Bach to construct musical objectivity themselves presupposed subjectivization. The art of fugue composition is one of motivic economy, of exploiting the smallest part of a theme in order to make it into an integral whole. It is an art of dissection; one could almost say, of dissolving Being, posited as the theme, and hence incompatible with the common belief that this Being maintains itself static and unchanged throughout the fugue. By comparison to this technique Bach employs the genuinely medieval one of polyphonic figuration, of imitation, only secondarily. In the passages and pieces where imitation triumphs—by no means frequent in Bach—in the *stretti* passages and fugues, such as the extremely dense D major fugue from the second book, the venerable technique is placed in the service of a driving, thoroughly dynamic, thoroughly 'modern' effect. The fact that the identity of the recurring themes in Bach was able to preserve itself at all, under the attack of the new compositional techniques that had been set free by polyphony, signifies nothing more static than do the dynamic Beethoven sonatas, which faithfully adhere to the tectonic demands of the reprise, yet of course only in order to develop the reprise itself out of the 'process' of the development. In his last book Schoenberg rightly speaks of Bach's technique of the developing variation, which then became the basic compositional principle in Viennese Classicism. A social deciphering of Bach would presumably have to establish the link between the decomposition of the given thematic material through subjective reflection on the motivic work contained therein, and the change in the work-process that took place during the same epoch through the emergence of manufacturing, which consisted essentially in breaking down the old craft operations into its smaller component acts. If this resulted in the rationalization of material production, then Bach was the first to crystallize the idea of the rationally constituted work, of the aesthetic domination of nature; it was no accident that he named his major instrumental work after the most important technical achievement of musical rationalization. Perhaps Bach's innermost truth is that in him the social trend which has dominated the bourgeois era to this very day is not merely preserved but, by being reflected in images, is reconciled with the voice of humanity which in reality was stifled by that trend at the moment of its inception.

4

If Bach was indeed modern, then why was he archaic? For there can be no doubt that his form-world, especially in the most powerful manifestations of his late work, so grotesquely misunderstood by Hindemith in recent years, evokes much that even in his own time sounded like something out of the past, and which seems to have been deliberately aimed at creating pedantic misunderstanding. It is impossible not to hear the seventeenth century tone in precisely such magnificent conceptions as the c-sharp minor triple fugue from the first book of the *Well-Tempered Clavichord*, where, in order to bring out the contrast between the three themes all the more drastically, Bach leaves everything not directly related to this contrast in a 'pre-schematic' state, so to speak, motivically undeveloped like the rudimentary pre-Bach fugues, one of which, the *Ricercata*, is alluded to by a word-play in the *Musical Offering*. Like the *Ricercata*, the *alla breve* fugue in E-major in the second book carries the archaic element down to its very score, as though it had been written in the vivacious spirit of a highly stylized past, itself naturally fictitious, the same procedure followed by Bach in writing his famous piano concerto in the Italian style. He frequently indulged an inclination, entirely incompatible with Existentialist dignity, to experiment with strange, arbitrarily chosen idioms and to awake their formative power for music construction. As early as Bach the rationalization of compositional technique, the predominance of subjective reason, so to speak, brings with it the possibility of freely chosing from all the objectively available procedures of the epoch. Bach does not feel himself blindly bound to any of them but instead always chooses that which best suits the compositional intention. Such liberty vis-à-vis the ancient however, can hardly be construed as the culmination of the tradition, which instead must prohibit just that free selection of available possibilities. Even less can the meaning of Bach's recourse to the tradition be described as restorative. For it is precisely the archaic-sounding pieces which are often the most daring, not merely in terms of their contrapuntal combinations, which indeed draw directly on the earlier polyphonic arrangements, but also with regard to the most advanced aspects of the general effect. The c-sharp minor fugue, which begins as though it were a dense network of equally relevant lines, the theme of which seems at first to be nothing more than the unobtrusive glue that holds the voices together, progressively reveals itself, starting with the entrance of the figured second theme, to be an irresistible crescendo, composed from beginning to end and climaxing with the mighty explosion of the main theme entering in the bass, the most extreme concentration of a pseudo-ten-voice *stretto* and the turning point of a heavily accented dissonance, in order then to vanish as though through a dark portal. No appeal to the acoustically static character of harpsichord and organ can cover over the basic dynamism of the compositional structure itself, regardless of whether or not it could be realized as a crescendo on the instruments of the time, or even, as some idly question, whether Bach could have 'thought' of such a crescendo. Nowhere is it written that the conception that a composer has of his music must coincide with its intrinsic nature, with the objective law peculiar to it. His work is 'baroque' far more in the sense given to that word by the seventeenth century theatre, that of excess, of allegorical expression heightened to the utmost, of reliance on perspective for effect, than in the sense of 'pre-classical', which inevitably fails to explain just that which is specific to Bach, above all, his archaic tendencies. In order to do them justice the question of their function within the fabric of composition must be raised. And here one stumbles upon an ambiguity of progress itself, one which in the meanwhile has taken on a universal aspect. In Bach's time to be modern was to throw off the burden of the *res severa* for the sake of *gaudium*, of the pleasing and playful, in the name of communication, of consideration for the presumptive listener who, with the decline of the old theological order, had also lost the belief that the formal vocabulary associated with that order was binding. It cannot be denied, either that it is historical necessity that art relinquish techniques once they are no longer validated by the objective spirit of the times, or that the faculties of human eloquence thereby set free in music ultimately produced a higher form of truth. But the price which had to be paid for the freedom of movement thus attained was the immanent coherence of music. Even the earliest products of the 'unskilled' style, most conspicuously, those of Bach's own sons, bore witness to that price. The enigma becomes suddenly visible when one compares the corresponding formal types in Viennese Classicism and in Bach, the rondo of a Mozart piano concerto and the presto of the Italian Concerto. Despite all its newly won compositional flexibility and effervescence, Mozart's proverbial grace is, as pure musical *peinture*, rather mechanical and crass in comparison with Bach's infinitely involuted, unschematic approach. It is a grace of tone rather than of score. The clearer the outlines of the form become, the more their dense and pure logic seems to be replaced by the appeal to a once-established schema. Anyone who has returned to Beethoven after prolongued, intensive study of Bach sometimes feels as though he were confronted by a kind of decorative light music, which only the culture-cliché could consider 'profound'. Such a judgement is distorted and biased, of course, and invokes external criteria. It is no accident that today's Bach apologists would endorse it. Yet it still includes elements of the historical constellation that constitutes Bach's essence. Among his archaic traits is the attempt to parry the impoverishment and petrifaction of musical language, the shadow-side of its decisive progress. Such traits represent Bach's effort to resist the inexorable growth of the commodity-character of music, a process which was linked to its subjectivization. Yet such features are also identical with Bach's modernity inasmuch as they always serve to defend the right of inherent musical logic against the demands of taste. Bach as archaist distinguishes himself from all subsequent classicists, up to and including Stravinsky, by his refusal to confront the historical level of the material with an abstract stylistic ideal. Rather what was becomes a means of forcing what is toward a future of its own making. The reconciliation of scholar and gentleman, which, as Alfred Einstein stressed, set the tone and aim of Viennese Classicism since Haydn, is in a certain sense also the dominant idea in Bach. He was not, however, interested in striking a mean between the two elements. His music strove to achieve the indifference of the extremes towards each other more radically than any other until that of the late Beethoven. Bach, as the most advanced master of *basso continuo*, at the same time renounced his obedience, as antiquated polyphonist, to the trend of the times, a trend he himself had shaped, in order to help it reach its innermost truth, the emancipation of the subject to objectivity in a coherent whole of which subjectivity itself was the origin. Down to the subtlest structural details it is always a question of the undiminished coincidence of the harmonic-functional and of the contrapuntal dimension. The distant past is entrusted with the utopia of the musical subject-object; anachronism becomes a harbinger of things to come.

5

This, if true, does not merely contradict the prevailing conception of Bach's music but also modifies the immediate relation to it. This relation defines itself essentially through the praxis of performance. Today, however, under the unholy star of Historicism, the performance of Bach has assumed a sectarian aspect. Historicism has incited a fanatical interest that no longer concerns even the work itself. At times one can hardly avoid the suspicion that the sole concern of today's Bach devotees is to see that no inauthentic dynamics, modifications of tempo, oversize choirs and orchestras creep in; they seem to wait with potential fury lest any more humane impulse become audible in the rendition. The critique directed at the late Romantics' inflated and sentimentalized Bach image need not be challenged, even though the relation to Bach apparent in Schumann's work proved to be incomparably more productive than the present punctilious purity. What calls for refutation, however, is that of which the purists are most proud—their 'objectivity'. The only objective representation of music is one which shows itself to be adequate to the essence of its object. This, however, is not to be identified—as Hindemith, too, took for granted—with the idea of the historically first rendition. The fact that the colouristic dimension of music had hardly been discovered in Bach's time, and had certainly not yet been liberated as a compositional technique; that composers did not make sharp distinctions between the different types of piano and organ, but rather abandoned the sound in large measure to taste, points in a direction diammetrically opposed to the desire to slavishly imitate the customary sounds of the time. Even had Bach been in fact satisfied with the organs and harpsichords of the epochs, with its thin choruses and orchestras, this would in no way prove their adequacy for the intrinsic substance of his music. The artists' consciousness—the 'idea' they had of their work cannot, of course, be reconstructed—may, it is true, contribute to elucidating certain aspects of their work, but it can never supply the canon. Authentic works unfold their truth-content, which transcends the scope of individual consciousness, in a temporal dimension through the law of their form. In addition, that which is known of Bach as interpreter absolutely contradicts the musicological style of presentation and points to a flexibility on the part of the composer which would much prefer to renounce the monumental than give up the chance of adapting the tone to subjective impulse. Of course, Forkel's famous report appeared too long after Bach's death to claim full authenticity; but what he writes about Bach the pianist is clearly based on precise statements, and there is no apparent reason why the picture should be falsified at a time when the controversy had not yet arisen and when there was little sympathy for the clavichord—'He loved best to play the clavichord. The so-called pianos (sc. harpsichords), despite a completely different action'—which can only mean the register—'were too soulless for him, and the pianofortes during his lifetime were still too undeveloped and much too primitive to have satisfied him. Hence, he held the clavichord for the best instrument for study as well as for private musical diversion. He found it most suitable for executing his finest ideas and did not believe that either the harpsichord or the piano could produce as great a variety of tonal nuances as this instrument, which despite its poor tone was extraordinarily pliable in its details.' What is true, however, for differentiating within the intimate sphere, is conversely all the more so for the extensive dynamics of the large choral works. No matter how it was done in the Church of St. Thomas, a performance of the *St. Matthew Passion*, for instance, done with meagre means sounds pale and indecisive to the present-day ear, like a rehearsal which a few musicians have by chance decided to attend, while at the same time it assumes a didactic-pedantic character. Yet even more important is that such a performance thereby contradicts the intrinsic essence of Bach's music. The only adequate interpretation of the dynamic objectively embedded in his work is one which realizes it. True interpretation is an x-ray of the work; its task is to illuminate in the sensuous phenomenon the totality of all the characteristics and interrelations which have been recognized through intensive study of the score. The favourite argument of the purists is that all this should be left to the work itself, which need only be performed ascetically in order to speak; interpretation, they contend, serves only to unduly emphasize music which can be expressed simply and which is all the more powerful without such frills. This argument completely misses the point. As long as music requires any kind of interpretation whatsoever, its form defines itself through the tension between the composition's essence and its sensuous appearance. To identify the work with the latter is only justifiable when the appearance is a manifestation of the essence. Yet, precisely this is achieved only through subjective labour and reflection. The attempt to do justice to Bach's objective content by directing this effort towards abolishing the subject is self-defeating. Objectivity is not left over after the subject is subtracted. The musical score is never identical with the work; devotion to the text means the constant effort to grasp that which it hides. Without such a dialectic, devotion becomes betrayal; an interpretation which does not bother about the music's meaning on the assumption that it will reveal itself of its own accord will inevitably be false since it fails to see that the meaning is always constituting itself anew. Meaning can never be grasped by the 'pure' rendition, allegedly purged of all exhibitionism; rather, such a presentation, which is meaningless in itself and not to be distinguished from the 'unmusical', becomes not the path to meaning, as which it sees itself, but a wall blocking the way. This does not mean, however, that the monstrously massive performances of Bach which were the order of the day up until the First World War are any better. The dynamics required are not related to the level of volume nor to the breadth of *crescendo* and *decrescendo*. The dynamics consist in the quintessence of all the compositional contrasts, mediations, subdivisions, transitions and relations which constitute the work; and at the time of Bach's greatest maturity, composition was no less the art of infinitesimal transitions than in any of the later composers. The entire richness of the musical texture, the integration of which was the source of Bach's power, must be placed in prominence by the performance instead of being sacrificed to a rigid, immobile monotony, the spurious semblance of unity that ignores the multiplicity it should embody and surmount. Reflection on style must not be permitted to suppress the concrete musical content and to settle complacently into the pose of transcendent Being. It must follow the structure of the musical composition that is concealed beneath the surface of sound. Mechanically squeaking *continuo*-instruments and wretched school choirs contribute not to sacred sobriety but to malicious failure; and the thought that the shrill and rasping Baroque organs are capable of capturing the long waves of the lapidary, large fugues is pure superstition. Bach's music is separated from the general level of his age by an astronomical distance. Its eloquence returns only when it is liberated from the sphere of resentment and obscurantism, the triumph of the subjectless over subjectivism. They say Bach, mean Telemann and are secretly in agreement with the regression of musical consciousness which even without them remains a constant threat under the pressures of the culture industry. Of course, there is also the possibility that the contradiction between the substance of Bach's compositions and the means for realizing it in sound, both those available at the time and those accumulated since, can no longer be resolved. In the light of this possibility, the much discussed 'abstractness' of sound in the *Musical Offering* and the *Art of the Fugue*, as works in which the choice of instruments is left open, acquires a new dimension. It is conceivable that the contradiction between music and sound-material—especially the inadequacy of the organ tone to the infinitely articulated structure—had already become visible at the time. If this were the case, Bach would have omitted the sound and left his most mature instrumental works waiting for the sound that would suit them. With such pieces it is not even remotely possible for philologists with no affinity for composition to write out the parts and assign them to unchanging instruments or groups. What is demanded is that they be rethought for an orchestra which neither squanders nor scrimps but rather which functions as a moment of the integral composition. In the case of the entire *Art of the Fugue*, the only such effort has been that of

Fritz Stiedry, whose arrangement did not survive its New York premiere. Justice is done Bach not through musicological usurpation but solely through the most advanced composition which in turn converges with the level of Bach's continually unfolding work. The few instrumentations contributed by Schoenberg and Anton von Webern, especially those of the great triple fugue in E flat major and of the six-part *Ricercata*, in which every facet of the composition is transposed into a correlative timbre and in which the surface interweaving of lines is dissolved into the most minute motivic interrelations and then reunited through the overall constructive disposition of the orchestra—such instrumentations are models of an attitude to Bach which corresponds to the stage of his truth. Perhaps the traditional Bach can indeed no longer be interpreted. If this is true, his heritage has passed on to composition, which is loyal to him in being disloyal; it calls his music by name in producing it anew.

146

ARNOLD SCHOENBERG 1874–1951

Heard melodies are sweet, but those unheard
Are sweeter; therefore, ye soft pipes, play on;
Not to the sensual ear, but, more endear'd,
Pipe to the spirit ditties of no tone.

Keats

In the public mind of today Schoenberg appears as an innovator, as a reformer, even as the inventor of a system. With grudging respect it is admitted that he prepared the way for others, a way, it is true, which they had no great desire to travel; yet this concession is linked to the implication that he himself was a failure and has already become obsolete. The one-time pariah is repressed, neutralized and absorbed. Not merely his early works but those of his middle period as well—which at the time earned him the hatred of all culture-lovers—are dismissed as 'Wagnerian' or 'late Romantic', although in forty years few have learned how to perform them properly. The works he wrote after the First World War are appraised as examples of the twelve-tone technique. In recent years, it is true, numerous young composers have taken up this technique again, but more in the search of a shell behind which to take refuge than as the necessary result of their own experience, and hence without troubling to worry about the function of the twelve-tone method within Schoenberg's own work. Such repression and dressing-up is provoked by the difficulties that Schoenberg poses to a listening public which has been kneaded into shape by the culture industry. If one does not understand something, it is customary to behave with the sublime understanding of Mahler's jackass, and project one's own inadequacy on to the object, declaring it to be incomprehensible. And it is true that Schoenberg's music demands from the very beginning active and concentrated participation, the most acute attention to simultaneous multiplicity, the renunciation of the customary crutches of a listening which always knows what to expect, the intensive perception of the unique and specific, and the ability to grasp precisely the individual characteristics, often changing in the smallest space, and their history, devoid of all repetition. The purity and sovereignty with which Schoenberg always entrusts himself to the demands of his subject-matter has restricted his influence; it is precisely because of its seriousness, richness and integrity that his music arouses resentment. The more it gives its listeners, the less it offers them. It requires the listener spontaneously to compose its inner movement and demands of him not mere contemplation but praxis. In this, however, Schoenberg blasphemes against the expectation, cherished despite all idealistic assurances to the contrary, that music will present the comfortable listener with a series of pleasurable sensations. Even schools such as Debussy's, despite the aesthetic atmosphere of art for art's sake, have met this expectation. The line dividing the young Debussy and salon music was fluid, and the technical accomplishment of the mature composer were adroitly incorporated by commercial mass music. With Schoenberg affability ceases. He proclaims the end of a conformity which had made music into the natural preserve of infantility within a society which had long been aware that it would be tolerated only as long as it allowed its inmates a quota of controlled juvenile happiness. He sins against the division of life into work and leisure; he insists on a kind of work for one's leisure that could easily call the latter into question. His passion points to a music of which the mind need not be ashamed, and which therefore shames the prevailing temper. His music strives to be mature at both its poles: it releases the threatening instinctual sphere which music otherwise presents only after it has been filtered and harmoniously falsified, and it demands great intellectual energy, the principle of an ego strong enough not to have to deny the instincts. Kandinsky, in whose 'Blue Rider' he published the *Herzgewaechse*, formulated the programme of the 'intellectual in art'. Schoenberg remained devoted to this, not by aiming at abstractions but by making the concrete form of music itself intelligible.

This gives rise to the most popular objection to Schoenberg— against his so-called 'intellectualism'. However, this either confuses the intrinsic force of intellectualization with reflection that remains external to the object, or it dogmatically exempts music from the demands of intellectualization which have become obligatory for all aesthetic media as a corrective against the transformation of culture into *biens culturels*. The truth is that Schoenberg was a naïve artist, above all in the often hapless intellectualizations with which he sought to justify his work. If anyone was ever guided by the tide of involuntary musical intuition it was he. Half self-taught, the language of music was self-evident to him. It was only with the greatest reluctance that he transformed it down to its most elementary levels. Although his music channeled all the energies of his ego towards objectifying its impulses, it nevertheless remained ego-alien to him for the duration of his life. He himself readily identified with the elect who resist their mission. Courage he considered the attribute of 'those who accomplish acts which exceed their confidence'. The paradoxical nature of the formula characterizes his attitude towards authority. It combines aesthetic avant-gardism with a conservative mentality. While inflicting the most deadly blows on authority through his work, he seeks to defend the work as though before a hidden authority and ultimately to make it itself the authority. In the eyes of the Viennese composer, coming from a parochial background, the norms of a closed, semi-feudal society seemed the will of God. Yet this respect was linked to an opposing element, although one no less incompatible with the notion of the intellectual. Something not integrated, not entirely civilized, indeed hostile to civilization, kept him outside the very order of which he was so uncritical. Like a man without origins, fallen from heaven, a musical Caspar Hauser, he hit the bullseye unerringly. Nothing was to be allowed to recall the natural milieu to which he nonetheless belonged, and the result was that his undeveloped nature became all the more evident. He who severed all ties so that he alone could be responsible for everything, was able precisely because of that isolation, to win contact with the collective undercurrent of music and to achieve that sovereignty which enables each one of his works to represent the entire genre. There was no greater surprise than when that hoarse and irritable speaker sang a few bars. His warm, free, sonorous voice was untroubled by the fear of singing which is burned into the civilized mind and which makes the pseudo-nonchalance of the professional singer all the more distressing. Music had taken over the role of parents; 'musically', he was borne along by the language of music, like the speaker of a dialect, and in that respect comparable to someone like Richard Strauss or the Slavic composers. From the earliest works—already manifest in 'Transfigured Night'—there flows from this language a specific warmth, both in tone and in the wealth of successive and simultaneous musical figures, uninhibitedly productive, virtually oriental in their fertility. Enough is not enough. Schoenberg's intolerance of all excess ornament stems from his generosity, from his reluctance to have the listener deprived of true riches by ostentation. His generous imagination and artistic hospitality, intent on providing each guest with the best, is probably more important for him than what is generally termed, dubiously enough, 'the need for expression'. Non-Wagnerian, his music springs from creative fervour, not consuming desire, and is insatiable in its giving. As though all the artistic materials with which he could prove himself were borrowed property, he produces his own material as well as its resistances, driven incessantly by the disgust of everything he produces which is not entirely new. The flame of untrammelled, mimetic creation, which came over Schoenberg from that subterranean heritage in the end also consumed the heritage. Tradition and fresh start are as interwoven in him as the revolutionary and conservative aspect.

The reproach of 'intellectualism' is linked to the lack of melody. Yet he was supremely melodic. Instead of the established formula he constantly produced new forms. His melodic imagination scarcely ever contented itself with a single melody; instead, all simultaneous musical events are treated as melodies, which makes them more difficult to grasp. Even Schoenberg's instinctive mode of reaction is melodic; everything in him is actually 'sung', including the instrumental lines. This endows his music with its articulate character, free-moving and yet structural down to the last tone. The primacy of breathing over the beat of abstract time contrasts Schoenberg to Stravinsky and to all those who, having adjusted better to contemporary existence, fancy themselves more modern than Schoenberg. The reified mind is allergic to the elaboration and fulfilment of melody, for which it substitutes the docile repetition of mutilated melodic fragments. The ability to follow the breath of the music unafraid had already distinguished Schoenberg from older, post-Wagnerian composers like Strauss and Wolf, in whom the music seems unable to develop its substance according to its intrinsic impulses and requires literary and programmatic support, even in the songs. By contrast, the works of Schoenberg's first period, including the symphonic poem, 'Pelleas and Melisande', and the 'Gurrelieder', are already fully composed. Wagnerian methods are as little related to Schoenberg as Wagnerian expression; by reaching its goal instead of breaking off and beginning anew the musical impulse loses the moment of crazed desire, of obsessive preoccupation. Schoenberg's original expression, generous and, in the meaningful sense, jovial, recalls the humane expression of Beethoven. From the very start, of course, it is prepared to turn into the defiance of a world which rejects its gifts. Scorn and violence seek to subdue the coolness, rebelliousness; and the sentiment of one who fails to reach human beings precisely because he speaks to them as such turns to fear. This is the origin of Schoenberg's ideal of perfection. He reduces, constructs, arms his music; the rejected gift will become so perfect that it will have to be accepted. By reaction, his love had to become hard, like that of all minds since Schopenhauer who have not been content to make do with the world as it is. Kraus' verse, 'what has the world done to us?' is emphatically true of the musician.

Schoenberg's nonconformity is not a matter of temperament. The complexion of his musical intuition left him no choice but to compose coherently. His integrity was forced on him; he had to work out the tension between Brahmsian and Wagnerian elements. His expansive imagination thrived on Wagnerian material, whereas the demands of compositional consistency, the responsibility of respecting the music's intrinsic tendencies drew him to Brahman methods. Out of this context, the question of Brahmsian or Wagnerian style was irrelevant to Schoenberg. The Wagnerian style with its compositional limitations could not satisfy him any more than the Brahmsian with its academic character. Both practically and then theoretically he steadfastly rejected the notion of 'style', in the sense of a category existing prior to the subject-matter and oriented on external consensus; instead, he spoke of the 'idea', meaning the pure elaboration of musical thoughts. On all levels his primary concern was the What, not the How, the principles of selection and the means of presentation. Hence, the different stylistic phases of his work should not be over-interpreted. The decisive point comes very early, certainly not later than the Songs op. 6 and the d minor quartet op. 7. These works provide the key to all the later ones. All subsequent innovations, which provoked such a sensation at the time, are nothing but the logical consequence for musical language of what was inherent in the individual musical events of the specific work. Dissonance and large intervals, the two most conspicuous elements of the mature Schoenberg, are secondary, mere derivatives of the inner structure of all of his music; besides, the large intervals are already present in his youth. The central problem is that of mastering the contradiction between essence and appearance. Richness and plenitude are to be made the essence, not mere ornament; the essence, in turn, will appear no longer as the rigid framework on which the music is draped but rather as concrete and evident in its most subtle traits. What he designated as the 'subcutaneous'—the fabric of individual musical events, grasped as the ineluctable moments of an internally coherent totality—breaks through the surface, becomes visible and manifests itself independently of all stereotyped forms. The inward dimension moves outward. Ordering categories, which reduce the difficulties of active listening at the cost of the pure elaboration of the work, are eliminated. This absence of all mediations introduced into the work from outside makes the musical progression seem fragmented and abrupt to the unnaïve-naïve listener, with the impression increasing in direct proportion to the actual degree of inner organization. The early song, *Lockung*, from op. 6, is the prototype of a characteristic that recurs continually, up into the twelve-tone phase. In its ten-measure introduction three sharply contrasting groups, also distinct in tempo, are juxtaposed; the first consisting of four measures, the other two of three each. None of the groups conspicuously repeats anything from the preceding ones, yet all are interrelated through intervening variation. The groups are also syntactically linked: turbulent question, insistence, and half-hearted, tentative and already transitional answer. There is an infinite amount taking place within the smallest space and yet everything is so totally formed that there is never any confusion. The second group, for instance, varies the first in retaining the diminished second and augmented fourth intervals while at the same time reducing the beat from 3/8 to 2/8, thus producing the general driven character. Amid radical change, melodic economy prevails. It is this organization of the musical structure that is the true Schoenberg, not the privileged use of striking techniques; what is crucial is the variegated alternation of distinct and contrasting figures with the general unity of motivic-thematic relations. It is music of identity in nonidentity. All the developments unfold more concentratedly and more rapidly than is deemed acceptable by the sluggish habits of culinary listening; polyphony functions with real parts, not with camouflaging counterpoint. The individual characteristics are intensified to the utmost; the articulation rejects all finished schemas, and contrast, repressed in the nineteenth century by transition, becomes, under the pressure of an emotional state polarized into extremes, the formative technique. Technically, the maturing of music means the protest against musical stupidity. Although Schoenberg's music is not intellectual, it does demand musical intelligence. Its basic principle is, to use his phrase, the 'developing variation'. Everything that appears strives to be developed logically, to be intensified and then resolved in an equilibrium. Universal responsibility and idiosyncrasy prevail against all musical traits which resemble journalistic language. Both fatuous rhetoric and the deceptive gesture that promises more than it fulfils are scorned. Schoenberg's music honours the listener by not making any concessions to him.

Hence, it is reproached for being 'experimental'. Underlying this criticism is the notion that progress in artistic technique proceeds in a steady, so to speak organic flow. Anyone who, acting on his own, discovers something new, without overt historical aid, is thought not merely to sin against the tradition but also to succumb to vanity and impotence. But works of art, including music, require consciousness and spontaneity, and these consistently destroy the semblance of continual growth. So long as the new music still had a clear conscience, resulting from its hostility to a tradition that Mahler had labelled as 'sloppy'; so long as it did not try anxiously

154

to prove that its intentions were really not that bad, it advocated the concept of experiment. It is only the superstitious belief which fetishistically confuses the reified, rigidified—precisely what is estranged from nature—with nature itself, that sees to it that nothing new is tried in art. All the same, artistic extremism must be held responsible for either following the logic of its subject-matter, an objectivity, however concealed, or succumbing to mere private caprice or an abstract system. It receives its legitimacy from the tradition it negates. Hegel taught that wherever something new becomes visible, immediate, striking, authentic, a long process of formation has preceded it and it has now merely thrown off its shell. Only that which has been nourished with the life-blood of the tradition can possibly have the power to confront it authentically; the rest becomes the helpless prey of forces which it has failed to overcome sufficiently within itself. Yet the bond of tradition is hardly equivalent to the simple sequence of events in history; rather, it is subterranean. 'A tradition,' writes Freud in his late work on *Moses and Monotheism*, 'which was founded only on communication could not produce the compulsive quality characteristic of religious phenomena. It would be heard, evaluated, eventually dismissed like every other piece of external information, and would never attain that privileged status necessary to liberate men from the sway of logical thought. It must have undergone the destiny of repression, the state of remaining in the unconscious, before it could develop a powerful enough influence, upon its return, to force the masses under its spell'. The aesthetic no less than the religious tradition is the recollection of something unconscious, indeed repressed. Where it does, in fact, unfold a 'potent influence', it is the result not of a manifest, direct consciousness of continuity but rather of unconscious recollection which explodes the continuum. Tradition is far more present in works deplored as experimental than in those which deliberately strive to be traditional. What has long been observed in modern French painting is no less true of Schoenberg and the Vienna School. The manifest sound-material of Classicism and Romanticism, the tonal chords and their normed associations, the melodic lines balanced between triad and second-intervals, in short, the entire façade of the music of the last two-hundred years is submitted to productive criticism. Yet what was crucial in the great music of the tradition was not those elements as such, but rather the specific function they assumed in the presentation of a particular compositional content. Beneath the façade there was a second, latent structure. The latter was determined by the façade in many respects, yet was continually producing and justifying it in its problematic character. The understanding of traditional music always meant the recognition not of the façade alone, but of that inner structure in its relation to that façade. As a result of the emancipation of the subject, this relation became so precarious that finally both structures split wide apart. Schoenberg's spontaneous productive power executed an objective historical verdict—he liberated the latent structure while disposing of the manifest one. Thus, it is precisely through his 'experiments'—through the anomalous character he gave to the appearances of his music—that he became heir to the tradition. He heeded the norms which were teleologically implicit in Viennese Classicism and then in Brahms, and thus, in this historical sense as well, he honoured his obligations. The objectification achieved under the primacy of 'total composition' had lost its authority by the time of Brahms because it had begun to function mechanically, had lost its hold on a resistant musical material and categorically repressed the impulse to rebel. In Schoenberg, however, each individual musical moment, down to the initial 'idea', is incomparably more substantial. His totality, true to the historical level of the mind, starts from the individual, not from a plan or architecture. As already had been done by Beethoven, although in rudimentary form, he includes the Romantic element in integral composition. Of course, this also has its place in Brahms, in lyrical melodies amid instrumental forms; there, however, it is neutralized, kept in a kind of equilibrium with the 'work', and this is the source of that illusoriness and resignation that characterize the Brahmsian form, which prudently smooths over oppositions rather than immersing itself in them. In Schoenberg the objectification of subjective impulses becomes crucial. He may have learned his motivic-thematic variations from Brahms, but the polyphony which gives his objectification of subjectivity its pungency belongs entirely to him; it is literally the recollection of something buried for over two hundred years. This stems from the fact that Beethoven's 'thematic work', particularly in the chamber music, incurred polyphonic obligations which it failed to meet, except for a few exceptions in his late period. Wilhelm Fischer, in his study, 'On the Stylistic Development of Viennese Classicism', arrived at this insight: 'In general, the development-section functions in Viennese Classicism as the playground for the melodic techniques of the old classical style which have been excluded from the exposition.' Yet this is true not merely of the 'baroque' principle of melodic elaboration, but to a far greater extent of polyphony, which continually appears in the development only to run aground. Schoenberg thinks Classicism's unfulfilled promise through to its conclusion and in so doing breaks down the traditional façade. He reasserted Bach's challenge, which Classicism, including Beethoven, had evaded, though without regressing behind Classicism. The Classic composers had neglected Bach out of historical necessity. The autonomy of the musical subject took priority over all other considerations and critically excluded the traditional form of object-ivization, at the same time making do with a semblance of ob-jectivization just as the unrestricted interplay of subjects seemed the best guarantee for society. Only today, when subjectivity in its immediacy can no longer be regarded as the supreme category since its realization depends on society as a whole, does the inadequacy of even Beethoven's solution, which extended the subject so as to cover the whole, become evident. The development-section, which even at its heights in Beethoven, in the *Eroica*, remains 'dramatic', not totally composed, is transformed through Schoenberg's poly-phony; the subjective melodic impulse is dialectically dissolved into its objective multivocal components. It is this organization, not capricious tolerance, that distinguishes Schoenberg's counterpoint from all the others of his epoch. At the same time it overcomes the burdensome harmonic emphasis. He is supposed to have said that no one thinks about harmony with truly good counterpoint. This, however, is characteristic not only of Bach, in whom the stringency of the polyphony distracts attention from the *continuo* schema within which it operates, but of Schoenberg as well, in whom such stringency ultimately makes all chord schemas and all façades super-fluous; his is music of the intellectual ear.

As 'developing variation', intellectualization becomes a technical principle. It overcomes all mere immediacy by accepting and following its inner dynamic. Schoenberg once ironically mentioned that musical theory is always concerned only with the beginning and the end and never with what comes between, namely, with the music itself. His entire work is a single effort to answer this question ignored by theory. Themes and their history, the musical progres-sion, have equal weight, indeed, the difference between the two is liquidated. This takes place within the group of works which ex-tends roughly from the *Songs* op. 6 to the *George Songs*, and which includes the first two Quartets, the *First Kammersymphonie* and the first movement of the *Second*. Only an obsessive concern with 'style' could consider such works 'transitional'; as compositions they are of the greatest maturity. The d minor Quartet, down to its last note, created an entirely new level of thematically coherent chamber-music composition. Its form is that of the later twelve-tone works; anyone who wants to understand them would do better to study this Quartet than to count series. Each 'idea', from the first beat on, is contrapuntal and contains within itself the potentiality of its development; each development preserves the spontaneity of the first idea. And that which still transpired successively in the First Quartet is then, within the scant dimensions and polyphony of the *First Kammersymphonie*, compressed into simultaneity. Thus, the façade, still tolerated to a degree in the Quartet, begins to disintegrate. In his last book, Schoenberg described and illustrated how, in the exposition of the *Kammersymphonie*, he followed the unconscious impulse—that is, the desideratum of the latent structure—sacrificed the usual conception of the logical 'consequence' of overt thematic references and instead drew the consequence from the inner consistency of the themes. The two, superficially independent main melodies of the first thematic complex reveal themselves to be related in the sense of the serial principle of the later twelve-tone technique; this is how far back in Schoenberg's development the technique reaches; it must be seen as an implication of the compositional procedure rather than of the mere material. The compulsion, however, to purge music of all preconceived notions leads not only to new sounds like the famous fourth-chord, but also to a new expressive dimension beyond the depiction of human emotions. A conductor has compared the resolution field at the end of the great development section with the joy of a glacier landscape. For the first time a break is made in the *Kammersymphonie* with what had been a basic stratum of music since the age of the *basso continuo*, from the *stile rappresentativo*, from the adjustment of musical language to the significative aspect of human language. For the first time Schoenberg's warmth turns into the extreme of coolness which expresses itself through the absence of all expression. Later he polemicized against those who demand 'animal warmth' of music; his dictum, which proclaims that what music has to say can be said only through music, suggests the idea of a language unlike that of human beings. The brilliant, dynamically reserved and yet barbed quality which increases throughout the *First Kammersymphonie*, anticipates fifty years beforehand and without preclassical gestures the later functionalism. Music which lets itself be driven by pure, unadulterated expression becomes highly allergic to everything representing a potential encroachment on this purity, to every tendency to ingratiate itself with the listener as well as the latter's efforts to ingratiate himself with it, to all identification and empathy. The logical consequence of the principle of expression includes the moment of its own negation as that negative form of truth which transforms love into the power of unremitting protest.

At first, and for many years thereafter, Schoenberg did not pursue this any further. The first movement of the *Second Kammersymphonie*, written at the same time, is thoroughly expressive and harmonic; with its vast wealth of qualitatively distinct and constructively employed chord intervals, it is one of the most consummate examples of total harmonization that Schoenberg's imagination wrung from the vertical dimension. The second movement, however, which was composed later in America at the urging of Fritz Stiedry, applies the experiences of the twelve-tone technique to the late tonality, thus resulting in an intermingling of expression and construction that is unique even for Schoenberg. The piece starts off playfully, like a serenade, but as it continues to condense contrapuntally the tragic knot is drawn ever more tightly until at the end it confirms the sombre tone of the first movement—and merges with it. The *Second Kammersymphonie* is technically closer to the f sharp minor Quartet op. 10 than to the First Symphony. This piece, as H.F. Redlich has remarked, represents in microcosm, retrospectively and prospectively, Schoenberg's entire development. The first movement, with its extraordinary abundance of intervals and thematic figures, balancing on one foot as it were, drains tonality of all it has left, exploiting it as a means of representation. The second movement, *scherzando*, unleashes all the glaring whites and the black caricatures of Strindbergian Expressionism; demons mangle the tonality. In the third movement, the lyric variations on George's 'Litany', music meditates on itself. The most essential motivic ingredients of the first two movements converge serially in the theme. Integral construction curbs the outburst of grief. The last movement, however, in song once again, sounds as though it came from another world, from the realm of freedom; it is the new music through and through, despite the F sharp major at the end, its first unadulterated manifestation, more utopian in its inspiration than any thereafter. The instrumental introduction of this 'withdrawal' has the sound of truth, as though music had been freed of all chains and was soaring above and beyond enormous abysses towards that other planet invoked in the poem. Schoenberg's encounter with George's poetry, which is diametrically opposed and yet inherently related to his work, is one of the few fortunate events in his sporadic and uncertain experiences with the non-musical life of his epoch. As long as he measured himself against George, he was protected against the literary temptations of paltry 'ur-sounds'.

George's maxim: 'The strictest standard is also the supreme freedom,' could have been his own. Of course, musical quality does not depend simply on that of the poetry, but authentic vocal music will succeed only when it encounters authentic poetry. The *Georgelieder* op. 15 already testify to the manifest break in style, which is why Schoenberg introduced them at their premiere performance with a programmatic declaration. But in their substance they belong to the f sharp minor Quartet, especially to its last movement. The compositional technique, at the time thoroughly unusual and provocative, recalls once again the idea of the great song cycles, of the *Fernen Geliebten*, the *Müllerin* and the *Winterreise*. With Schoenberg, 'the first time' is always 'once again'. The brevity, pregnancy and character of each individual song is equal in stature to the architecture of the whole, with the caesura after the eighth song, the adagio climaxing in the eleventh and the intensification of the last to the finale. The piano ascetically abandons the conventional resonance and thus creates the muted charm of cosmic distance. The lyrical warmth of *Saget mir auf welchem pfade*, the unconcealed nakedness of *Wenn ich heut nicht deinen leib berühre*, the pulsating pianissimo at the climax of the almost unbearable expressive intensity of *Als wir hinter dem beblümten tore*—all this sounds as though it could not have been otherwise and had always existed. The sombre parting at the end, however, expands symphonically like the rejoicing of *Und ein liebend Herz erreichet/was ein liebend Herz geweiht* before it.

With the *Georgelieder* the phase of 'free atonality' begins. This brought Schoenberg the fame of a subversive after the public scandal which had already been caused by the *Kammersymphonie* and the *Second Quartet*. What at the time seemed a radical break may be seen today as ratification of the inevitable. Schoenberg overturned the vocabulary, from the individual sounds to the schemas of the large forms, but he continued to speak the idiom and to strive for the kind of musical texture which is inseparably tied to the means he eliminated, not merely through common genesis but through its very meaning. Such a contradiction hindered Schoenberg's further development as much as it furthered it. Even in his most advanced works he remained traditional; he excluded the material of musical language which had provided musical structure with its basis since the beginning of the seventeenth century, and yet retained the structural categories, the bearers of the 'subcutaneous' moment in his music, virtually intact. The idiom was as self-evident and beyond question to him as to Schubert, and this is at least partly responsible for the conviction inherent in his work. Yet at the same time, the familiar categories of musical structure, like theme, elaboration, tension, resolution, no longer suit the material he has set free. Purged of all prior implications, the idiom is neutralized. Actually, each instant and each tone should be equally near the centre, and this would preclude the organization of musical time-progression which prevails in Schoenberg. Occasionally, in particularly unruly pieces such as the third one of op. 11, he did compose accordingly; otherwise, however, he composed as though he were still using prestructured material. Perhaps the innermost intention of the twelve-tone technique was to endow, on its own, the material with that prestructured quality. Otherwise, the coordination of the material assumes an external, arbitrary, indeed blind character. Nowhere is this more striking than in Schoenberg's relation to musical drama. It was determined directly by Wagernian aesthetics, despite the extreme expressionism of the first two dramatic works. As late as *Moses and Aaron*, the relation of music to text is scarcely different from any post-Wagnerian opera no matter how little attention is paid to the music-dramatic scores. In Schoenberg different historical moments collide. The composer who, in immanent-musical terms, was light-years ahead of his epoch, remained a child of the nineteenth century where its *terminus ad quem*, its function, was concerned. To this extent Stravinsky's critique of Schoenberg is not simply reactionary; it defines the bounds set by Schoenberg's naïveté.

This is, of course, opposed by the antiartistic, explosive element in Schoenberg. The piano pieces op. 11 are antiornamental to the point of gesticulating destructively. Unadorned, naked expression and hostility to art are united.[1] Something in Schoenberg, perhaps

[1] The gesture traces the direction of Schoenberg's development, before the listener's ears—the revelation of the subcutaneous, not unlike contemporary Cubism, which transposed similar latent structures into the immediate phenomenon. The analogy is particularly relevant to the elimination of traditional perspective in painting and of tonal—'spatial'—harmony in music. Both result from the anti-ornamental impulse. Artistic perspective, not without reason called 'trompe-l'oeil', contains an element of deception which is also present, in a manner it is difficult to define, of course, in tonal harmony, which creates the illusion of spatial depth. It is precisely this illusion that the movement of the piano pieces op. 11 destroys. The illusionary moment in harmony became intolerable and the reaction it produced contributed decisively to externalizing the inner dimension. The illusionary moment, however, was profoundly linked to the very *stile rappresentativo* from which Schoenberg distanced himself. In so far as art imitates, it has always involved illusion. But like painting, music does not simply abolish space; rather it replaces the illusion, the pretence of it, with an, as it were, expanded, peculiarly musical space.

161

allegiance to the command cited in the text of the choral pieces op. 27—'Thou shalt make no graven images'—seeks to eradicate the depictive-aesthetic features of music, the imageless art. At the same time, this feature characterizes the idiom in which every one of Schoenberg's musical ideas is conceived. He laboured under this contradiction to the very end. Repeatedly, even in the twelve-tone phase, he made heroic efforts to forget, to demolish concealing musical layers, but the musical idiom always maintained its opposition. Hence, his reductions are always followed by complex, richly woven works in which musical language emerges out of the effort to eliminate such language. Thus, the first atonal piano pieces were followed by the orchestral pieces op. 16, which sacrifice nothing of the emancipation of the material but which, amid their 'prose', develop anew in polyphony and thematic work. This results in 'basic figures', long before the twelve-tone technique. *Pierrot lunaire*, too, has similar elements, such as the 'moon spot', which became famous through the *tour de force* of a fugue accompanied by two simultaneous crablike canons; yet in addition, the theme of the fugue and of the woodwind canon is strictly derived from a series, whereas the canon in the strings forms an 'accompanying system', of the kind that then became virtually the rule in the twelve-tone technique. Just as free atonality developed out of the fabric of large tonal chamber music, the twelve-tone procedure in turn stemmed from free atonal composition. The fact that the orchestral pieces discover the serial principle without rigidifying it into a system ranges them among the most successful of his works. Some of them —the intricate lyric of the second, and the last, culminating in a finale of unparalleled perspective power—are the equals of the great tonal chamber music works and of the *Georgelieder*. As compositions, the stage works, *Erwartung* and *Glückliche Hand,* are no worse. But Schoenberg's anti-artistic tendency becomes unartistic in them and so upsets the conception. It is true that he scarcely ever composed anything which was freer than *Erwartung.* It is not merely the means of presentation which emancipates itself, but the syntax as well. Webern did not exaggerate when, in the first published collection on Schoenberg, he wrote that the score is 'an unheard-of event. In it a break is made with all traditional architectonics; there is always something new coming, with the most abrupt changes in expression'. Every moment abandons itself to the spontaneous impulse, and the object—the representation of dread—conserves Schoenberg's historical innervation, which was related to the most profound elements in Expressionism immediately preceding 1914. But Schoenberg was not capable of discriminating in his choice of text. Marie Pappenheim's monodrama is second-hand Expressionism, dilettante in its language and structure, and this rubs off on the music as well. However ingenious Schoenberg is in dividing the whole into three sections, search, outbreak and concluding lament, the music still draws inner form from the text, and, in adapting itself to it, is forced to repeat continually the same gestures and configurations. It thus violates the postulate of incessant innovation. In the *Glückliche Hand*, a no less Expressionist attitude turns compositionally to the objective symphonic form, designing pastose formal surfaces; yet here, too, such objectivity is hopelessly compromised by the foolish, narcissistic subject-matter. The symphony into which Schoenberg's work ought to coalesce was never written.

The Orchestral Songs op. 22 conclude with the words, *Und bin ganz allein in dem grossen Sturm* [*And am all alone in the great storm*]. At the time, Schoenberg must have experienced the height of his powers. His music expands like a giant, as though the totality, the 'great storm', were about to emerge from self-oblivious subjectivity, 'all alone'. To these years belongs *Pierrot lunaire*, the best known of all of Schoenberg's works after his abandonment of tonality. The objectivist, expansive tendencies are happily balanced by what the subject is capable of filling. A cosmos of every conceivable musical and expressive characteristic is created, yet one reflected in the mirror of isolated inwardness, in a hothouse of souls like that mentioned shortly before in the Maeterlinck song; a cosmos which is both fanciful and absurd. The restorative element—passacaglia, fugue, canon, waltz, serenade and strophic song—enters the *paradis artificiel* only ironically, as though it were denatured, and the aphoristically abbreviated themes sound like the distant echo of literal ones. This discontinuity is not to be separated from the anachronistic subject-matter. Albert Giraud's poems, translated by Hartleben, regress behind Expressionism to the level of commercial art, figured ornament and stylizing. The form and content which confront the subject remain its unconscious projection. It is not the subject-matter alone that brings Schoenberg's masterwork into paradoxical proximity to *kitsch*, thus jeopardizing everything exquisite in the piece; rather, through its propensity for isolated flowing and flashy *pointes*, the music itself sacrifices something of what Schoenberg had accomplished since *Erwartung*. All virtuoso spirituality notwithstanding and despite the fact that some of Schoenberg's most complex compositions are included in *Pierrot*, the musical project—the production of surface connections—retreats inconspicuously from his most advanced position. Yet this can in no way be attributed to a decline in compositional power. Schoenberg was never more sovereign in his use of technique than in the Arabesques, which playfully overcome all musical gravity. But he collides with the very historical necessity which he, more than any other composer of the epoch, embodies. He became entangled in the aporia of the false transition. Nothing spiritual has ever escaped this fate since Hegel, perhaps because non-contradiction can no longer be attained in the self-satisfied realm of the mind, if indeed it ever could. The aesthetic subject, like the philosophical subject, having developed fully and in control of itself, cannot stop at that self and its 'expression'; it must aim at objective authority, as Schoenberg's bestowing gesture intended from the very first. Yet this authority cannot be derived from mere subjectivity, even if the latter has drawn its sustenance from the entire dynamics of society, unless it is already present in society, from which the aesthetic subject must detach itself today precisely because that substantial content is lacking in society. In Schoenberg, the destiny of Nietzsche's 'New Table' repeated itself, as well as that of George, who invented a new god in order to ensure the possibility of cultic poetry; it was no accident that Schoenberg felt himself drawn to both men. After *Pierrot* and the *Orchestral Songs*, he began composing an Oratorio. The musical fragments that were published display again Schoenberg's ability to achieve the most extreme effects unfailingly, such as the hammer-stroke in the *Glückliche Hand*. But the text reveals the desperate nature of the enterprise. The literary inadequacy discloses the impossibility of the object itself, the incongruity of a religious choral work in the midst of late capitalist society, of the aesthetic figure of totality. The whole, as a positive entity, cannot be antithetically extracted from an estranged and splintered reality by means of the will and power of the individual; if it is not to degenerate into deception and ideology, it must assume the form of negation. The *chef d'oeuvre* remained unfinished and Schoenberg's admission of failure, his recognition that it was 'a fragment, like everything else', says perhaps more for him than any success. There is no question that he could have forcibly completed what he had in mind, but he must have sensed something false in the project itself; the idea of the masterpiece has today been twisted into the genre of masterpiece. The break between the substantiality of the ego and the over-all structure of social existence, which denies the ego not merely external sanction but its necessary preconditions as well, has become too profound to permit works of art a synthesis. The subject knows itself to be objective, removed from the contingency of mere existence, yet this knowledge, which is true, is at the same time also untrue. The objectivity that inheres in the subject is barred from reconciliation with a state of things which negates that objective substance precisely by aiming at full reconciliation with it, and yet which that objectivity must nevertheless become if it is to be saved from the impotence of mere 'being-for-itself'. The greater the artist, the stronger the temptation of the chimerical. For, like knowledge, art cannot wait, but as soon as it succumbs to impatience it is trapped. In this respect Schoenberg resembles not merely Nietzsche and George, but also Wagner. The sectarian stimga that adhered to him and his circle is a symptom of the false transition. His authoritarian nature is so constructed that, having followed musical logic in making himself the principle of all music, he then had to enthrone that principle above himself and obey it. The idea of freedom is blocked in his music by the desperate need to submit to a heteronomous authority, a need that arises because the effort to transcend mere individuality and reach objectivity is futile. The inner impossibility of music objectifying itself is manifested in the compulsive traits of its aesthetic complexion. It cannot truly go outside of itself and hence must elevate its own arbitrary will, which failed to attain objectivity, to a position of authority over itself. The iconoclast becomes the fetishist. Cut off from its realization, the principle of music which is both rationally transparent and inclusive of the subject becomes an abstraction, a rigid, unquestioned precept.

Schoenberg's pause in creation, of Biblical length, cannot be adequately explained in terms of his private destiny in the war and inflation. His forces regrouped as though after a mortal defeat. He busied himself with extraordinary intensity in those years with the 'Society for Private Musical Performances', which he had founded. His significance for musical interpretation can scarcely be over-estimated. Schoenberg, who as composer had turned the subcutaneous outwards, discovered and taught a mode of presentation that rendered the subcutaneous structure visible, making the performance the integral realization of the musical construction. The ideal of interpretation converges with that of composition. The dream of the musical subject-object concretized itself technologically after the composer had abandoned the conclusion of *Jacob's Ladder*. He no longer looks to superpersonal ideas and forms to lead the way to aesthetic authority, but instead recognizes that this can be achieved only through the immanent movement of the subject-matter in the form of logically coherent composition. He thus showed himself to be incorruptibly superior to the blandishments of all the usurpatory and restorative tendencies that emerged in post-Expressionist music,

165

even at points where he brushed the neo-Classical music he despised. But the stubborn loyalty of the later Schoenberg to the method, as a guarantee of comprehensive totality, merely deferred the aporia. Something almost imperceptible happened to his music under the primacy of the highly ingenious twelve-tone technique. Of course, the experiences and rules that precipitated necessarily and convincingly out of the compositional process were comprehended, codified and systematized. But this act does not leave the truth-content of those experiences untouched. They are no longer open and accessible to dialectical correction. Schoenberg is threatened by the nemesis of what Kandinsky, in an article written in 1912 and dedicated to him, describes as follows: 'The artist thinks that, having "finally found his form", he can now continue to create works of art in peace. Unfortunately, even he himself does not usually notice that from this moment (of "peace") on, he very rapidly begins to lose this finally found form.' This is so because each work of art is a force-field, and just as the act of thought cannot be separated from the truth-content of the logical judgement, works of art are true only in so far as they transcend their material preconditions. The element of delusion shared by both technical-aesthetic and cognitive systems does, it is true, assure them of their suggestive power. They become models. But in denying themselves self-reflection and making themselves static, they become moribund and cripple the very impulse that produced the system in the first place. There is no middle way that avoids the alternative. To ignore the insights that have coalesced into the system is to cling impotently to what has been superseded. Yet the system itself becomes a fixed idea and universal recipe. It is not the method itself that is false—no one can compose any longer who has not sensed with his own ears the gravitational pull towards twelve-tone technique—but rather its hypostasization, the rejection of all that is otherwise, of anything not already analytically assimilated. Music must not identify its methods, a part of subjective reason, with the subject-matter, which is objective. The pressures to do just this, however, increase as the aesthetic subject is less and less able to orient itself on something which is both distinct from it and yet in harmony with it—the magic formula replaces the comprehensive work which prohibits itself. To be true to Schoenberg is to warn against all twelve-tone schools. Devoid of experimentation as well as prudence, these schools no longer involve any risk, and hence have entered the service of a second conformity. The means have become ends. Schoenberg himself benefited greatly through his bond to the tradition of musical language; by means of the twelve-tone procedure he was able to organize music which was both highly complex and in need of such supports. With the composers that followed, the method gradually loses its function and is abused as a mere substitute for tonality; it does nothing more than to glue together musical phenomena which are so simple that such great pains are hardly worthwhile. For this turn of events, however, Schoenberg again is not wholly innocent. At times he wrote twelve-tone gigues and rondos, forms in which the twelve-tone technique becomes superfluous, while remaining fundamentally incompatible with musical types that so unmistakably presuppose tonal modulation. In the beginning he glaringly exposed the inconsistency of all too consistent music which depended on just this kind of borrowing, only to spend years thereafter striving to find a corrective.

To this day the potentiality of the twelve-tone technique has remained open. It does in fact permit the synthesis of a procedure which is completely free and yet completely strict. Inasmuch as thematic work wholly dominates the material, the composition itself can become truly athematic, 'prose', without succumbing to contingency in the process. But the reification of the method becomes flagrant when Schoenberg claims that the twelve-tone series, which solely predispose the material, have the power of creating large forms. What tonality was once able to achieve by virtue of modulatory proportions cannot be repeated by a technique, the very sense of which lies in its not appearing outwardly. When twelve-tone rows and relations become as evident in larger forms as key relations were in traditional music, the form rattles mechanically. The twelve-tone rows do not describe a musical space within which the work unfolds and which predetermines intuition. They are rather the smallest units which enable the construction of an integral whole comprising the most variegated relations. If they become manifest, the whole disintegrates into its atoms. It was self-evident therefore for Schoenberg's variative imagination to have concealed the rows behind the real musical progression. Thus hidden, however, they could not exercise the architectonic influence for which he hoped. The contradiction between latent organization and manifest music reproduces itself at a higher stage. Schoenberg invoked traditional formal means in order to exorcise it. Because he saddled the twelve-tone technique with the burden of objectivity as a kind of universal, conceptual order—a burden it could not bear—he was compelled to introduce external categories without regard for the material, so as to produce that order. Faith in organizational musical categories was something he never lost. Many of the large twelve-tone pieces, especially those composed in America, are convincingly successful.

The best, however, rely neither on the twelve-tone rows nor on the traditional types. They are characterized by the free use of authentic compositional techniques, as for instance, stacking thematic surfaces, which are based on distinct but disparate models, one on top of the other. The logic of construction is intensified anew; the main theme from the first movement of the Violin Concerto, for instance, is more pregnant in its construction than anything prior to the introduction of the twelve-tone technique. Schoenberg's compositional faculties were heightened through such resistances. For the disciples, however, the technique came to be regarded as 'natural', as the musical *ordo*, and in this sense, it became the bad heir of tonality, which itself was not natural any more but rather the product of rationalization; Schoenberg's followers thus succeeded only in displaying their own weakness, their impotent longing for security. This can be drastically demonstrated in the relation of twelve-tone technique to the octave. The technique tacitly accepts the identity of the octave, without which one of the most important twelve-tone principles, the interchangeability of each tone in any octave range, becomes inconceivable. Yet at the same time the octave retains something 'tonal' about it, and disturbs the equilibrium of the twelve half-tones; whenever octaves are doubled there is the association of the triad. The contradiction manifested itself in Schoenberg's fluctuating praxis. Earlier, beginning already to a large extent in the works of free atonality, the octave was avoided. Then, however, Schoenberg wrote octaves, probably to clarify the bass sounds and main thematic parts; the first time came in a piece which played with tonality, the *Ode to Napoleon*—here, just as in the Piano Concerto, it is impossible not to hear a certain forced, impure quality. The pseudo-nature betrays itself entirely in the early days of the technique in a tendency to the apocryphal, the shabby and the absurd. At times, music constructed according to formulas, essentially meaningless, threatens to undo all its sublimation and revert to raw material. Like the dogma of astrologers, which links the movement of the stars to the progress of human destinies while both remain unaffected by the cognitive act and are thus fortuitous, the sequence of twelve-tone events, determined down to its final note, contains vestiges of contingency for lived experience. As though to mock the potential synthesis of freedom and necessity, the latter, having been made absolute, reveals itself to be contingent.

The great composer triumphed once again over the inventor, as Schoenberg in later life devoted all his energies to the task of eliminating the apocryphal elements in twelve-tone technique. The first serial compositions, which were not strictly twelve-tone, were still

168

free of such elements. In the first four pieces of op. 23, the eruptive forces of the Expressionist phase echo tremulously. There are hardly any rigid sections. The second piece, for instance, a peripatie which in Schoenberg's hands became heir to the scherzo, is only a totally composed diminuendo of supreme originality; the outburst dies away rapidly, leaving a nocturnally tranquil, comforting concluding postlude. The spirited fourth piece comes closer to the idea of an athematic twelve-tone composition than almost any other work. The Piano Suite op. 25 and the Woodwind Quintet op. 26 are thoroughly twelve-tone. They bring out the element of constraint with particular emphasis, a kind of Bauhaus-music, metallic constructivism which derives its force from precisely the absence of primary expression; even where expressive characteristics appear, they are 'totally constructed'. The Quintet, probably the most difficult piece to listen to of any that Schoenberg wrote, brusquely drives sublimation, in one dimension, to an extreme—it declares war on colour. The basic impulse against everything infantile, against musical stupidity, takes hold of the medium which, more than any other, seems culinary, mere sensuous excitation this side of intellectual activity. Of all of Schoenberg's accomplishments in integrating musical means, not the least was that he conclusively separated colour from the decorative sphere and elevated it to a compositional element in its own right. It changes into a means for the elucidation of musical interrelations. By being thus included in the compositional process, however, it is also condemned. In a passage from *Style and Idea* Schoenberg explicitly repudiated it. The more nakedly construction represents itself, the less it requires colouristic help. The principle thus turns against Schoenberg's own achievements, comparable perhaps to the late Beethoven, in whom all sensuous immediacy reduces itself to mere foreground, to allegory. It is easy enough to imagine this late form of Schoenberg's asceticism, the negation of all façades, extending to all musical dimensions. Mature music becomes suspicious of real sound as such. Similarly, with the realization of the 'subcutaneous', the end of musical interpretation becomes conceivable. The silent, imaginative reading of music could render actual playing as superfluous as, for instance, speaking is made by the reading of written material; such a practice could at the same time save music from the abuse inflicted upon the compositional content by virtually every performance today. The inclination to silence, which shapes the aura of every tone in Webern's lyrics, is related to the tendency stemming from Schoenberg. Its ultimate result, however, can only be that artistic maturity and intellectualization abolish not only sensuous appearance, but with it, art itself. In Schoenberg's late work, artistic intellectualization moves emphatically towards the dissolution of art, and so converges abysmally with anti-artistic, barbaric tendencies. For this reason, the efforts of Boulez and the younger twelve-tone composers in all countries to achieve total abstraction are by no means 'youthful blundering', but rather the continuation and development of one of Schoenberg's intentions. He never, however, made himself completely the slave of his own intention or of objective tendencies. Paradoxically enough, the composer who forcibly organized and co-ordinated his material, with ever-increasing severity as he aged, in many respects broke through the systematic constraints of the logic he had unleashed. His composing never simulated the primitive unity of composition and technical procedure. The experience that no musical subject-object can constitute itself here and today was not wasted on him. On the one hand, it saved his subjective freedom of movement; on the other, it kept the demon of the composing machine distant from the objective form. He regained that freedom as soon as he could function in the twelve-tone technique as in a familiar 'language', in the school of the untroubled, gay Chamber Suite op. 29 and of the almost didactic Orchestral Variations, from which Leibowitz distilled a compendium of the new technique. His close contact with the text and with the *pointes*, however modest, of the comic opera, *From Today to Tomorrow*, returned to him all the flexibility of the musical idiom. With the latter fully in mind, he tosses off a masterpiece for the second time, again postponing the conclusion with that enigmatic faith in an endless life behind which his despair at the 'it-shall-not-be' is concealed. The fact that his powers actually rose to a highpoint once again in the early thirties was brought out by the unforgettable Darmstadt première of the *Dance of the Golden Calf* in the summer of 1961, only a few days before Schoenberg's death. The performance, under Scherchen, was met with wild enthusiasm and marked the first time that a twelve-tone piece had received the approval which its creator both scorned and needed more than anyone else. The expressive intensity, disposition of colour and constructive power sweep away all obstacles. To judge from the text of the fragment, as a finished opera, *Moses and Aaron* would have been lost; unfinished, it ranks among the great fragments of music.

Schoenberg, who resisted all conventions within the sphere of music, accepted the role assigned to him by the social division of labour, which restricted him to the sphere of music. His impulse to go beyond it as painter and poet was frustrated; the division of labour is not to be revoked by the claims of universal genius. He thus took his place among the 'great composers', as though this notion was eternal. The slightest criticism of any of the masters since Bach he found intolerable. Not only did he reject qualitative differences within the work of each, but also, whenever possible, stylistic distinctions between works written in different genres, even those which are beyond question, such as that between Beethoven's symphonic and his chamber music. That the category of the great composer was susceptible to historical variation did not occur to him any more than the doubt that his own work would be established as a classic when the time came. Against his will, that which crystallized in his work embodied immanent musical opposition to such socially naïve conceptions. The impatience with sensuous appearance in his late style corresponds to the emasculation of art faced with the possibility of its promises being fulfilled in reality, but also to the horror which, in order to suppress that possibility, explodes every criterion of that which might become an image. In the midst of the blindness of specialization, his music suddenly saw the light that shines beyond the aesthetic realm. His incorruptible integrity once attained this awareness when, during the first months of the Hitler dictatorship, he unabashedly said that survival was more important than art. If his late work has been spared the fate of all art since the Second World War with the exception of Picasso's, it is because of this relativizing of the artistic, to which Schoenberg's anticultural element sublimated itself. Perhaps this is only fully revealed in his didactic traits. When Valéry remarked that the work of great artists has something of the quality of finger exercises, of studies for works that were never created, he could have used Schoenberg as his model. The utopia of art transcends individual works. Moroever, it is this medium alone which produces the characteristic consensus among musicians which holds that the distinction between production and reproduction is indifferent. Musicians sense that they labour on music and not on works, even if such labour progresses only through works. The late Schoenberg composed not works, but paradigms of a possible music. The idea of music itself grows all the more transparent as the works insist less and less on their appearance. They begin to acquire the character of the fragment, the shadow of which followed Schoenberg's art throughout his life. His last pieces give a fragmentary impression, not merely in their brevity but in their shrivelled diction. The dignity of the great works devolves on splinters. Oratorio and Biblical opera are outweighed by the tale of the *Survivor from Warsaw*, which lasts only a few minutes; in this piece, Schoenberg, acting on his own, suspends the aesthetic sphere through the recollection of experiences which are inaccessible to art. Anxiety, Schoenberg's expressive core, identifies itself with the terror of men in the agonies of death, under total domination. The sounds of *Erwartung*, the shocks of the *Music for the Film*, of 'impending danger, anxiety, catastrophe', finally meet what they had always prophesied. That which the feebleness and impotence of the individual soul seemed to express testifies to what has been inflicted on mankind in those who represent the whole as its victims. Horror has never rung as true in music, and by articulating it music regains its redeeming power through negation. The Jewish song with which the *Survivor from Warsaw* concludes is music as the protest of mankind against myth.

VALÉRY PROUST MUSEUM

In memory of Hermann von Grab

The German word, '*museal*' ['*museumlike*'], has unpleasant overtones. It describes objects to which the observer no longer has a vital relationship and which are in the process of dying. They owe their preservation more to historical respect than to the needs of the present. Museum and mausoleum are connected by more than phonetic association. Museums are like the family sepulchres of works of art. They testify to the neutralization of culture. Art treasures are hoarded in them, and their market value leaves no room for the pleasure of looking at them. Nevertheless, that pleasure is dependent on the existence of museums. Anyone who does not have his own collection (and the great private collections are becoming rare) can, for the most part, become familiar with painting and sculpture only in museums. When discontent with museums is strong enough to provoke the attempt to exhibit paintings in their original surroundings or in ones similar, in baroque or rococo castles, for instance, the result is even more distressing than when the works are wrenched from their original surroundings and then brought together. Sensibility wreaks even more havoc with art than does the hodge-podge of collections. With music the situation is analogous. The programmes of large concert societies, generally retrospective in orientation, have continually more in common with museums, while Mozart performed by candlelight is degraded to a costume piece. In efforts to retrieve music from the remoteness of the performance and put it into the immediate context of life there is not only something ineffectual but also a tinge of industriously regressive spite. When some well-intentioned person advised Mahler to darken the hall during the concert for the sake of the mood, the composer rightly replied that a performance at which one didn't forget about the surroundings was worthless. Such problems reveal something of the fatal situation of what is called 'the cultural tradition'. Once tradition is no longer animated by a comprehensive, substantial force but has to be conjured up by means of citations because 'It's important to have tradition', then whatever happens to be left of it is dissolved into a means to an end. An exhibition

175

of applied art only makes a mockery of what it pretends to conserve. Anyone who thinks that art can be reproduced in its original form through an act of the will is trapped in hopeless romanticism. Modernizing the past does it much violence and little good. But to renounce radically the possibility of experiencing the traditional would be to capitulate to barbarism out of devotion to culture. That the world is out of joint is shown everywhere in the fact that however a problem is solved, the solution is false.

One cannot be content, however, with the general recognition of a negative situation. An intellectual dispute like the one on museums must be fought out with specific arguments. Here two extraordinary documents are available, for the two authentic French poets of the last generation have expressed themselves on the question of the museum. Their positions are diametrically opposed, but the statements are not directed polemically against each other, nor in fact does either betray any acquaintance of the other. In a contribution to a volume of essays dedicated to Proust, Valéry emphasized that he was not very familiar with Proust's novels. Valéry's remarks on museums are entitled 'Le problème des musées' and appear in the volume of essays *Pièces sur l'art*. The passage from Proust occurs in the third volume of *A l'ombre des jeunes filles en fleurs*.

Valéry's appeal is obviously directed against the confusing overabundance of the Louvre. He is not, he writes, overly fond of museums. The more marvellous the treasures which are preserved in them, the more all delight disappears. The word Valéry uses, 'délices', is one of those which are utterly untranslatable. 'Delicacies' sounds too journalistic, 'joys', too heavy and Wagnerian. 'Delights' is perhaps closest to what is intended, but none of these words expresses the faint reminiscence of feudal pleasure that has been associated with *l'art pour l'art* since Villiers de l'Isle Adam. The only echo of it in German is the 'deliziös' ['delicious'] of the *Rosenkavalier*. In any case, in the Louvre the seignorial Valéry feels himself constrained from the first by the authoritarian gesture that takes away his cane and by the 'No Smoking' sign. Cold confusion, he says, reigns among the sculptures, a tumult of frozen creatures each of which demands the non-existence of the others, disorder strangely organized. Standing among the pictures offered for contemplation, Valéry mockingly observes that one is seized by a sacred awe; conversation is louder than in church, softer than in real life. One does not know why one has come—in search of culture or enjoyment, in fulfilment of an obligation, in obedience to a convention. Fatigue and barbarism converge. Neither a hedonistic nor a rationalistic civilization could have constructed a house of such disparities. Dead visions are entombed there.

The ear, Valéry argues, which is further removed from music than the eye is from painting and can therefore harbour illusions, is better off—no one can ask it to listen to ten orchestras at once. Furthermore, the mind is certainly not capable of performing all possible operations simultaneously. Only the mobile eye is forced to apprehend in the same moment a portrait and a seascape, a kitchen and a triumphal march, or, worst of all, styles of painting completely incompatible with one another. The more beautiful a picture is, the more it is distinct from all others; it becomes a rare object, unique. This picture, one sometimes says, kills the ones around it. If this is forgotten, Valéry warns, the heritage of art will be destroyed. Just as man loses his abilities through an excess of technical aids, so an excess of riches impoverishes him.

Valéry's argumentation bears the stamp of cultural conservatism. He certainly did not concern himself with the critique of political economy. It is therefore all the more astounding that the aesthetic nerves which register false wealth should react so precisely to the fact of over-accumulation. When he speaks of the accumulation of excessive and therefore unusable capital, Valéry uses metaphorically an expression literally valid for the economy. Whether artists produce or rich people die, whatever happens is good for the museums. Like casinos, they cannot lose, and that is their curse. For people become hopelessly lost in the galleries, isolated in the midst of so much art. The only other possible reaction to this situation is the one which Valéry sees as the general, ominous result of any and all progress in the domination of material—increasing superficiality. Art becomes a matter of education and information; Venus becomes a document. Education defeats art. Nietzsche argues along very similar lines in his *Untimely Meditation*, 'On the Use and Abuse of History for Life'. The shock of the museum brings Valéry to historical-philosophical insight into the perishing of art works; there, he says, we put the art of the past to death.

Even afterwards, in the street, Valéry cannot free himself from the magnificent chaos of the museum (a metaphor, one could say, for the anarchical production of commodities in fully developed bourgeois society), and he searches for the basis of his malaise. Painting and sculpture, the demon of knowledge tells him, are like abandoned children. 'Their mother is dead, their mother, architecture. While she lived, she gave them their place, their definition. The freedom to wander was forbidden them. They had their place,

177

their clearly defined lighting, their materials. Proper relations prevailed between them. While she was alive, they knew what they wanted. Farewell, the thought says to me, I will go no further.' With this romantic gesture, Valéry's reflection ceases. By breaking it off, he avoids the otherwise inevitable conclusion of the radical cultural conservative: the renunciation of culture out of loyalty to it.

Proust's view of the museum is woven most skilfully into the fabric of the *Recherche du temps perdu*. Only there can its meaning be interpreted. Proust's reflections, which represent a return to the techniques of the pre-Flaubertian novel, are never mere observations on the material represented. They are bound up with it through subterranean associations and hence fall, like the narrative itself, within the great aesthetic continuum of his inner dialogue. In speaking of his trip to the sea resort Balbec, Proust remarks on the caesura which voyages make in the course of life by 'leading us from one name to another name'. The caesuras are particularly manifest in railway stations, 'these utterly peculiar places ... which, so to speak, are not part of the town and yet contain the essence of its personality as clearly as they bear its name on their signs'. Like everything surveyed by Proust's memory, which seems to drain the intention out of its objects, the stations become historical archetypes and, as the archetypes of departure, tragic ones. Of the glass dome of the Gare St.-Lazare he writes: 'Over a sprawling city it stretched its wide, wasted heaven full of ominous dramas. Certain skies of Mantegna or Veronese are as modern, almost Parisian— under such a vaulting sky only terrible and solemn things can happen, the departure of a train or the raising of the cross.'

The associative transition to the museum is left implicit in the novel; it is the picture of that station painted by Claude Monet, whom Proust loved passionately, which now hangs in the collection of the *Jeu de Paume*. Briefly, Proust compares the station to a museum. Both stand outside the framework of conventional pragmatic activity, and, one might add, both are bearers of a death symbolism. In the case of the station, it is the ancient symbolism of the voyage; in that of the museum, the symbolism associated with the work of art—'l'univers nouveau et périssable', the new and fragile cosmos the artist has created. Like Valéry, Proust returns again and again to the mortality of artifacts. What seems eternal, he says at another point, contains within itself the impulse of its own destruction. The decisive lines on the museum are contained in Proust's physiognomy of the station. 'But in all areas our age is obsessed with the desire to bring things before our eyes in

their natural surroundings and thus to suppress what is essential—
the mental event that raised them out of those surroundings. Today
one "shows" a picture amidst furniture, small art objects, and
curtains "of the epoch", in a trivial decorative display produced by
the hitherto ignorant lady of the house after having spent her days
in archives and libraries. But the masterpiece observed during
dinner no longer produces in us the exhilarating happiness that can
be had only in a museum, where the rooms, in their sober abstinence
from all decorative detail, symbolize the inner spaces into which the
artist withdraws to create the work.'

It is possible to compare Proust's thesis with Valéry's because
they share the presupposition that works of art should be enjoyed.
Valéry speaks of 'délices', Proust of 'joie enivrante', exhilarating
joy. Nothing is more characteristic than that presupposition of the
distance not merely between the present generation and the previous
one but also between the German and the French attitudes towards
art. As early as the writing of *A l'ombre des jeunes filles en fleurs*,
the expression *Kunstgenuss* [*aesthetic pleasure*] must have sounded
as touchingly philistine in German as a Wilhelm Busch rhyme. This
aesthetic pleasure, furthermore, in which Valéry and Proust have
as much faith as in a revered mother, has always been a questionable matter. For anyone who is close to works of art, they are no
more objects of delight than is his own breathing. Rather, he lives
among them like a modern inhabitant of a medieval town who
replies with a peremptory 'yes, yes', when a visitor remarks on the
beauty of the buildings, but who knows every corner and portal. But
it is only when the distance necessary for enjoyment to be possible
is established between the observer and works of art that the question of their continuing vitality can arise. It would probably never
occur to anyone who was at home with art and not a mere visitor.
But since they both continually reflect upon their own work as well
as produce it, Valéry and Proust are certain of the pleasure their
works provide those on the outside. They agree even to the point
of recognizing something of the mortal enmity which exists among
works and which accompanies the pleasure of competition. Far
from recoiling before it, however, Proust affirms this enmity as
though he were as German as Charlus affects to be. For him, competition among works is the test of truth. Schools, he writes at one
point in *Sodom and Gomorrah*, devour each other like micro-
organisms and insure through their struggle the survival of life. This
dialectical attitude, which transcends fixation on the individual as
such, brings Proust into conflict with Valéry, the *artiste*. It makes

179

his perverse tolerance of museums possible, whereas for Valéry the duration of the individual work is the crucial problem.

The criterion of duration is the here and now, the present moment. For Valéry art is lost when it has relinquished its place in the immediacy of life, in its functional context; for him the ultimate question is that of the possible use of the work of art. The craftsman in him, fashions poems with that precision of contour which embodies attention to the surroundings, has become infinitely sensitive to the place of the work of art, including its intellectual setting, as though the painter's feeling for perspective were intensified in him to a feeling for the perspective of reality, in which it becomes possible for the work to have depth. His artistic standpoint is that of immediacy, but driven to the most audacious consequences. He follows the principle of art for art's sake to the verge of its negation. He makes the pure work of art the object of absolute, unwavering contemplation, but he scrutinizes it so long and so intensely that he comes to see that the object of such pure contemplation must wither and degenerate to commercialized decoration, robbed of the dignity in which both its *raison d'être* and Valéry's consist. The pure work is threatened by reification and neutralization. This is the recognition that overwhelms him in the museum. He discovers that the only pure works, the only works that can sustain serious observation, are the impure ones which do not exhaust themselves in that observation but point beyond, towards a social context. And since, with the incorruptibility of the great rationalist, Valéry must recognize that this stage of art is irrevocably past, there is nothing left for the anti-rationalist and Bergonian in him but to mourn for works as they turn into relics.

Proust, the novelist, virtually begins where Valéry, the poet, stopped—with the afterlife of works of art. For Proust's primary relationship to art is the precise opposite of that of the expert and producer. He is first of all an admiring consumer, an amateur, inclined to that effusive and for artists highly suspect awe before works that characterizes only those separated from them as though by an abyss. One could almost say that his genius consisted not least of all in assuming this attitude (which is also that of the man who conducts himself as a spectator even in life) so completely and accurately that it became a new type of productivity, and the power of inner and outer contemplation, thus intensified, turned into recollection, involuntary memory. The amateur is incomparably more comfortable in the museum than is the expert. Valéry feels himself at home in the studio; Proust strolls through an exhibition. There is something exterritorial about his relation to art, and many of his false judgments, as in questions of music, display traces of the dilettante to the end (what, for instance, has the conciliatory kitsch of his friend, Reynaldo Hahn, to do with Proust's novel, where each sentence puts an established attitude out of business with remorseless gentleness). But he moulded this weakness into an instrument of strength as only Kafka could. However naïve his enthusiastic judgements of individual works of art, especially those of the Italian Renaissance, may sound in comparison to Valéry's, he was far less naïve in his relation to art as such. To speak of naïveté in an artist like Valéry, in whom the process of artistic production is so indissolubly merged with reflection upon the process, may sound like a provocation. But he was in fact naïve in having no doubts about the category of the work of art as such. He took it for granted, and the force of his thought, his historical-philosophical energy, increased as a result. The category becomes the criterion in terms of which Valéry can see changes in the internal structure of works of art and in the way they are experienced. Proust, however, is entirely free of the unconditional fetishism of the artist who makes the things himself. For him works of art are from the outset something more than their specific aesthetic qualities. They are part of the life of the person who observes them; they become an element of his consciousness. He thus perceives a level in them very different from that of the formal laws of the work. It is a level set free only by the historical development of the work, a level which has as its premise the death of the living intention of the work. Proust's naïveté is a second naïveté. At every stage of consciousness a new and broader immediacy arises. Whereas Valéry's conservative belief in culture as a pure thing in itself affords incisive criticism of a culture which tends by its very historical nature to destroy everything self-subsistent, Proust's most characteristic mode of perception, his extraordinary sensitivity to changes in modes of experience, has as its paradoxical result the ability to perceive history as landscape. He adores museums as though they were God's true creation, which in Proust's metaphysics is never complete but always occurring anew in each concrete experience, each original artistic intuition. In his marvelling eye he has preserved something out of childhood; Valéry, by contrast, speaks of art like an adult. If Valéry understands something of the power of history over the production and apperception of art, Proust knows that even within works of art themselves history rules like a process of disintegration. 'Ce qu'on appelle la postérité, c'est la postérité de l'oeuvre' might well be translated as, 'What is

called posterity is the afterlife of the work.' In the artifact's capacity for disintegration Proust sees its similarity to natural beauty.
He recognizes the physiognomy of decomposing things as that of
their second life. Because nothing has substance for him but what
has already been mediated by memory, his love dwells on the
second life, the one which is already over, rather than on the first.
For Proust's aestheticism the question of aesthetic quality is of
secondary concern. In a famous passage he glorified inferior music
for the sake of the listener's memories, which are preserved with
far more fidelity and force in an old popular song than in the self-
sufficiency of a work by Beethoven. The saturnine gaze of memory
penetrates the veil of culture. Once they are no longer isolated as
domains of the objective mind but are drawn into the stream of
subjectivity, distinctions between levels of culture lose the pathetic
quality that Valéry's heresies constantly accord them. Valéry takes
offence at the chaotic aspect of the museum because it distorts the
works' expressive realization; for Proust this chaos assumes tragic
character. For him it is only the death of the work of art in the
museum which brings it to life. When severed from the living order
in which it functioned, according to him, its true spontaneity is
released—its uniqueness, its 'name', that which makes the great
works of culture more than culture. Proust's attitude preserves, in
adventurously sophisticated form, the saying from Ottilie's journal
in Goethe's *Elective Affinities*: 'Everything perfect of its kind must
go beyond its kind,' a highly unclassical thought which does art the
honour of relativizing it.

Yet anyone who is not satisfied with intellectual history alone
must face the question: Who is right, the critic of the museum or
its defender? For Valéry the museum is a place of barbarism. His
conviction of the sanctity of culture (which he shares with Mallarmé)
underlies this judgement. Since this religion of spleen provokes so
much opposition, including objections with a simplistic social orientation, it is important to affirm its moment of truth. Only what exists
for its own sake, without regard to those it is supposed to please,
can fulfil its human end. Few things have contributed so greatly
to dehumanization as has the universal human belief that products
of the mind are justified only in so far as they exist for men—the
belief itself bears witness to the dominance of manipulative rationality. Valéry was able to show the objective character, the immanent
coherence of the work in contrast to the contingency of the subject
with such incomparable authority because he gained his insight
through the subjective experience of the discipline of the artist's
work. In this he was unquestionably superior to Proust; incorrupt-

ible, he had greater resistance. In contrast, the primacy Proust assigns the flux of experience and his refusal to tolerate anything fixed and determinate have a sinister aspect—conformity, the ready adjustment to changing situations which he shares with Bergson. Proust's work contains passages on art which approach in unbridled subjectivism the philistine attitude that turns the work into a battery of projective tests. In contrast, Valéry occasionally complains—and hardly without irony—that there are no tests which can determine the quality of a poem. Proust says in the second volume of *Le temps retrouvé* that the work is a kind of optical instrument offered to the reader in order that he makes self-discoveries perhaps not otherwise possible. Proust's arguments in favour of museums also have as their point of reference not the thing itself but the observing subject. It is not coincidental that it is something subjective, the abrupt act of production in which the work becomes something different from reality, that Proust considers to be preserved in the work's afterlife in the museum. For him, the moment of production is reflected in the same isolation of the work that Valéry considers its stigma. Proust, in his unfettered subjectivism, is untrue to objectifications of the spirit, but it is only this subjectivism that enables him to break through the immanence of culture.

In the litigation implicitly pending between them, neither Proust nor Valéry is right, nor could a middle-of-the-road reconciliation be arranged. The conflict between them points up in a most penetrating way a conflict in the matter itself, and each takes the part of one moment in the truth which lies in the unfolding of contradiction. The fetishism of the object and the subject's infatuation with itself find their correctives in each other. Each position passes over into the other. Valéry becomes aware of the intrinsic being of the work through unremitting self-reflection, and, inversely, Proust's subjectivism looks to art for the ideal, the salvation of the living. In opposition to culture and through culture, he represents negativity, criticism, the spontaneous act that is not content with mere existence. Thus he does justice to works of art, which can be called art only by virtue of the fact that they embody the quintessence of this spontaneity. Proust holds on to culture for the sake of objective happiness, whereas Valéry's loyalty to the objective demands of the work forces him to give up culture for lost. And just as both represent contradictory moments of the truth, so both, the two most knowledgeable men to have written about art in recent times, have their limits, without which, in fact, their knowledge would not have been possible. Quite obviously Valéry agrees with his teacher,

Mallarmé in finding, as he wrote in his essay. 'The Triumph of Manet', that existence and things are here only to be devoured by art, that the world exists to produce a beautiful book and finds its fulfilment in an absolute poem. He also saw clearly the escape to which *poésie pure* aspired. 'Nothing leads so surely to complete barbarism', another of his essays begins, 'as complete absorption in what is purely spiritual'. And his own attitude, the elevation of art to idolatry, did in fact contribute to the process of reification and dilapidation which, according to Valéry's accusation, art undergoes in museums. For it is only in the museum, where paintings are offered for contemplation as ends in themselves, that they become as absolute as Valéry desired, and he shrinks back in terror from the realization of his dream. Proust knows the cure for this. In a sense works of art return home when they become elements of the observer's subjective stream of consciousness. Thus they renounce their cultic prerogative and are freed of the usurpatory aspect that characterized them in the heroic aesthetics of Impressionism. But by the same token Proust overestimates the act of freedom in art, as would an amateur. Often, almost in the manner of a psychiatrist, he understands the work all too much as a reproduction of the internal life of the person who had the good fortune and the misfortune to produce it or enjoy it. He fails to take full account of the fact that even in the very moment of its conception the work confronts its author and its audience as something objective, something which makes demands in terms of its own inner structure and its own logic. Like artists' lives, their works appear 'free' only when seen from the outside. The work is neither a reflection of the soul nor the embodiment of a Platonic Idea. It is not pure Being but rather a 'force field' between subject and object. The objective necessity of which Valéry speaks is realized only through the act of subjective spontaneity which Proust makes the sole repository of all meaning and happiness.

It is not merely because the protestations of culture against barbarism go unheard that Valéry's campaign against museums has a quixotic aspect—hopeless protests are nevertheless necessary. But Valéry is a bit too ingenuous in his suspicion that museums alone are responsible for what is done to paintings. Even if they hung in their old places in the castles of the aristocrats (with whom Proust is in any case more concerned than is Valéry), they would be museum pieces without museums. What eats away at the life of the art work is also its own life. If Valéry's coquettish allegory compares painting and sculpture to children who have lost their mother, one must remember that in myths the heroes, who represent the emancipation of the human from fate, always lost their mothers. Works of art can fully embody the *promesse du bonheur* only when they have been uprooted from their native soil and have set out along the path to their own destruction. Proust recognized this. The procedure which today relegates every work of art to the museum, even Picasso's most recent sculpture, is irreversible. It is not solely reprehensible, however, for it presages a situation in which art, having completed its estrangement from human ends, returns, in Novalis' words, to life. One senses something of this in Proust's novel, where physiognomies of paintings and people glide into one another almost without a break and memory traces of experiences fuse with those of musical passages. In one of the most explicit passages in the work, the description of falling asleep on the first page of *Du côté de chez Swann*, the narrator says, 'It seemed to me that I was the thing the book was about: a church, a quartet, the rivalry between Francis the First and Charles the Fifth.' This is the reconciliation of that split which Valéry so irreconcilably laments. The chaos of cultural goods fades into the bliss of the child whose body feels itself at one with the nimbus of distance.

The museums will not be shut, nor would it even be desirable to shut them. The natural-history collections of the spirit have actually transformed works of art into the hieroglyphics of history and brought them a new content while the old one shrivelled up. No conception of pure art, borrowed from the past and yet inadequate to it, can be offered to offset this fact. No one knew this better than Valéry, who broke off his reflections because of it. Yet museums certainly emphatically demand something of the observer, just as every work of art does. For the *flaneur*, in whose shadow Proust walked, is also a thing of the past, and it is no longer possible to stroll through museums letting oneself be delighted here and there. The only relation to art that can be sanctioned in a reality that stands under the constant threat of catastrophe is one that treats works of art with the same deadly seriousness that characterizes the world today. The evil Valéry diagnoses can be avoided only by one who leaves his naïveté outside along with his cane and his umbrella, who knows exactly what he wants, picks out two or three paintings, and concentrates on them as fixedly as if they really were idols. Some museums are helpful in this respect. In addition to light and air they have adopted the principle of selection that Valéry declared to be the guiding one of his school and that he missed in museums. In the *Jeu de Paume*, where the Gare St.-Lazare now hangs, Proust's Elstir and Valéry's Dégas live peacefully near each other in discrete separation.

THE GEORGE–HOFMANNSTHAL CORRESPONDENCE, 1891–1906

In Memory of Walter Benjamin

Anyone who comes to the George–Hofmannsthal correspondence in the hope of learning something about the situation of German poetry during the fifteen years covered by the volume is liable to be disappointed. Although the two writers conceal themselves from each other with a stringency and discretion that borders on total reticence, their personal discipline hardly ever encourages material discussion. Rather, thought itself seems infected by the general rigidity. The pages are filled with technical details concerning publication and publishing houses, punctuated by irritated, reserved attacks and stereotyped defences. Passages such as George's criticism of a superfluous word in one of Hofmannsthal's verses, George's polemics against Dehmel and his, as it were, non-negotiable verdict on 'Venice Saved' are exceptions. The gesture of the letters tends to imply that the artist's profound immersion in his material renders extensive reflection unnecessary, or that the writers are too secure in their shared experiences and attitudes to have to talk them to death.

This implication, however, rests more on a tacit agreement than on its actual justification in the letters themselves. It is contradicted by the formal character of the reception accorded by each to the other's work, above all, by George's attitude to Hofmannsthal's poetry; throughout the correspondence George plays the role of the younger poet's editor. It is not from George, but from a well-meaning reviewer that one would expect lines such as the following: 'I have received and read your poems and I thank you. You can hardly write a verse which does not make one richer with a new sensation, indeed a new sensibility.' At issue are two of Hofmannsthal's most memorable lyrical models, 'Manche freilich müssen drunten sterben, ['Some of Them, Of Course, Must Die Below'], and 'Weltgeheimnis' ['World Mystery'] which George remembers even in his last volume, in the 'Song'. To his perfunctory praise George adds the incredible question: 'Is it your intention to have the poem, "Some of Them . . ." follow "World Mystery"? Or is it part of it? There is no mention of this.' The assumption of even the possibility that the two poems—the one, trochaic, organized in four and six-line stanzas, the other, iambio-dactylic, tetrameter throughout, in three-line rhymed stanzas—could be combined into one refutes the assumption of an artistic understanding between the two writers. The poverty of theoretical content must thus be explained in terms of the position of the authors, neither of whom can be considered naïve.

The plans for their collaboration on the periodical, *Blätter für die Kunst* [*Folios for Art*], as discussed in 1892 by Hofmannsthal, with George's permission, in letters to Carl August Klein, are not utterly indifferent to theoretical publications. On July 26, Hofmannsthal inquires: 'With what shall the individual "issues" be filled, in view of the necessarily small number of collaborators and the quantitatively small production of real works of art? Or shall criticism and technical theory be included and if so, how much?' He is told that 'ordinary critical essays are out of the question', but Klein adds the rather vague qualification: 'We will not exclude the possibility that each of us may offer his judgement on a particular work of art. For—in the old Franconian language of the German *décadence*—it is "very interesting to hear all sorts of new or piquant opinions about paintings, about a theatrical or musical piece".' Hofmannsthal, longstanding collaborator in periodicals like *Moderne* and *Moderne Rundschau* [*Modern Review*], is not satisfied: 'By prose articles what I meant was not so much ordinary critical essays as rather reflections on questions of technique, contributions to the colour-theory of words and similar by-products of the artistic work-process, which each of us could communicate to the others and which, I believe, would be mutually beneficial.' The 'colour-theory of words' refers presumably to 'Voyelles', one of three poems by Rimbaud which George later included in his translations of contemporary poets. 'Voyelles' is a litany to modernity, and exercised influence even upon the Surrealists. The poem, in which Rimbaud promises that the vowels' *naissances latentes* will be revealed in the future, reveals in the meanwhile its own secret. It is the exactitude of the inexact, first demanded in Verlaine's 'Art Poetique' as the combination of the *indécis* and the *précis*. Poetry becomes the technical mastery of something which does not allow itself to be mastered by consciousness. The endowment of sounds with colours, depending solely on the gravitation of language away from meaning, liberates the poem from the concept. Yet at the same time language, as supreme tribunal, delivers the poem over to technique —the characterization of the vowels is less their associative disguise than an indication of their proper linguistic use in the poem.

'Voyelles', too, is a didactic poem. Verlaine's poem is in accord with it. The nuance which Verlaine proclaims as the rule is of the same cast as Rimbaud's correspondence of sound and colour; their subordination of the latter under the primacy of music conserves its remoteness from meaning and makes technical coherence the criterion of the nuances themselves, as the correctly or falsely chosen tone.[1] The tacit procedure of George and Hofmannsthal appeals to nothing other than Rimbaud's and Verlaine's manifesto—to the incommensurable. This is not the metaphysical Absolute which formed the core of German Romanticism and its philosophy. It is no accident that the tone is bearer of the incommensurable, since it is not intelligible but sensuous. Poetry inherits those sensual moments of the object—one could almost say, of the object of the natural sciences—which elude exact measurement. The poetic contrast between life and its technical distortion is itself technical. The excessively praised exquisite sensibility of the artist makes him in a certain sense the complement of the natural scientist; it is as though his sensory apparatus enabled him to register smaller differences than those accessible to that of the scientist.[2] He sees himself as a precision instrument. Sensibility becomes an experimental procedure, indeed an arrangement designed to grasp the basic stimuli which otherwise elude subjective domination and make them legible on the scale of sensation. Like the technician, the artist is in full control of his sensibility; he can turn it on and off as Niels Lyhne does with his talent. He appropriates the unexpected, that which has

[1] The young George had not yet pronounced his verdict on music, which he later permitted his followers to execute although he himself avoided it in the Beethoven Proverb of the *Seventh Ring*. Instead he replaced the word music by 'tone' or 'tones'. Out of protest against the cliché of assigning a single aesthetic dimension to the muse, he was led into the Romantic error of transposing a highly developed art to its mythic ur-stage. And, indeed, this was then made part of the official doctrine of the Circle. At the same time, however, the reduction of music to tones also points to the technical element. Closely related is George's custom of using the word 'poet' in the plural.

[2] This was observed very early in Jacobsen, who studied natural science and propagated Darwinism before his literary production began. In an extraordinarily incisive introduction, written in 1898, to the edition of his collected works published in 1905 by Eugen Diederichs, Marie Herzfeld observes: 'J.P. Jacobsen is both a man of dreamlike imagination and a wide-awake realist.' The unity of both moments in the complexion of Neo-Romanticism could not be perceived at the time. The authoress of this introduction was one of four readers whom Hofmannsthal wished 'to inform personally of our intentions' (August 24, 1892). The first volume of George's translation of contemporary poets includes Jacobsen with Rossetti and Swinburne.

not yet been included in the current material of expression; new snow in which no intention has as yet left its trace.[3] When, however, naked sensation resists the poet's interpretation, he subdues it by enlisting the incalculable sensation in the service of calculated effect.

The secret of sensory data is no secret at all but rather blind intuition without concept. It is of the same cast as, for instance, the theory of empirio-criticism formulated contemporaneously by Ernst Mach, which combines the ideal of scientific exactitude with the sacrifice of independent categorical form. The pure data which this philosophy distills remain as opaque as the thing-in-itself it rejects. The datum can only be 'had', not held. As recollection it is no longer itself, as words even less; it becomes an abstraction under which life in its immediacy is subsumed in order solely to manipulate it better through technology. The categorical forms are no longer capable of fixing subject and object; both sink in the 'stream of consciousness', the truly modern Lethe. The poem to George which opens the correspondence has for its title, 'Einem, der vorübergeht' ['To One Who Passes By']. George immediately recognizes the elements of insubordination: 'But am I nothing more for you than "one who passes by"?'[4] From the very beginning, he is intent on preserving Being from the stream of oblivion on whose banks he erects his works.[5] The esoteric serves as a shield; that which other-

[3] In music it was Berlioz, the chief advocate of the 'modern style' among the older Romantics, who employed the orchestra as a palette in the name of the *imprévu*. He is the first orchestral technician. The notion of the *imprévu* goes back to Stendhal. The young Hofmannsthal refers to this: 'It is nothing other than Stendhal's craving for the "imprévu", for the unforeseen, for that which is not "revolting, shallow, insipid and intolerable" in love, in life' (Loris, *Die Prosa des jungen Hofmannsthal*, Berlin 1930). The *imprévu* suspends the monotonous mechanism of bourgeois life and yet is itself mechanically produced—through tricks. The interpretation of music written prior to Berlioz in terms of its technique belongs to a later aspect and could be disclosed only historically. The phrase, 'compositional technique' occurs rarely in the times of Mozart or Beethoven. Beethoven, of course, began to recognize the importance of technical means as opposed to the 'natural genius' of the composer.

[4] The wilful manipulation of the past is one of the oldest elements in the inventory of aestheticism. In the Diapsalmata from *Either-Or* Kierkegaard wrote in 1843: 'On each experience I perform the baptism of oblivion and consecrate it to the eternity of memory.'

[5] This impulse is evinced in a passage from the letters in which, after discussing an issue of the *Blätter für die Kunst* for a few lines, George continues: 'Forgive me for again amplifying the historical part of my letter so little.' For him the transitory immediately becomes eternal as history. This distortion of the 'historical' is a reaction to the disintegration of the object. Hofmannsthal's 'organic' and George's 'plastic' sense of form, usually contrasted to each other, stem from the same historical-philosophical complex.

wise would elude control is held fast as mystery. Hence, the non-existent tacit agreement. Because the ordained mystery itself does not exist. The bombastic analogy used to designate it in the correspondence remains entirely devoid of content: 'Later I would have certainly collapsed had I not felt myself bound through the Ring—that is one of the mysteries!' writes George. The mystery must be seen, not so much to prevent its being profaned as its being unmasked. The pure materials are gathered in the mystic cell. Yet should the technique which processes the materials be revealed to the public, it would end the poet's claim to an authority which had long since been ceded to the event itself. A mystery is made of the non-mysterious; technique itself is initiated into the rationale. The more that questions of poetry are translated into questions of technique, the more readily exclusive circles are formed. The tapestry, intentionless inter-weaving of materials, poses a technical puzzle; its 'solution', however, 'will never be granted to the multitude through talk'. The justification of the Circle, however, as it emerged for George through his collaboration on *Blätter für die Kunst*, is by no means participation in concealed regions nor the substantiality of the individual; rather, it is technical competence. 'And I will not even overlook the most minute points—the accidental flourishes and ornaments—which, observed in themselves, I fully abandon. The fact, however, that these minute objects could have been the occasion of such work; the fact that despite all their thinness they cannot be accused of the bungled character so often present in more famous works, this seems to me, in temporal and spatial terms, to be of far greater significance for our art and culture than all the organizations and theatrical pieces in which you presently set all such great hopes.' The question whether technique as arcana, treated sacramentally, does not necessarily turn into technical inadequacy, into that routine which vulgar criticism has in mind when it prattles about formalism—this question remains unanswered.

The emptier the mystery, the more its guardians must rely on 'bearing'. Besides technique, it is this that George sees fit to laud in his pupils: 'But you, with your grand feeling for style, must at least have been fascinated, at least found graceful the sight of those "who did not go along", "who never sought attention", that elegance of bearing as embodied in our common friend, Andrian, in your circle.' However much the not going along and the distance from the business of everyday life speaks in favour of such bearing, the notion is at the same time compromised by the epithet 'elegance', meant to define that distance positively. Indeed, the notion itself is not to be trusted. Its role in the intelligible world is like that of smoking in the profane. To have 'bearing' is lean back with one's personality; the coolness which it evinces makes a good impression. Monads which are repelled from one another by their material interests can still attract each other through the gesture of being blasé. The necessity of estrangement is twisted into the virtue of self-sufficiency. Hence, all are united in the praise of bearing. It is extolled wherever it is found, in a revolutionary as readily as in Max Weber; and in the *Nationalsozialistischen Monatsheften* [*National Socialist Monthly Magazine*] the hunting dogs already struck a trim, collected, resolute pose. The victorious individual transforms the wrongs he is compelled to do to all the others in a competitive society into moral profit through bearing. It is not merely the taut, aggressive stance that is stigmatized but nobility as well, and even that grace which, in George's hierarchy of ideas ranks supreme, as the beauty of simple, statuesque being. If grace was once the expression of man's gratitude—gratitude granted by the Gods for being able to move about without fear and without arrogance in the creation, as though it still were such—today it is distorted, the expression of man's gratitude granted by society because he is able to move about in it securely and without resistance, giving it his undivided obedience. Charm, grace and their heir, the attractive person, serve precisely to conceal privilege. Nobility itself is noble by virtue of the ignoble. This emerges clearly in George, and not merely in sinister formulations such as: 'I have never wanted anything but your best. I hope you realize that before it is too late.' Anyone who has the presence of mind while reading George's poetry not to forget its pragmatic content in favour of its pretended identity with the lyrical aspect is often struck by a base element in the most elevated passages. As early as the famous introductory cycle in the *Jahr der Seele* [*Year of the Soul*], in 'Nach der lese' ['After the Harvest'], a degrading substitute for love is depicted which does not stop short of insulting the beloved. The most tender verses are followed by those of thoughtless crudity. Few businessmen would allow themselves to tell their girl friends 'und ganz als glichest du der Einen Fernen' ['and just as though you were she, so far away'], and other such meagre compliments. The thought of the businessman is no accident; the ideal which can never be allowed oneself, which is just good enough to devalue what one actually has, belongs to the stock and trade of the bourgeois. Such ideality is the other side of Being, substance and *kairos*. 'Der heut nicht kam bleib immer fern!' ['He who did not come today, let him ever stay away!']. He must press his nose flat against the park gate and, in addition, be told he has a flat nose. The price of George's culture is always barbarous.

The contrast between George and Hofmannsthal revolves around the postulate of bearing, repeatedly emphasized by George through example and language and evaded by Hofmannsthal with the aid of incessantly varied devices, such as the outburst: 'I find it extremely difficult to hear ideas such as the mastery of life, royalty of spirit expressed in a tone which at the same time fails to fill me with true awe'; or the evasive retort: 'Perhaps in me the poetic power combines with other intellectual instincts to yield a duller mixture than in you.' In place of bearing, however, he offers a laxity which reveals itself to be hardly more human than its implacable opposite. It is the diligent cosmopolitanism of the young gentleman of good family, the model which Hofmannsthal later used in stylizing his own past, a legend from the very first. His is the laxity of one who does not need bearing since he 'belongs' anyway. He convulsively identifies with the aristocracy, or at least with that kind of upper-class society which shares most of its interests and knows its way around: 'So much about me; otherwise I am well, plan to spend several days this summer in Munich looking at paintings, autumn probably hunting in Bohemia. And you? At least a few lines when you have the chance would be most welcome.' The Bohemian forests captivated him. Concerning 'one of my friends'. he writes: 'He is utterly immersed in life, not art. He will give you a fine idea of Austrian life, with a broad survey of the manifold internal and external aspects, including those of other countries as well. He is Count Josef Schoenborn of the Bohemian line of the family.' The 'line' is nonchalantly tossed in at the end. George, more versed in chthonic matters and sufficiently sober to recognize the hopelessness of such hobnobbing calls it by its true name: 'You write, my dear friend, that "he is utterly immersed in life, not art", which seems to me a virtual blasphemy. Can anyone who is completely detached from art imagine that he is immersed in life? How is that possible? At best during times of semibarbarism.' Hofmannsthal's laxity assimilates the criticism in less than a half-year: 'I have in mind a letter to a very young friend who is wholly immersed in life and who must be shown that he can never be properly bound to life until he has estranged himself from it in the mysterious manner which works through the appreciation of poetry.' What kind of life the young friend is to be prepared for remains undetermined. There is reason, however, for the assumption that what is intended is the higher life of attachés and officers who are on a first-name basis with the sons of bankers and industrialists, a life in which all concerned tactfully refrain from mentioning their nobility.[6] The desire for happiness inherent in snobbism should not be overlooked; it inspires the snob in his efforts to escape from the practical sphere and reach a social dimension which, in its rejection of utility, appears to be on the side of the mind. The girls of Hofmannsthal's poetry were not to be found in the middle-class. But the mind which permits itself to participate in this social adventure does not have an easy time of it. It cannot content itself with the splendour of the good life, and is thus compelled to repeat the 'that's not what I meant at all' experience from which it had originally fled. Proust alone did this problem justice. The photographs of his youth resemble those of Hofmannsthal, as though history had arranged the same experiment twice, in different places. With Hofmannsthal the experiment failed. The intellectual, surrounded by his dogs, anticipating gay diversions or much 'riding through the dusk, wind and starlight', can hardly be on good terms with himself. The mind is *reçu* at the price of self-denunciation. Hofmannsthal's Bohemian affiliations correspond to the secret passion the *bon vivant* has for keeping his distance from other intellectuals. There is no Bergotte and Elstir in his *paradis artificiel*: 'Unfortunately my society is so totally unliterary that I cannot think of any serious collaborator worth proposing to you.'

The tortured self-rejection of the *literati* stems from the problematic relations between power and the intellectuals. Without automatic charm and agile cunning there is no moving ahead. German society, recruited from the rural gentry and the big industrialists, was less closely bound to the artistic and philosophical tradition than Western European society. After 1870 the leisure class was in

6 The young Hofmannsthal did not wholly deny himself insight into this aspect of his world. Of Marie Bashkirtzev, the patron saint of the *fin du siècle*, he says: '*En attendant* she is as proud as possible. Everything which suggests power and royalty enchants her—the palaces of Colonna and Chiarra, the Swiss Guard of the Vatican, every sort of triumphal carriage in every sort of museum, every proud, quietly superior word, all refined and legitimate arrogance. She herself is too vivacious and too nervous for this grand style of elegance despite all the inner nobility of her character. Hence her strongly pronounced affinity for such elegance has something of the envy Napoleon felt when he saw that he could never learn how to walk properly. She speaks too loudly and is too excitable; the tone of her diary is also louder, less reserved than is fitting for conversation in good society.' These lines may also be read as an unintentional piece of self-criticism. The reproach for being too loud reveals a prototypical gesture of the snob, one which Proust described—calling the other person a snob. It is a characteristic of competitiveness. Elegance never forbide the *élan vital* to climb with the use of its elbows.

196

general nervous and unsure of itself in its relations to culture; the intellectuals it saw were nervous and unsure of themselves, unable to forget how ready their patrons were to throw out anyone who became troublesome. The few writers who insisted on representing the 'nation' had to choose between glorifying the prevailing crudity as substance and 'life' and substituting a dream-society for the real one which they obeyed and feared, a dream-society organized to suit them and to serve as a pedagogical model for reality. Hofmannsthal tried to do both: he seized on substantial moments in the Austrian tradition to create an ideology of high life, attributing to it precisely the humanistic frame of mind trampled under foot by the hunter's boot, and he also conceived a fictitious aristocracy in which his nostalgia was realized. Kari Buehl, 'The Difficult Man', is the product of this effort. The young Hofmannsthal was not yet capable of such artistic creations. He made himself popular with the feudal gentry as a middleman of the *fin du siècle*. Sometimes laudatory, sometimes apologetic, he introduced them to the tone set by the elites in England, France and Italy. It is as though he sought to express his gratitude towards those he courted by giving them instruction in intellectual manners. At the same time, this gave him access to the market. The tidbits he imparted to the Viennese *monde* concerning d'Annunzio, Bashkirtzev and the modern style were perfectly suited, as cultural journalism, to make the average man—excluded from all this—smack his lips, just as the esotericism that followed was to include the flattering appeal to those not allowed to participate.[7] Here, too, the secrets of aestheticism reveal

[7] Oscar Wilde is the clearest example of this. *Dorian Gray* propagates art and is a bestseller. In Germany this trend made its mark on the stage. Its models were d'Annunzio's *Giocanda* and Maeterlinck's *Monna Vanna*. Hofmannsthal was involved in this sphere even before his collaboration with Richard Strauss. George recognized this quickly and reproached Hofmannsthal for 'sensationalism', especially in his criticism of *Venice Saved*: 'The whole new historical and morality drama suffers—for me—from badly applied Shakespeare. In him the plot is formed out of figures from his passionate soul; today, they are formed out of concepts, out of ramifications stemming from this or that presupposition. In Shakespeare everything is rough and raw necessity—today, however, it consists in bungling afterthoughts or even in mere scribbling...' Sensationalism makes public the technical secret of the artist. Yet with his ascetic ideology, George is still more sensational, especially in the late works, than he would like to admit; not merely in the provocations of *Algabal*, but also in poems like 'Porta Nigra' from the *Seventh Ring*. The Roman boy and paramour, Manlius, who curses modern civilization, suggests Hugenberg's *Night Extra* in its thundering against the *Kurfürstendamm*. From time immemorial it has been customary to seek allies against depravity by displaying a close familiarity with it.

themselves to the public. The garrulous Loris abandons the *Zeitgeist* to the audience which produced it in the first place. That segment of the German Right with which Hofmannsthal sympathized either joined the National Socialists in so far as it was permitted to or spent its energies in intellectual handweaving, of which Lorenz and Cordula are the most typical figures. They do service to propaganda in their own way—their sober moderation belies the limitless horror. In 1914 the forces of barbarism were content with rhymes, to which Hofmannsthal, of course, also contributed. By the time of the concentration camps the scribes have learned discrete silence, rugged speech and elegaic abundance.

The less worldly George School summoned up greater resistance. In this respect, the sorely taxed notion of bearing still demonstrated its superiority to that 'majesty', the glance 'from above' that Borchardt singled out for praise. George himself, at least, remained impervious to a *mondanité* which was able to conduct international dialogues even about Hitler. The 'secret Germany' proclaimed by George was less compatible with the New Order than was the exquisite conformity which from the very first felt itself above all those national boundaries that were later to be revised. George was suspicious of the fatal tolerance that the modish salons sought to bestow upon him. He preferred conventicles towards which he gravitated anyway—as an outcast. The correspondence bears witness to this. The reason for the excitement produced by George in the house of the seventeen-year-old Hofmannsthal is not mentioned. Robert Boehringer relates the affair to a kick that George is supposed to have given a dog with the words, 'sale voyou'. The area of conflict is probably more accurately described in the letter in which George—intending to emigrate to Mexico—bids farewell to Hofmannsthal's father: 'Your son and I may never wish to know each other for the rest of our lives, he may turn away, I may turn away, he will always remain for me the first person on the German side to have understood and appreciated my work without first having been close to me personally, and that at a time when I had begun to tremble on my solitary cliff it is difficult to explain to a non-poet the enormous importance this had. Small wonder, then, that I threw myself at such a person (Carlos? Posa?) and found nothing disreputable about it.' Two days earlier, in a letter to Hofmannsthal himself, he writes: 'So, because of something—god knows what—"that you think you have understood" you hurl a sanguine insult at a gentleman who was about to become your friend. How could you have been so negligent, even with a criminal one does not close one's ears to his shrieking hints.' This is the language of the outlaw. Nothing but the fear of being caught in the machinery of morality can have impelled George to call himself a gentleman. He must have known better than anyone else that the rules of language exclude anyone who claims to be a gentleman from being one. But the word reveals a second aspect for him. Overwhelming anxiety demands the image of the gentleman as the historical model for the timeless George—the phantasma of the *fin du siècle*. Just as the monstrous is cited here in sacerdotal-incognito garb, the railroad before the end of time is cited in his Dream Reports—and only in these—from *Tage und Taten* [*Days and Deeds*].[8] English titles serve the same function in Verlaine's poetry. The 'sanguine insult', it appears, was not really hurled at the gentleman; rather, his insulting face bore traces of blood from the very first. In George's mouth the word 'gentleman' looks like a murderer. Its propriety calls for sacrilege as the dandy's suit demands a gardenia. In George's era, the outlaw assumes the burden of unproductive resistance. He experiences the social catastrophe through the destruction of the family which society forces upon him. This is preserved in the aphoristic poem, 'Vormundschaft' ['Tutelage'], from the *Seventh Ring*:

> Als aus dem schönen sohn die flammen fuhren
> Umsperrtest du ihn klug in sichern höfen.
> Du hieltst ihn rein für seine ersten huren . . .
> Od ist dies haus nun: asche deckt die öfen.

[8] The name of the fiend appears in the *Stern des Bundes* [*Star of the League*] as the symbol of 'powers, not wholly formed'. It should probably be understood as being outside the polarity of the sexes, rather like the witches in *Macbeth*. The poem ascribes to them precisely that possibility which the epoch failed to realize:

> Unholdenhaft nicht ganz gestalte kräfte:
> Allhörige zeit die jedes schwache poltern
> Eintrug ins buch und alles staubgeblas
> Vernahm nicht euer unterirdisch rollen—
> Allweis und unkund des was wirklich war.
> Euch trächtig von gewesnem die sie nutzen
> Sich zur belebung hätte bannen können
> Euch übersah sie dunkelste Verschollne . . .
> So seid ihr machtlos rückgestürzt in nacht
> Schwelende sprühe um das innre Licht.

'Monstrous powers, not wholly formed,/That watchful time recorded every murmur, every blast of dust/But did not hear your subterranean rumbling—/Omniscient, yet not knowing what was real./You pregnant with the past,/How it could have used you,/Brought you back to life,/And yet it did not see you, shrouded in oblivion . . ./Thus, powerless, you fell back into night,/Smouldering sparks around the inner light.'

['As flames flared forth from the handsome son,/ You cleverly shut him up in safe courts./You kept him pure for his first whores.../ Barren is this house now; ashes cover the stove.'] The son, shut up by his family, falls prey to the very world, a market and desert, from which moral decay might have protected him. In the safe courts, however, George recognizes the possession that keeps this world alive, and he pointedly expresses his opposition to it in the maxim to Derleth:

> In unsrer runde macht uns dies zum paare:
> Wir los von jedem band von gut und haus.[9]

['In our round 'tis this that makes us one: /We free from every bond to house and home.'] He is kept from Bohemianism by its sloppiness, which trusts in the world as it is; he is bound to it by the possibility of criminality serving as a mode of opposition which renounces all faith in the world. The beginning of the poem to the friend of his youth, Carl August—

> Du weisst noch ersten stürmesjahres gesell
> Wie du voll trotz am zaun den hagelschlossen
> Hinwarfst den blanken leib auf den blauschwarz
> Die trauben hingen?

['Do you still recall, friend of that first tempestuous year/How, full of defiance, by the gate/You hurled your bare body at the hail,/Where, blue-black, grapes hung in clusters']—recalls Haenschen Rilow's

[9] Borchardt contrasts Hofmannsthal to the 'worthless riffraff who know no house but the coffeehouse, the pawnbroker's house and the house of ill repute'. Such abominable praise could not have been bestowed upon George, even if one overlooks the fact that according too all witnesses the Viennese setting for his friendship with Hofmannsthal was the café. While complaining of a visit Hofmannsthal failed to make, George finds a phrase which all by itself is enough to make him unusable for this sort of agitation againt the literati—'landscape as house'. The chthonian experience that it suggests its fundamentally related to that of he homeless wanderer. Homer spun his entire epic out of the nostalgia of Odysseus to see Ithaca one last time. The chthonians of today are no longer nostalgic. They are always at home with themselves. In poems such as 'Return' from the *Year of the Soul*, George shows his superiority to them: 'Du wohntest lang bei fremden stämmen./Doch unsre liebe starb dir nicht.' ['You lived long with foreign tribes,/Yet for you our love did not die.' Such verses, of course, stem rather from the strong feelings evoked in children by stories of cowboys and indians than from the thought of elegant forms of society, which the early George so despised: 'I have nothing to say against that gullibility you find so attractive, if it forms the soil in which something can grow... but where you emphasize it, closer scrutiny will convince you that nothing could be more spurious, more putrid, more worm-eaten than such vulgar and idiotic doings.'

vineyard in Wedekind's *Frühlings Erwachen* [*Spring Stirrings*]. The tradition according to which George is said to have esteemed Wedekind highly is illuminating. George's great poem about the 'Taeter' ['Culprit'] does far more than merely describe criminality as one possibility among others; it enters into direct collusion with it. This is joined by petrified verses such as the third 'Jahrhundertspruch' ['Centenary Maxim'] from the *Seventh Ring* and the 'Gehenkte' ['Hanged Man'] from the *Neuen Reich* [*The New Imperium*]. This alone legitimizes George's 'bearing'—it is the Baudelairean arrogance of the pariah, 'trésor de toute gueuserie.'[10] When, of course, the hanged man lauds himself in an unyielding metaphor —'und ehe ihrs euch versahet, biege/Ich diesen starren balken um zum rad' ['and before you knew it/I bent this rigid beam

---

[10] Baudelaire, 'Le vin du solitaire', *Les fleurs du mal*. Not the least of Gundolf's perfidies is his attempt to turn the outcast into a lawyer's tidbit. In the third edition of his book on George there is the pompous but soothing statement, that 'whatever is seen to be virtue, order, power demands a subterranean destroyer who also preserves and renews, the bearer of the divine history of the future. More exactly, what is proclaimed here is a doctrine of George's which is already announced in the *Seventh Ring*—his belief in the renewal of the world through the most remote factors, its reconstruction at its sorest point. The keystone is laid ... through the wholesome act of the criminal, or even convict'. For renewal, reconstruction and similar cultural aims criminals are just fine in Gundolf's eyes—as though what George had had in mind was their forced labour and not their murderous assault on society. George's 'Gehenkte' is equivocal enough, yet in any event it still expresses the most bitter contempt for that morality, in whose service the Commentator seeks to place immorality: 'Als ich zum richtplatz kam und strenger miene/die Herrn vom Rat mir beides: ekel zeigten/Und mitleid musst ich lachen: "ahnt ihr nicht/Wie sehr des armen sünders ihr bedürft"/Tugend—die ich verbrach—auf ihrem antlitz/Und sittiger frau und maid, sei sie auch wahr,/so strahlen kann sie nur wenn ich so fehle!' ['As I came to the gallows, and with stern mien/The men of the council showed me both—disgust/And pity I had to laugh: "Don't you know/How much you need the poor sinner"/Virtue—which I spurned —however true/Can only shine so brightly on their face/ And on that of righteous woman and of maid/ If I so err!'] Gundolf continues: 'In such poems (to which the "Taeter" in the *Teppich des Lebens* [*Tapestry of Life*] belongs) George reveals the abyss out of which his much praised and much derided sense of beauty emerges. This has nothing to do with Epicureanism; rather, just as the Greek Apollo presupposes the Titans, Dante's Paradise his Inferno, Shakespeare's comedies his tragedies, it presupposes a voyage into the realms of merciless terror.' The Literary Historian, however, can only imagine this voyage as a sojourn. Immorality is first neutralized as mythical amorality and then assimilated into the victorious march of positive development as the very 'threshold', the concept of which George rejected as idealistic. On the map of 'divinely structured Being', Hell becomes a tourist attraction.

into a wheel']—the heretic disintegrates into a hero, in accordance with the founding spirit of the late George. The protest against marriage and family turns into its opposite once the totalitarian state, which cast its shadow over George's last books, repudiates marriage and family and assumes their functions. The firebrand then becomes standardized as the inflammatory agitator, the culprit becomes prophet of the executioner. The iconoclast who described himself as 'free from every bond to house and home', now sees himself as a freelance mercenary: 'Wir einzig können stets beim ersten saus/Wo grad wir stehn nachfolgen der fanfare' ['We alone are always ready, at the very first din/Wherever we may be, to follow the fanfare']. The fateful purity which tainted the young George as early as *Algabal*, and which made the 'Culprit' as well as the Group Spirit attractive to wayward schoolmasters, perverted him finally into a figure of light. In transcending society George reveals its humanity. His inhumanity, however, is what society absorbs.

Hofmannsthal also claimed to transcend society, and the thought of the outsider is never foreign to one who must simulate his own society. But he is a conciliatory outsider, too self-infatuated to be truly angry with the others. 'From my childhood on I was possessed with the most feverish desire to get through to the spirit of our confused epoch, through the most varied methods and guises. I was drawn to a certain kind of journalism, in the most elevated sense, such as perhaps only Ruskin represents; we have no such figure. By publishing in the daily newspapers and in assorted reviews, I was heeding an urge which I would rather explain clearly than deny.' The desire to use disguises, which is oriented towards a prestabilized harmony with the demands of the market, is that of the actor. This, too, was very quickly recognized by George. In a letter dated May 31, 1897, he writes verse which then recur in a milder form, with Hofmannsthal's initials, in the *Year of the Soul*: 'Finder/Des fluessig rollenden gesangs und spruehend/Gewandter zwiegespräche. frist und trennung/erlaubt dass ich auf meine daechtnis/Den alten hasser grabe, thu desgleichen!' ['Discoverer/Of the fluidly rolling song and sparkling/Deft dialogue. time and separation/let me bury the old hatred/in my memory. do the same!'] This characterizes not the dramatist but the 'actor of your self-created dreams', the page in 'The Death of Titian', who is defended and apostrophized by his friend the poet.[11] What Hofmannsthal's

[11] Borchardt feels obliged to add his defence of aestheticism to the words of the Page: 'He, whom they try to dismiss as the sated cultural decadent, as the aesthete, the connoisseur of sound—and this is how he is still portrayed by the audacious and moronic breed that judges literature and

poetry composes—more than the stylistic costuming, more even than the dramatic intention—is the rolling voice of the actor. It is as if the poem were the objectification of this voice just as particular instruments are assigned to objectify the lyrical immediacy of the subject. Verses like: 'Er glitt durch die Floete/Als schluchzender Schrei,/An daemmernder Roete,/Flog er vorbei' ['He glid through the flute/As a sobbing cry,/In the violet of twilight/He flew by'] have the tone of Josef Kainz, for whom Hofmannsthal wrote the obituary.[12] Alls psychologistic reductions notwithstanding, Hofmannsthal's histrionics have their origins in the technical demands involved in the writing of poetry. His poems recite themselves as though to perfect their self-control. Their discursive 'spoken' character allows the verses to listen to themselves.[13] Hence his preference for the discursive form of poetry, blank verse. Its syncopation, the best known of Hofmannsthal's stylistic devices, was taken from the English writers. It is designed by the poet-technician to serve the needs of the actor inherent in the theatrical form; it introduces the freedom that is otherwise present only in

---

theatre in Germany—he is the first German poet since Goethe who has been able to give universal validity and artistic quality to problematic and personally endured situations, through his profound seriousness, his visionary power and his participation in all the higher aspects of contemporary existence.' However banal the objections against which Borchardt protests may be, concepts like profound seriousness and the higher aspects of existence are no better. Hofmannsthal cannot be saved from slander as an aesthete—aestheticism itself must be saved. What Borchardt calls the 'moral dramas', such as 'Death and the Fool', and 'The Emperor and the Witch', in which all appearances are abandoned and delivered up to that profound seriousness for correction, may well prove to embody the same kind of betrayal of his basic experience on the part of Hofmannsthal as that committed by George in his 'turn' which began with the 'Tapestry'.

[12] George presents a parallel phenomenon. The final line of the description of the anemonae at the end of 'Betruebt als fuehrten sie zum totenanger' assumes acoustically the Rhenist intonation which may well have been George's own: 'Und sind wie seelen die im morgengrauen/Der halberwachten wuensche und im herben/Vorfruehjahrswind voll lauernden verderben/Sich ganz zu oeffnen noch nicht recht getrauen' ['And are like souls, which in the morning grey/Of half-roused wishes and in the rough/Wind of early spring full of lurking ruin/Can hardly bring themselves to open'].

[13] Hofmannsthal's listening to himself tends towards self-adulation. At times poems shut their eyes and taste themselves with their tongues, as though eager to display their own uniqueness. The verse 'Dein Antlitz war mit Traeumen ganz beladen./Ich schwieg und sah dich an mit stummen Beben' ['Your face was filled with dreams. Silently/I looked at you with voiceless trembling'], is followed by the line: 'Wie stieg das auf!' ['How that rose!']. It is repeated three times.

recitation into the closed form of poetic metre itself. It is also, however, the verse bequeathed to the child by a theatre which, since Hofmannsthal's youth, had reserved Hamlet and Schiller for school. Hofmannsthal has reason to trace his efforts at intellectual disguise back to his childhood. The child playing theatre arranges words and their resistances like heirlooms, bedecking them with colourful jewels and rhinestones. What may prove to endure in Hofmannsthal is his untiring imitation of the childhood gestures which, as it were, reproduce the only stage in which tragic drama can still be experienced. In the hands of his voice every subject is bewitched into childhood, and it is this transformation which enables him to avoid the pitfalls of bearing and responsibility. The magical power to manipulate childhood is the strength of the weak;[14] it eludes the impossibility of its task like the Peter Pan of poetry. Impossible indeed. Hofmannsthal's theatricality, from its Alexandrine end-results to the pseudo-morphoses of his later period, stems from an eminently real insight: that language no longer allows anything to be said as it is experienced.[15] Language is either reified and banal, as the designation of commodities, falsifying thought in

[14] This determines the tone of second naïveté in Hofmannsthal's poetry. The notion originates with Jacobsen. It is found in the small prose work, 'There Should Have Been Roses', a treasure-chest of characteristic Hofmannsthal motifs. The characters in the 'Proverb', dreamt in a southern garden, are two pages. The description of them jumps to the two actresses who are to portray the pages: 'The actress who is to be the younger of the two pages is in thin silk, tightly bound, pale blue with embroidered heraldic lilies of the lightest gold. This, and as much lace as possible, is the most conspicuous element of the costume, which is designed not so much to suggest a particular century as to bring out the youthful, full figure, the magnificent blonde hair and the transparent tinge. She is married but her marriage survives only for a year and a half; then she is divorced from her husband and is said to have acted badly towards him. And this may well be so; nevertheless, it would be difficult to find anything more innocent. This means that hers is not that uncommonly attractive, first-hand innocence, which certainly has its charm, but is on the contrary, the deliberate, cultivated innocence about which there can be no mistake, which goes directly to the heart and enthralls with all the power wih which perfection is endowed.'

[15] This insight is formulated, however corrupted by vitalistic jargon, in Hofmannsthal's Chandos Letter: 'In brief, my situation is this: I have completely lost the capacity to speak or think coherently about anything. First, it became gradually impossible for me to discuss a higher or more general theme, and thereby to utter those words which are used habitually and without a second thought by all men. I felt an ineffable uneasiness at even saying the words "mind", "soul", or "body"... abstract words which the tongue must employ, of course, in order for any sort of judgement to see the light, disintegrated in my mouth like mouldy mushrooms.'

advance. Or it enthrones itself, ceremonious without ceremony, empowered without power, self-appointed—in short, in the manner that Hofmannsthal attacked in the George school. Language utterly rejects the object in a society in which the force of facts assumes such an overwhelming aspect that even the true word sounds like a mockery. Hofmannsthal's children's theatre is the attempt to emancipate literature from language. Refused recognition as something substantial, language falls silent; ballet and opera are the necessary results. Among the tragic and comic masks no human face remains. Hence, the truth of Hofmannsthal's appearances. His language takes on the aspect of horror and uncertainty precisely when it pretends to speak with epic rationality: 'Circe, kannst du mich hören?/Du hast mir fast nichts getan' ['Circe, can you hear me?/You've done almost nothing to me'], he writes in the text of *Ariadne*. The epic 'almost', which, even in the face of mythical metamorphosis, stops short with characteristic reserve, deprives the very myth of its foundations with modern lassitude.

Confronted by Hofmannsthal's play-acting, no objection is too trivial for George: 'Your most painful problem is a certain rootlessness . . .' He thus seems to dabble in the vocabulary of antisemitism, traces of which can be found in his work, despite his rejection of Klages. The translator of Baudelaire's *Malabaraise*, proclaimed, in the *Star of the League*: 'Mit den frauen fremder ordnung/Sollt ihr nicht den leib beflecken/Harret! lasset pfau bei affe! /Dort am see wirkt die Wellede/Weckt den mädchen tote kunde: /Weibes eigenstes geheimnis' ['With women from alien strains/Do not besmirch your bodies/Be strong! Leave peacocks to apes! /There on the lake rules Veleda/Waking maidens to dead tidings: / Women's deepest, secret'].—verses which would not have fared badly in the *Turnhalle* of Rhenish *Gymnasien*. However, George recoiled at having anything to do with this atmosphere: 'It was an outrage for the literary rabble to have thrown these highly distinct people into a heap simply because they all distanced themselves from the rabble in a similar manner a selection much like that made by the Rhenish Jan Hagel, who screamed "jew" at all those who behaved differently.' It was not George's intention to hold up his own empirical 'rooted' existence to Hofmannsthal's lack of roots: 'For Christmas I have little to offer you here . I scarcely even know whether I will be here then. The intimate winter companionship which you depict, whether in the country or in the city, can only be experienced by one who, like yourself, has a home, not by one, who is always a visitor as I am.' In a letter written on August 27, 1892, this is formulated in an even more astonishing manner, one which George can hardly have meant ironically: 'I do not believe that you should allow yourself to be swept away so completely by your passion for something beautiful and sonorous. That is the granite-German in you, the Latin in me. Through constant contact with people of foreign tongues you will notice that they are far more active . more genuine in their likes and dislikes.'[16] From the very beginning George interprets his contrast to the 'rootless' Hofmannsthal not as one of origins but of decision.[17] He does not appeal to the 'soil', the power of Being or to unconscious elements. The definitive letter that he writes Hofmannsthal in July 1902 is inspired by strategic considerations, namely of the literary situation, yet without their leading him to exclude the opposite position from the out-

[16] As late as March 26, 1896, George writes Hofmannsthal: 'Who knows if I would have continued writing poetry in my mother tongue, had I not found a poet in you or in Géraudy!' As late as February 1893 he published the original French version of a poem in *Floréal*. The patriotic Gundolf would have none of this: 'Those who seek to interpret him as a disciple of the French Parnassiens and Symbolists and to situate him with Swinburne or d'Annunzio mistake the surface for the foundation; these poets were important for him—whatever they may mean to their countries as literary movements or whatever new motifs or techniques they may have introduced—solely as the embodiments of the richest, purest and most refined linguistic complexes of their people existing at the time. Baudelaire's infernal consecration and Verlaine's morbid grace and fatigue, d'Annunzio's sensual splendour, Swinburne's intoxicating psychic oscillations, Rossetti's Celtic-Italic, melancholy fire, even the poetry of his personal friends, Verwey and Lieder, all were important for him only in so far as they enriched language with new masses, weights, resistances, movements, depths and lights. To interpret these poets in relation to George in terms of "movements" or of emotional values, as embodying certain moods or styles, is a mistake of the literati and confuses the supreme synthesizer of all these movements with their disciple.' Only dilettants can isolate the poetic 'foundation' from mere 'motifs or techniques'; only philistines are incapable of mentioning Baudelaire without immediately adding Verlaine.

[17] It is to decision—in the final instance, to political action—that George looks for precisely what cannot be a matter of decision: the presence of what has been. Decision, however, is thereby transformed into an enemy of whatever it is that is decided. The neo-chthonians forgot that Rumpelstilskin tears himself into pieces as soon as he is confronted by his name. Such is the calamity prepared by the agitatory cult of primordial powers. In this George and Klages anticipate fateful tendencies of National Socialism. The mythologists unceasingly destroy what they take to be their substance through the act of naming. They heralded the sell-out of allegedly primal words like 'death', 'inwardness' and 'genuineness' which subsequently was consummated in the Third Reich. Phenomenology, which in a certain sense puts essences on display, helped to pave the way for this sell-out. The book, *Die Transzendenz des Erkennens* [*The Transcendance of Knowledge*] by Edith Landmann, establishes the connection between the George and the Phenomenological schools.

set as inferior or of less dignity: 'Now that you have had your say, let me have mine. If you find it admirable for you to allow yourself to be swept along by the colourful flow of events, the fact remains that for me they are meaningless without selection and discipline. Which attitude is superior is a question which is outside this discussion. only this is certain: the fact that something happens at all is only made possible by the latter form of conduct . of course I know that all the bearing and conduct possible will not produce a masterwork—yet it is equally true that much, if not everything, is suppressed without them. You, too, will have already been struck by how our entire art has been confounded by the trend towards the fragmentary and the volatile . through the series of "men-of-power" who were always denied the final touch—all that has its roots in that way of mind . . . And now the higher journalism that you praise and which should be furthered—this demands not the tepid sensitivity and mollusklike sensibility which is absorbed in "Berlin Naturalism" today, in "Viennese Symbolism" tomorrow; what is needed is the opposite: rigorous concentration on a single point . . .' Concerning the disintegration of language he has as few illusions as does Hofmannsthal: 'Everything can be said today; dross and empty straw.' But where Hofmannsthal chooses the feint, he resorts in desperation to force. He strangles words until they can no longer elude him; dead, he feels them safely in his grasp, whereas they are as lost to him as when they were evanescent. Thus George's heroism turns into its opposite. Its mythical features are diametrically opposed to the heritage in whose name they were appropriated by political apologists. They are features of defiance. 'It has grown late.' There is no trace of the archaic in George's work which is not directly related to this 'late' as its contrary. He scrutinizes words, so close and so alien, as though he hoped thus to see them as they were the day they were made. Such estrangement is no less completely determined by the liberalist epoch than is the anti-liberalist politics which in Germany so appealed to George as the needed authority. The extent to which he combines the liberal notion of security of law, the obstinate drive to dominate and a conception of prehistorical, archetypal relations is indicated in several lines from a letter of July 9, 1893: 'Every society, including the smallest and most loosely organized, is built on contracts. Your voice counts as much as any other it must however in every case make itself heard without dissembling.' If contracts apparently presuppose the full legal equality of the contracting parties, their introduction into questions of intellectual solidarity nevertheless remains an instrument for the suspension of equality and for subjugation, and presupposes a condition in which the individual subjects are in mortal enmity with one another, by means of which competitive society becomes increasingly like the primal horde. George's insistence that Hofmannsthal 'make (him)-self heard without dissembling', in connection with the *Blätter für die Kunst*, could only produce calamity when heeded. Whenever Hofmannsthal actually did allow himself to be lured into criticism of George and his followers he came off badly.

Against a world which seemed rootless to him, George appealed to the unequivocal character of nature. But this modern nature became unequivocal only through its domination by man. This endows the famous concluding stanzas of 'Die Templer' ['Templars'], which outline George's theory of form, with their historical-philosophical meaning, which was not part of the original intention: 'Und wenn die grosse Näherin im zorne/Nicht mehr sich mischend neigt am untern borne,/In einer weltnacht starr und müde pocht: /So kann nur einer der sie stets befocht/Und zwang und nie verfuhr nach ihrem rechte/Die hand ihr pressen, packen ihre flechte,/Dass sie ihr werk willfährig wieder treibt: /Den leib vergottet und den gott verleibt.'[18] ['And when the great seamstress in

---

[18] In his conception of the compulsion which the 'great seamstress' is said to have encountered, George is as opposed to Klages as he is similar to him in his neo-heathen invocation of the earth. This indicates how greatly his relation to Klages fluctuated. In the correspondence with Hofmannsthal, he defends the Pelasgian. As early as 1902 Hofmannsthal recognized the bizarre inconsistency between the pedantic sobriety of expression and the dogma of intoxication which Klages' philosophy unceasingly disavows and compares it to the masked-ball poetry of Alfred Schuler: 'I must frankly confess, however, that Klages' study of you seemed to me to fall short at innumerable important points, to lack the power to embody its intuitions. It contained metaphors which I am still endeavouring to forget.' George's reply is exceedingly general: 'Concerning K. and his book, let me just say at this point that in them we have a subject worthy of dispute. He has great nobility, a consuming drive for the highest values, but is also a titan who moves mountains.' In the *Star of the League* of 1913 the chthonians are dealt a rebuff that also applies to National Socialism, the langue of which it employs: 'Ihr habt, fürs reckenalter nur bestimmte /Und nach der Urwelt, später nicht bestand./Dann müsst ihr euch in fremde gaue wälzen/ Eur kostbar tierhaft kindhaft blut verdirbt/Wenn ihrs nicht mischt im reich von korn und wein./Ihr wirkt im andern fort, nicht mehr durch euch,/ Hellhaarige schar! wisst dass eur eigner Gott/ Meist kurz vorm siege meuchlings euch durchbohrt.' ['Meant for an age of heroes,/After primeval times you cannot endure,/Then you must hurl yourselves through foreign lands/Your precious bestial childlike blood turns bad/If you do not mix it in the realm of liquor and wine/Your works live on in others, no longer in you,/Lighthaired band! know that your own God/Often on the eve of victory, turns assassin, runs you through.'] The

wrath/No longer bends to mix at the lowest gate,/Beats in a world-night rigid and weary/Then only one who always fought her/And compelled and never heeded her laws,/ Can press her hand, seize her braid,/That she submissively take up her work again: /To deify the body and embody the divine.'] One who can only conceive of nature as the object of his violence should not justify his own being as nature. This contradiction is the counterpart in George to Hofmannsthal's fiction. George would like to dominate Hofmannsthal. What is said of Austria in the poem, 'Den Brüdern' ['To the Brothers'], dedicated to Andrian, designates the relationship: 'Da wollten wir euch freundlich an uns reissen/Mit dem was auch in euch noch keimt und wächst.' ['We sought as friends to snatch you to us/With the seed of future growth in you as well.'] Hofmannsthal is on the defensive. Just as in private life he evades all offers of friendship and closeness, in literary matters as well he assumes the standpoint of the period—aloofness. It does not even cause him great concern to see his poems published in obscure magazines, whereas George throws bearing to the winds as soon as his literary métier is affected and shows himself to be as passionate as any of his Paris friends. Hofmannsthal's defensive manoeuvres prudently manifest the most varied imaginative powers. He adopts the ceremonial character of the elder Goethe or of the letters written by Hoelderlin during his madness; he coquettishly deserts to the 'mass of readers'; he conciliates through sympathy, even for the otherwise despised friends of George; and he insults through the *pathos* of gratitude which distances itself. Even his 'closeness' to George, affirmed countless times to the very end, is made remote through the stereotyped quality of the many assurances. He conceals himself close by and slips into George's language; the letters he wrote to others would never be thought to have the same author. The most dependable technique, however, is that of self-accusation. The 'humble evasion'—recognized and labelled as such by George—with which he reacts to George's proposal to edit the *Blätter für die Kunst*, is not to be excelled. Hofmannsthal even parries insulting rebukes made by George, such as the condemnation of his solidarity with 'delirium', by appealing to his own bad condition. His compliance and openness are so limitless—even in the last letter he writes that

dialogue between man and druid, however, in the *New Imperium*, can no longer be distinguished from the school of Klages. The more George's abstractly glorified 'deed' was transposed to the realm of fatal political praxis, the more necessarily it required undisturbed nature and 'life' as its ideology.

he had 'gradually' come to accept fully George's annihilating 'evaluation of *Venice Saved*', although it had seemed severe at first—that he appears incorrigible: only someone who is untouched by criticism can accept it all without resistance.

The friendship of the two is on the decline before it ever attains reality. Already at this time friendship on the basis of mere sympathy or mere taste was no longer possible, even between men of the most extraordinary productive power; rather its sole remaining foundation was that of binding common knowledge—friendship from solidarity, which embraces theory as an element of its praxis. In the correspondence knowledge is anxiously excluded from the preconditions of friendship—the trauma of their first meeting in Vienna continues to have its effect and makes every attempt at explication a new act of confusion: 'Perhaps I judged you too strongly before . not because of repented deed but because of the uttered sentiment. I paid far too little attention to your utterly different manner of feeling as well as to your utterly different education in another clime: I believed that the principle that great and distinguished men have at all times recognized each other with noble suddenness suffered no exceptions and in my mind I assigned you the place 'where the rudders graze the ship'. Yet as excuse for you I always had the incomprehensibility of madness and I have never ceased to love you with that love whose basic feature is awe and which only comes into consideration for higher humanity. So much for the personal.' It is hardly to be expected that the personal was promoted through these vague lines which are both flattering and biting. They come from George's ceremonious letter of reconciliation, the same one to which the verses on the 'old hatred' are appended. Through the correspondence, George varies the always fatal intention of forgiving and forgetting. Each amiable intermittent letter seeks to extinguish a debt while the liabilities mount irresistibly through obstinate consideration: a gesture of concession by the one is all that is required for the other to be moved to attack or to withdraw. Behind the casuistry of the letters stand questions of prestige, of controlling rights over the work—be it intellectual—of others, and finally, questions of intellectual property and of a kind of originality which contradicts the concept of style emphatically advocated by both authors. In 1892 Hofmannsthal writes George: 'In the *Death of Titian* you will see a familiar detail—I mean the picture of the infante.' This is an allusion to a poem from the *Hymns*. With irritated, ostentatious noblesse George replies: 'Since you did not prefix a motto to the 'Prologue', and since in the same issue excerpts from my books are printed, I had my 'infante' deleted. The masses could easily misunderstand.' Scorn for the masses did not protect George from a jealousy common to just those circles which lack his exclusiveness. Nothing, however, could more glaringly illuminate the absurdity of such concerns than the object of the controversy. The cultural experience of the *infante* was had first by neither George nor Hofmannsthal—it stems from Baudelaire.[19] It is calculations of this kind which exclude solidarity and cast a shadow over acts such as the journalistic intervention of the one on behalf of the other. Hofmannsthal wrote repeatedly about George while George never wrote about Hofmannsthal, and yet the reproach for lack of solidarity always comes from George. George almost wrote a piece on Hofmannsthal once, but the exploratory discussion of the plan—which implicitly reproached Hofmannsthal for his fame—leaves no doubt as to why the essay was never completed. 'For some time now I have been contemplating an article on you—although I will have to find a large foreign journal to publish it—one in which artistic events really count as events—I will not speak about you after every savage tribe, every spice and money broker has had his say.' In the decline of the friendship between the two the market prevails, in the negation of which lyric poetry has its origins. Those who disdain to compete lose out as competitors.

George was less naïve in relation to the market than was Hofmannsthal. But he was hardly less naïve towards society. Thus, he opposes the market as a phenomenon without touching its underlying conditions. He would like to emancipate poetry from the demands of the public, yet at the same time he remains within a social framework which he will later mythologize with words like 'league' and 'hero', 'folk' and 'deed'. To place oneself above 'regard for the mass of readers' means, for George, to transform the mass of readers into a mass of coerced consumers through a technique of domination closely allied to artistic technique. Hence his ambivalent attitude towards success. The draft of a letter to Hofmannsthal, since lost, contains the following lines; 'On no account will I begin before I have settled everything contractually with everyone—delivery and remuneration, format and bearing. With some of my friends this is unnecessary, with others, however, all the more imperative, for as you know, not to seek success is magnificent, to seek it and not attain it, disreputable.'[20] His scorn of success applies solely to the

[19] 'Je suis comme le roi d'un pays pluvieux./Riche, mais impuissant, jeune et pourtant très vieux.' George translated the poem.
[20] The draft is from 1897. This is the year in which the *Year of the Soul* appeared. The turn which took place between the *Book of the Hanging*

market mechanism which subjects the competing parties to reverses. He strives for success while avoiding the market. The grandeur that proudly led him not to seek success is that of the literary tycoon, as which George previously saw himself and the model of which he could have easily taken from the German economy of the time. 'I was firmly convinced that we—you and I—could have exercised a very wholesome dictatorship for years through our writing—that this did not happen is solely your responsibility.' It is not easy for dictators to make mistakes. Those who live dangerously have true security. In the long run they are spared disreputable failure. With the acumen of hatred, Borchardt saw the monopolistic traits of the George school in his polemics against the *Jahrbuch für die geistige Bewegung* [*Yearbook for the Spiritual Movement*]: 'The central journal for German industrialists must proclaim that economic power is free only when man binds himself to man for the sake of man, that the hermit should not complain about economic ruin, and the like. . . . The friends of Herrn Wolfskehl make this necessity into both a virtue and a dogma of what they punitively term 'isolation', which is said to wither and lay waste to everything; they modify

---

Garden and the *Year of the Soul* can be placed in its proper context by regarding it in relation to success and the techniques for achieving it. This turn has its model in Verlaine, to which the *Year of the Soul* is substantially indebted. The title, 'Traurige Tänze' ['Sorrowful Dances'], poems like 'Es winkte der abendhauch' ['The Evening Breeze Waved'] with the concluding lines: 'Meine trübste stunde/Nun kennst du sie auch' ['My darkest hour/Now you know it too'] are inconceivable without Verlaine. The apotheosis from *Days and Deeds* describes what for George is the definitive event: 'After his first Saturnian poems, in which the youth was intoxicated with Persian and Papal splendour, yet still played with familiar Parnassian sounds, he leads us into his own rococo garden of the *feste galante*, where powdered knights and painted ladies stroll about or dance to graceful guitars, where quiet couples row in boats and little girls in concealed corridors look up lasciviously at the naked marble gods. Over this light alluring France, however, he breathes a never-felt breath of painful inwardness and deathly melancholy. . . . But what most gripped an entire poetic clan was the *Songs without Words*—stanzas of suffering and celebrating life . . . here, for the first time, we heard our souls, free of all discursive addition, throbbing; knew that it no longer needed buskin or mask and that the simple flute was enough to betray what is most profound to man. One colour magically evokes figures, while three spare strokes form a landscape and a shy sound gives the experience.' The turn consists in the attempt to evade the interior and to step into the 'landscape as house'. It involves the greatest simplification of technique: the language of the solitary resounds as the echo of the forgotten language of all. This simplification opens poetry once more to a circle of readers; but the solitary is the dictator of those who resemble him (cf. Walter Benjamin, *Uber einige Motive bei Baudelaire*, Schriften I, Frankfurt 1955, p. 426 ff.).

Schiller's heroic maxim to suit their modernity: "The strong man is most powerful in a group", in the syndicate of souls.'[21] An effort is made to transform competition into domination, and the competitive motive is cynically cited when it serves the cause of domination. By 1896 George offers Hofmannsthal co-editorship of the *Blätter für die Kunst*. He lends emphasis to the offer with the words: 'Since this is a matter of a serious collaboration involving all your talents, your occasional collaboration (which you could surely offer) would be meaningless. In the latter case we would have to endeavour to fill your place with someone else, but I prefer not to think about this severe loss.'

The *Blätter für die Kunst* embody most conspicuously the differences between George and Hofmannsthal. In the attitude of each towards the *Blätter* and its party[22] a true antinomy becomes manifest. It subsequently reasserted itself in the realm of politics, in places of which the two authors would never have dreamed. In 1893 Hofmannsthal writes Klein: 'The prospect of writing a newspaper article on the *Blätter* is no pleasant one for me; for my taste past issues have contained 1. too few really worthwhile items, 2. too much of me. Both these facts would so restrict what I could say that I prefer to be silent.' The background of this utterance may be discovered in an early letter of Hofmannsthal to Klein: 'In general, your proposal to discuss our undertaking in another public journal completely astonishes me. To what end? In that case, why not simply publish my pieces elsewhere, with strangers? Apparently I have completely misunderstood the entire point of the enterprise. I have absolutely no fear of 'compromising' myself and in artistic matters I am free of all personal obligations and ties. But please, tell me clearly what you want and to what end!' The matter is dialectical enough: George's exclusiveness strives dictatorially towards public, even journalistic pronouncements, and thus virtually negates itself; this, however, allows Hofmannsthal to appeal precisely to the esoteric quality of the circle which has been transgressed,

[21] By contrast to the George school, Borchardt's criticism assumes the standpoint of the ultra-right. At times this position permits materialist insights. The important article on the Toscan villa develops the latter as an art form out of the underlying economic condition of land-tenure.

[22] But sectarian groups formed at the same time in other spheres as well, from the Bayreuthian Round to the psychoanalysts. Despite divergences in content, notable similarities in their structure are evident. Common to all is an ambiguous notion of purgation and renewal which feigns resistance to the existing order while collaborating with it. Political solidarity is replaced by faith in panaceas. The efficacy of this catharsis proved itself in the guerilla warfare of competition as well as in the one-party system.

gressed, and to publish his pieces 'elsewhere, with strangers', thus completely abandoning the esoteric position. His attitude is determined by the fear of compromising himself, which he denies; what he is afraid of, however, is not so much the actual danger of lowering himself to the level of the commercial public, but rather of ruining his chances with it. His isolation within the circle makes him an understanding spokesman for the *profanum vulgus* against which the *Blätter* were founded: 'What I would like to do is not so much persuade as to experience less sparingly. On the basis of my far from perfect insight, I anticipate the virtual bewilderment of the public in face of such a strange and bitterly taciturn undertaking.' Through his critical insight Hofmannsthal surpassed the public's aversion. There was no equivocation in his rejection not merely of the bad poems which filled the *Blätter* but of the imitators of George himself. The following formulation is one of the more polite ones: 'If you had the friends and companions you deserved I, too, would be delighted.' There is no question that George was as well aware of the quality of the *Blätter* as was Hofmannsthal. He could easily reproach Hofmannsthal in return for the inferior literary quality of his friends, except that Hofmannsthal had never committed himself so decisively to them as George had to his collaborators. But George was not content with this: 'I maintain my attitude in opposition to yours, which rejects all work except for yours and mine. Not to speak of foreigners like Lieder · Verwey I do not understand how you can pass over artists and thinkers like e.g. Wolfskehl and Klages—the sombre ardour of the one, the brisk steady air of the other are so unique so primordial that I cannot even remotely compare anyone from your circle (in so far as it has manifested itself). . . . If you speak of the lesser stars, it is easy to make the judgement that they themselves know—but you make a great mistake if you suspect them of what you allege to be dishonesty and false poise—they are all men of good intellectual stamina with whom, if you knew them · you would live most pleasantly · to behave like geniuses—is something they never did, unlike those whom in contrast to ours you choose to protect. . . . In the *Blätter* everyone knows what he is · there is a sharp line drawn here between the work which is made and that which is born · all those who hate the *Blätter* seek to blur this line . . . If, however, you were to tell me that all you saw there was a collection of more or less good verse—and not the constructive element, to which, of course, little attention is paid today—you would present me with a great new disappointment.' The constructive element includes the co-ordination of the dominated no less than the unity of the consciously propagated technique—the suppression and intensification of productive power. Hofmannsthal sees the suppression but has nothing to oppose to it except for current conceptions of tradition and individuality: 'I would thereby exchange much of value, homogeneous to the individual, in forms, relations, insights, for more shallow things.' Each is right with respect to the other. In Hofmannsthal's aloofness George senses 'cleverness ready to seize any opportunity to suit the needs of the market'. Hofmannsthal, in turn, reveals the spurious quality of the collective held together by command, divest of all spontaneity, and the fate of the 'plebeian' who eludes this collective. The solitary and the organization man are both threatened by the existing order, the former through his own impotence which speciously installs itself as supreme tribunal and in reality cedes its rights to the inimical powers, the latter through the power which he obeys and which thereby carries the injustice which ought to be resisted into the ranks of those who resist. For both must live in a world of universal injustice. George's bearing is marked by this stigma down to its very language. During the days of their initial conflict he challenged Hofmannsthal: 'How much longer must we play hide-and-seek? If you want to speak freely (which is also my aim), then I invite you once more to appear on neutral territory. Your letter which was also so diplomatic—but was it my fault that you had to come into just that unfortunate café . . .' As the talk of contracts does later, here that of neutral territory and diplomacy inflates the private sphere to the general, as though it possessed political relevance. That reflects the newspapers which report the general, politically significant events to the private man. Esoteric pathos can easily have originated in the world of commodities: the dignity of the individual is borrowed from that of the headlines. George's expansive gestures have the naïveté of one who clothes himself in big words without blushing. He is incapable of regarding any matter, even the most private, as though it were anything else but public. His literary strategy stems from political impulses gone astray.

These impulses had at least one opportunity to realize themselves in their proper object. In 1905 Hofmannsthal, acting on behalf of Count Harry Kessler, of whom he himself was highly critical in several letters to Bodenhausen, made himself spokesman of that glittering pacifism of the ruling class; already at this time such pacifism embodied teleologically the attitude of those who later, during the occupation of Paris, acted as though the whole affair had been arranged by the PEN club merely to allow them to dine with their French colleagues at Prunier. The plan was to include

George. Hofmannsthal's letter, dater Weimar, December 1, 1905, reads as follows:

My dear George,

I have been asked to write you concerning a most serious matter, one which transcends the personal sphere. The fearful, inconceivable danger of an English-German war—although it was evident in the summer—is closer now, remains closer than newspaper reporters and most politicians care to believe. The few persons on this side who are aware of the seriousness of the situation and the few on the other side who wish to ward off the impending explosion have joined together, knowing how much force imponderables bear in such epochs, in order to exchange open letters, each signed by forty to fifty of the absolutely first names of the country (excluding professional politicians). The English open letter (signed by Lord Kelvin, George Meredith, A. Swinburne etc.) will be addressed to the editors of German newspapers, the German letter to the English papers (since the newspapers are the real powderkegs). In this exceptional situation and with full knowledge of your distaste for publicity, you are being asked to lend your name to this project, whereas e.g. there is no intention of including that of the well known Sudermann. The aim is to unite the most serious intellectual powers of the nation in this profoundly grave matter. If you would care to sign the enclosed letter, please return within ten days to Harry Count Kessler, Weimar, Cranachstrasse 3.

Yours,
HOFMANNSTHAL.

The all-star cast of 'absolutely first names', the exclusion of the unfortunate Sudermann, required to reinforce the included in their sentiment of superiority, and the vague impersonality in phrasing, suggesting that the powerful forces which are behind the important doings are so powerful that their emissary, intoxicated with awe, does not dare to name them—all that has as much style as the Joseph legend. George did not answer the unworthy letter. But an outline of his answer has been preserved and included in the correspondence, first without the most important sentence because of pressure from the Hitler régime, and now unabridged:

'If this message had not come from someone for whose understanding I have the greatest admiration, I would have held it for a joke. The two sides have no relations, whether in intellectual or in tangible matters, how can this help? And then the situation is

216

hardly as simple as this note would have it, war is only the last consequence of senseless economic activities on both sides which have lasted for many years, glue consisting of a few men seems to me utterly ineffective and in the long run who knows whether any genuine friend of the Germans should not hope for a vigorous naval catastrophe, so that they can thus recover that patriotic humility which would enable them once again to engender spiritual values. I would have replied with greater tranquillity had I not been overtaken with sorrow at the fact that there seems hardly to be any point remaining in which we do not misunderstand each other.'

Shortly thereafter a publishing matter provided the occasion of the final break.

The fact that George recognized the relationship between international aggressiveness and imperialistic ambitions, that the future emigrant already was speaking of Germany in words that must have sounded blasphemous to his own circle, indeed, that without theoretical insight into society he nevertheless perceived the objective necessity which leads to war—all this cannot be adequately explained by what Borchardt terms his 'important international affiliations'. Rather the true cause of his awareness is to be found in the substance of his poetry. In the working-class movement it has become habit, especially since the time of Mehring, to view naturalistic and realistic tendencies in art which tend to reflect social life in its immediacy as being inherently progressive and everything opposed to this as reactionary. Any artist who does not depict backyards, pregnant mothers and, more recently, prominent figures, is deemed a mystic. This badge may occasionally fit the consciousness of the censored authors. But to insist on the rendering of social reality in its immediacy is to adopt the empirical bias of the bourgeoisie which is supposed to be the object of criticism. Society, based on exchange, impels its off-springs to go about their business incessantly, to organize their lives around it, to have eyes solely for personal advantage, which is made the object of blind pursuit. Whoever steps out of line faces ruin. The force of immediacy prevents men from becoming conscious of the very mechanism which mutilates them—it reproduces itself in their pliant minds. This consciousness is hypostasized in the postulate which insists on the observation and reflection of the immediate at the same time, its complement, the fetishized theory, is betrayed through loyalty. The realist, in literature sworn to the palpable, writes from the mentally retarded perspective of the person whose impulses are limited to reflex actions. The realist tends to become a reporter who runs after striking events like a businessman after profit. Literary works,

217

classed today as luxuries and disdained as such, stand outside of this sphere. Today the doctrine of socialist realism, having become official ideology, is devoid of value. Even in regard to the conservative George and Hofmannsthal, talk of a flight from reality is not even half-true. First of all, the work of both is pointedly turned against mystical inwardness: 'Schwärmer aus zwang weil euch das feste drückt/Sehner aus not weil ihr euch nie entfahrt/Bleibt in der trübe schuldlos...die ihr preist—/Ein schritt hinaus wird alles dasein lug!' ['Forced to become enthusiast, because oppressed by the fixed/Dreamer, because unable to escape yourself/Stay in the gloom guiltless... which you praise—/One step beyond and life becomes a lie!'] In Hofmannsthal's 'Conversations about Poems', his definitive utterance about George's poetry, he strives for an adequate theory: 'If we wish to find ourselves we must not descend within us; it is outside that we are to be found, outside. Like the insubstantial rainbow, our soul bends over the irresistible torrent of existence. We do not possess ourself; it wafts over us from outside, it flees us for long times and returns to us in a breath of wind.' Just as reconstructive Empirio-criticism is led, by way of the immanence of subjectivity, to deny the subject and adopt a second, naïve realism, inwardness is led to extinguish itself in Hofmannsthal's conception. If it is true that the Symbolists' secret is not so much one of inwardness as one of *métier*, it is certainly not permissible to assign them a progressive function in regard to technique, as 'formalists', while insisting on the reactionary content of their poetry. Many progressives have transposed the crude form-content schema of positivism to the sphere of art as though its language were the dispensable semiotic system which even scientific language is not. But even were this schema true, it is completely false to suppose that all the light would fall on the sovereign form and all shadow on the subordinate content.

It would be false, to George and Hofmannsthal as well as to the movements designed as Symbolism and Neo-Romanticism, to praise or blame them for what they themselves would have readily admitted—that they preserved the beautiful while the Naturalists resigned themselves to the barren life of industrial society. The renunciation of the beautiful can preserve its idea more powerfully than the illusory conservation of disintegrating beauty. Conversely, nothing is as ephemeral in George and Hofmannsthal as the beautiful that they celebrate—the beautiful object. It tends towards the commercial *objet d'art*, which George did not deny his blessing. In the preface to the second edition of the *Hymns* he approvingly cites the 'fortunate rise of activity in painting and decoration', and similarly, in a letter to Hofmannsthal from 1896 which was never sent: 'After decades of pure physical or scientific effort a new yearning for higher art has become evident at many points in Germany. It passes from painting tone and poetry through decoration and architecture and finally even reaches fashion and life.' On the way to fashion and life, beauty fraternizes with the very same ugliness against which it, being outside the sphere of utility, had declared war. The communal life which George desired has handicraft character: 'Today this is all easier to forget, since our efforts have turned out well (despite everything) and we have behind us a youth full of confidence self-discipline and the ardent desire for beauty.' This defines the 'great and distinguished persons', who, ever since Charcot and Monna Vanna, flee their families into illness. The depravation into handicrafts affected not merely things, but individuals as well; handicrafts are the stigma of emancipated beauty. It succumbs once the newly won and technically controlled materials, manufactured at will, become marketable. George came very close to recognizing this in the concluding poem of the *Pilgerfahrten* [*Pilgrimages*], which leads into *Algabal*. The ideal of the beautiful is represented through the metaphor of the clasp: 'Ich wollte sie aus kühlem eisen/Und wie ein glatter fester streif,/Doch war im schacht auf allen gleisen/So kein metall zum gusse reif./Nun aber soll sie also sein:/Wie eine grosse fremde dolde/Geformt aus feuerrotem golde/Und reichem blitzenden gestein.' ['I wanted it of iron cool/And smooth like a hard solid plate,/But in all the tunnels of the shaft/There was no metal ready to cast,/Now however it must be:/Like a large strange cluster/Formed of fire-red gold /And rich shimmering stones.'] If 'there was no metal ready to cast', if the conditions of material life did not contain the objective possibility of the beautiful, which manifests itself instead 'like a large strange cluster' in the negation of material life, then it follows that material life draws the chimera back into itself through imitation. The simple clasp of commercial handicrafts, consisting of inexpensive metal, represents allegorically the golden clasp, which had to be cast because the proper metal was lacking. The correspondence leaves no doubt as to the chimerical character of the exquisite. It emerges even out of the economic machinations. George's bibliophilic passion led him to invent a typeface which imitated his handwriting. 'I am sending you new samples of the binding, as well as of the type (my own which I have been working for some time to improve) I think you will like them. You will see that they have been modelled on my handwriting—in any case, a good solution after all the recent designers of type merely added a few frills to the already existing characters to get away from the old ones.' The phoneyness inherent in a product of mass production pretending to be unique results from the attempt to create beauty without any objective criterion for it other than the withered programmatic intention 'to get away from the old'. The spurious singularity, however, is at the same time planned for the sake of material value: 'The first aim of our circle (expanded through the fixed readership of the dealers) is to produce truly beautiful books that people can afford · which will also not sacrifice what is essential to the connossieur—rarity · the reader with little understanding of us, who simply follows us from afar, may then pay the raised price ... A way other than subscription does not exist.' The mere fact that the exquisite allure can be expressed in terms of value, that the unique can be compared—this abstractness of malachite and alabaster makes the exquisite interchangeable. The symbolically beautiful is doubly distorted—through naïve faith in the material and through allegorical ubiquity. Everything can signify everything on the handicrafts market. The less familiar the materials, the less limited their intentionality. Page after page can be devoted to a jeweller's catalogue in Oscar Wilde, countless interiors of the *fin du siècle* resemble a curiosity shop. Even George and Hofmannsthal display an enigmatic lack of taste concerning the painting and sculpture of their era. Among the painters praised in the correspondence the favourites are Burne-Jones, Puvis de Chavannes, Klinger, Stuck and the incredible Melchior Lechter. The great French painting of the epoch is never mentioned.[23] When George, in an entirely different context, of course, speaks with regret of the fact that 'our better minds ... can no longer distinguish brash dabblers in colour from painters', it should be remembered that the Wilhelmian judgement of impressionism and toilet-art is not so very different. The paintings which embody the true impulses of the poem 'Frühlingswind' ['Spring Wind'], or of the ice landscapes in the *Year of the Soul*,

---

[23] Once again this recalls Marie Bashkirzev. She lacked the slightest understanding of advanced art. Her horizon in painting was determined by the salon; she admired Bastien-Lepage. Her paintings are like early picture postcards. With a candour which suggests the obsessive need to confess and which, above all, sacrifices the sick person's healthy craving for success, she occasionally characterizes herself as a raw and ignorant barbarian. Her judgement of the art she has journeyed to see is that of the cultural tourist; she is incapable of apprehending nuances since she brutally subordinates everything she beholds to her interest in status. This did not hinder the mixture of naïveté, *morbidezza* and the cult of power which she ostentatiously displayed from making her the heroine of a movement with which she objectively had little in common.

are placed under a taboo. The seal of approval is given to photo-graphically accurate ideal figures, beautiful creatures in the erotic taste of the time, which assume sublime significance without the allegorical intention being burdened with the demands of autono-mous painting. Nothing less important is neglected than the dictate of form, under which George's own poetry stands.

George retreats from his principle, however, when he strives to subordinate the material to meanings in order to purge him-self from the reproach of aestheticism. In his youth he was as indifferent to meaning as the Rimbaud of 'Voyelles': 'You need not regret the one mistake, "sing" instead of "suck". It does not harm anything; in fact it fits very well.' True symbolism is a *lucus a non lucendo*. In Hofmannsthal's George dialogue, the student of language says: 'It is full of images and symbols. It sets one thing in place of another.' Hofmannsthal corrects him with the words: 'What a repulsive thought! Are you talking seriously. Poetry never set one thing in place of another, for it is precisely poetry which fervently strives to set the thing in its own place, with an energy which is utterly distinct from the dull language of every-day, with a magical power utterly distinct from the feeble termino-logy of science. If poetry does anything, it is this: out of every phenomenon in the world and in dreams it extracts, with passionate thirst, that which is most peculiar, most essential to it.' And to the protest, 'are there no symbols?'—'Why, of course, there is nothing but them.' The desired aim is to explode a reality which has rigidi-fied into conventional meanings through the use of material foreign to intention; that which could be flees to fresh data, lest it be drawn through ordinary communication down into the sphere of that which is. Such poetry compromises itself through every gesture which signifies and thus goes beyond the mere materials; Melchior Lechter triumphs with the Angel of the 'Prologue'. But it is not George's particular blindness which is responsible. What he asked of the pure material was beyond what it could achieve. Both as the abstract relics of the thing-world and as the subject's 'exper-ience', they belonged to the very sphere they were intended to leave behind. Ironically, Hofmannsthal is right: the unsymbolic neces-sarily turns into the all-symbolic. In this there is no difference be-tween Rimbaud's pure sounds and the noble materials of the later poets. One can, it is true, call the early, aesthetic George 'real', and the later, realistic George a bad aesthete—but the latter is already present in the former. The beauty, from whose blind eyes stare sparkling jewels already contains the ideology of the 'young *führer* in the First World War', who covers over the business side, the curse of which is supposed to be lifted by magic. The jewels acquire their value from surplus labour. The secret of non-intentional materials is money. Baudelaire is superior to all those who followed because he nowhere inclined towards beauty as something positive and immediate, but only as that which has been irrevocably lost, or as that which is its most radical negation. Satan, the *deus absconditus* betrayed by fate, is for him 'le plus savant et le plus beau des Anges'; he is not saddened by the rosy angel of the Beautiful Life, to whose faithful image beauty abandons itself in George. Through beauty George communes with the realistic copyists.

What drew him to this beauty was not primarily the poetic will to form, but rather an aspect of its content. Like a shibboleth, the object is held up to impending ruin while appeals are made to its beauty. The correspondence with Hofmannsthal offers a remarkable example of this. Discussing the publication of *The Death of Titian* in the *Blätter für die Kunst*, George writes: 'I completed the bookmarks wherever they had been omitted unintentionally, in accordance with your meaning ... and then, on my own (there was so little time), in the note deleted "since Titian died of the plague at the age of ninety-nine". Otherwise you would have introduced an injurious tone into your work, obviously by accident'. According to this, the mere mention of the plague in a work of art could do damage to it, and not just to it alone. Symbolism is dominated by the magic of tortured beauty. In the George dialogue Hofmannsthal seeks to grasp the aesthetic symbol as a sacrificial rite: 'Do you really know what a symbol is?... Will you try to imagine how sacrifice originated?... It seems to me that I can see the first person who sacrificed. He felt that the Gods hated him ... then, in the dual darkness of his lowly hut and his heartfelt dread, he seized his sharp, curved knife and was ready to let the blood run from his throat to please the fearful, invisible deity. And then, drunk with dread and savagery and the nearness of death, his hands clutched once again, half unconsciously, at the woolly warm fleece of the ram. And this animal, this life, this thing breathing in the dark, bloodwarm, so close to him, so familiar—suddenly the knife tore through the throat and the warm blood spurted över both the animal's fleece and the man's breast, then his arms—and for one moment he must have thought that it was his own blood; for that moment, in which a sound of voluptuous triumph issued from his throat to mix with the dying moans of the animal, he must have mistaken the voluptuousness of a heightened life for the first convulsion of death; for a moment he must have died in the animal, for only thus could the animal die for him.... Henceforth, the animal died the symbolic sacrificial death. But everything rests on the fact that he, too, died in the animal, for one moment. . . . That is the root of all poetry . . . He died in the animal. And we dissolve in symbols. Is this how you meant it?'—'Certainly. In so far as they have the power to enchant us.' This gory theory of the symbol, which comprehends the sinister political possibilities of neo-romanticism, says something about its own motives. Dread compels the poet to worship the inimical powers of life; Hofmannsthal uses it to justify the symbolic act. In the name of beauty he consecrates himself to the preponderant thing-world as a sacrifice. If the primitive man, to whom Hofmannsthal attributes his ideology, did not really die but instead slaughtered the animal, the non-committal sacrifice of modern man must be taken all the more drastically. He seeks to save himself by throwing himself away and making himself the mouthpiece of things. The estrangement of art from life urged by George and Hofmannsthal, intended to elevate art, changes into unlimited, adaptable proximity to life. In truth, it is not the aim of symbolism to subordinate all material moments as symbols of an inner sphere. It is just this possibility that is subjected to doubt, whereas it is the absurd, the estranged thing-world itself, in its impenetrability for the subject, which endows the latter with its dignity and meaning on the condition that the subject dissolve itself in the world of things. Subjectivity no longer regards itself as the animating centre of the cosmos. It abandons itself to the miracle that would happen if the mere material, divested of meaning, were on its own to animate waning subjectivity. Instead of things yielding as symbols of subjectivity, subjectivity yields as the symbol of things, prepares itself to rigidify ultimately into the thing which society has in any case made of it. Thus, for the unsuspecting faith of the early Rilke, the very word, 'thing', became the formula of a cult. Such anxiety embodies experiences of society which are concealed in its immediate appearance. They relate to the composition of the individual. In the past, autonomy demanded that the inviolable externality of the object be overcome by subjecting it to one's own will. The economic competitor survived by anticipating fluctuations in the market, even if he could not do anything about them. The modern poet lets himself be overwhelmed by the power of things as though he were an outsider being swallowed by a cartel. Both win the semblance of security; the poet, however, without sensing its opposite. The 'ciphers, which language is powerless to dissolve'—namely those, which exhaust themselves in the signification of their objects—become a *menetekel* to Hofmannsthal. The estrangement of art from life has a dual meaning.

It comprises not merely the refusal to accept the *status quo*, in contrast to the naturalists who are always tempted to affirm the horrors seen by their acute artistic eye, as simply existing—now and always. George and Hofmannsthal curried favour equally with the established order. But it remained an order which was estranged from them. Organized estrangement reveals as much of life as can be revealed without theory, since the essence itself is estrangement. The others represent capitalist society, but allow human beings to speak fictitiously as though they could still talk to each other. Aesthetic fictions speak the true monologue, which communicative speech merely conceals. The others narrate experiences, as though it were still possible to narrate anything about capitalism. All neo-romantic words are final.[24] The others employ psychology as glue to paste together the inner dimension and the estranged outer one; but it is a psychology which is inadequate for the social tendencies of the age while at the same time, as Leo Lowenthal has remarked, remaining behind the scientific advances developed since the end of the nineteenth century.[25] Instead of psychology, its aesthetic opponents invoke the inextinguishable image, which—however lacking in transparency—still designates the powers which drive towards the catastrophe. It is the configuration of that which psychology can only suggest in derivative and scattered hints, just as the individuals with which it is occupied themselves are only derivatives of the historical reality. Baudelaire's 'Petites Villes', and even George's 'Culprit', or 'You Walked to the Oven', are closer to the insight of the collapse, to its necessity, than are the assiduous description of slums and mines. If the historical hour echoes obscurely in the latter, the poems, by contrast, know what the hour means. It is in this knowledge, not in the unheard prayer to beauty, that form originates—in defiance. The passionate effort to express oneself in language, keeping banality at a distance, is the attempt, however hopeless, to extricate experience from its mortal enemy, which engulfs it in late bourgeois society—oblivion. The banal is consecrated

[24] The executor of the will was Wedekind. His dialogue rests on the principle that no speaker ever understands the other. Wedekind's plays are permanent misunderstandings. This was pointed out, astoundingly enough, by Max Halbe in his memoires. As acrobats, the *dramatis personae* resemble mechanisms. Although they do not know it yet, it is no longer possible for them to speak—hence the profound justice of Wedekind's artificial German.

[25] Hofmannsthal, who was a friend of Schnitzler's, was interested in psychoanalysis but his work remained unaffected by it. He distanced himself from the psychological novel. The George school, like phenomenology, is utterly anti-psychological.

to oblivion; that which is given form is to endure as secret historio-graphy. Hence, the blindness to impressionism; they failed to under-stand that no power on earth can resist transience which is not itself a transient power. Defiance of society includes defiance of its language.[26] The others share the language of men. They are 'social'. The aesthetes are as far ahead of them as they are asocial.[27] Their works measure themselves against the recognition that the language of men is the language of their degradation. To steal language from them, to renounce communication, is better than to adjust. The bourgeois glorifies the existing order as nature and demands that his fellow citizens speak 'naturally'. This norm is overturned by aesthetic affectation. The affected aesthete speaks as though he were his own idol. He thus makes himself an easy target. Anyone can prove to him that he is no different from everyone else. But he re-presents the utopia of not being oneself. Of course, the others may criticize society. But they remain as true to themselves as to their notion of happiness as a healthy, well organized, rationally ordered life. The utopia of aestheticism abrogates the social contract of happiness. Happiness lives off an antagonistic society, a world 'où l'action n'est pas la soeur du rêve'.[28] As faithful if moderate pupils of Baudelaire, George and Hofmannsthal established happiness where it was defamed. Confronted with the defamed, what is

[26] Hence the priority of translation from Rossetti and Baudelaire to George and Borchardt. They all seek to save their own language from the curse of banality by viewing it from the standpoint of a foreign language and thus letting its everydayness freeze under the Gorgon glance of strange-ness; every poem of Baudelaire as well as of George must, according to its own linguistic form, be judged solely against the ideal of translation.

[27] Of course, only this far; as long as they offend by their 'degeneracy', for which they have been reproached since Max Nordau's book. Every turn to the positive is in fact disintegration. One example will serve for many: the great Baudelairean motif of sterility. The sterile woman escapes from the procreative order of the detested society. Baudelaire cele-brates her together with the lesbian and the whore. He compares the *froide majesté de la femme sterile* to the useless starlight which is outside the sphere of social purposes. Hofmannsthal adopts the motif in order to turn it to patriotic and at the same time trivial ends. 'From all these things/ And from her beauty—that was sterile,' he takes leave, for the sake of the beloved. In the 'Woman Without Shadow' sterility is a curse which must be lifted.

[28] George translates: 'I am truly happy to flee this race/Which refused to join dream and deed.' The translation is a betrayal. Baudelaire speaks of the *monde*, of the total structure of reality which keeps the dream far from active hands. George makes a 'race' out of it, as though it were a question of degeneration, of 'decadence', whereas Baudelaire's revolt strikes at the principle of order itself. In George scandal is replaced by that 're-newal' which always associates itself with 'race'.

allowed withers and vanishes for them. The unnatural is charged with the task of recreating the multitude of instincts which were distorted by the primacy of procreation; irresponsible play seeks to overcome the ruinous seriousness of whatever one happens to be. Both shake personal identity to the roots with a silent roar, identity, the walls of which comprise the innermost prison cell of the existing order. Whatever they may choose to provide a positive contrast to the ruling society is subordinate to it as a reflection of the individual, just as George's angel resembles the poet, just as the lover in the *Star of the League* finds 'my own flesh' in the beloved. What survives is determinate negation.

A PORTRAIT OF WALTER BENJAMIN

... and listen to the sounds of the day as though they were
chords of eternity.

Karl Kraus

The name of the philosopher who took his life while fleeing Hitler's executioners has, in the more than twenty years since then, acquired a certain nimbus, despite the esoteric character of his early writings and the fragmentary nature of his later ones. The fascination of the person and of his work allowed no alternative other than that of magnetic attraction or horrified rejection. Everything which fell under the scrutiny of his words was transformed, as though it had become radioactive. His capacity for continually bringing out new aspects, not by exploding conventions through criticism, but rather by organizing himself so as to be able to relate to his subject-matter in a way that seemed beyond all convention—this capacity can hardly be adequately described by the concept of 'originality'. None of the ideas which flowed from his inexhaustible reserve ever pretended to be mere inspiration. Benjamin, who as subject actually lived all the 'originary' experiences that official contemporary philosophy merely talks about, seemed at the same time utterly detached from them. Nothing was more foreign to him, and above all to his flair for instantaneous, definitive formulations, than what is traditionally associated with spontaneity and ebullience. The impression he left was not of someone who created truth or who attained it through conceptual power; rather, in citing it, he seemed to have transformed himself into a supreme instrument of knowledge on which the latter had left its mark. He had nothing of the philosopher in the traditional sense. His own contribution to his work was not anything 'vital' or 'organic'; the metaphor of the creator is thoroughly inappropriate for him. The subjectivity of his thought shrank to its own specific difference; the idiosyncratic moment of his mind, its singularity—something which, according to conventional philosophical mores, would have been held for contingent, ephemeral, utterly worthless—legitimized itself by giving his thought its compelling character. The thesis that where knowledge is concerned the most individual is the most general, suits him perfectly. Had all analogies drawn from physics not become profoundly suspect in an age which has been characterized by the radical divergence of social and scientific consciousness, his intellectual energy might well be described as a kind of mental atomic fission. His insistence dissolved the insoluble; he grasped the essential precisely when walls of sheer facticity sealed off illusive essences. To speak in terms of formulae, he was impelled to break the bonds of a logic which covers over the particular with the universal or merely abstracts the universal from the particular. He sought to comprehend the essence where it did not permit itself to be distilled by automatic operation or reveal itself to dubious intuition, by subjecting it to methodic conjecture within a configuration of individually opaque elements. The rebus is the model of his philosophy.

The deliberate digressiveness of his thought, however, is matched by its gentle irresistibility. This resides neither in magical effects, which were not foreign to him, nor in an 'objectivity', denoting the disappearance of the subject in those constellations. It stems rather from a quality which intellectual departmentalization otherwise reserves for art, but which sheds all semblance when transposed into the realm of theory and assumes incomparable dignity—the promise of happiness. Everything that Benjamin said or wrote sounded as if thought, instead of rejecting the promises of fairy tales and children's books with its usual disgraceful 'maturity', took them so literally that real fulfilment itself was now within sight of knowledge. In his philosophical topography, renunciation is totally repudiated. Anyone who was drawn to him was bound to feel like the child who catches a glimpse of the lighted Christmas tree through a crack in the closed door. But the light, as one of reason, also promised truth itself, not its powerless shadow. If Benjamin's thought was not creation *ex nihilo*, it had the generosity of abundance; it sought to make good everything, all the pleasure prohibited by adjustment and self-preservation, pleasure which is both sensual and intellectual. In his essay on Proust, a writer for whom he felt the strongest of affinities, Benjamin defined the desire for happiness as the basic motif; one would scarcely be misled in suspecting this to be the origin of a passion which produced two of the most perfect translations in German—those of *A l'ombre des jeunes filles en fleurs* and of *Le côté de Guermantes*. However, just as in Proust the desire for happiness acquires profundity only through the onerous weight of the novel of disillusion, which is fatally completed in *La Recherche du temps perdu*, in Benjamin the devotion to happiness which has been denied is won only through a regretful sorrow, the like of which is as rare in the history of philosophy as the utopia of cloudless days. His relation to Kafka is no less intimate than that to Proust. Kafka's remark, that there is infinite hope except for us, could have served as the motto of Benjamin's metaphysics, had he ever deigned to write one, and it is no accident that at the centre of his most elaborate theoretical work, *The Origins of the German Tragic Drama, [Ursprung des deutschen Trauerspiels]* there is the construction of 'sorrow' ['Trauer'] as the last self-negating, self-transcending allegory, that of Redemption. Subjectivity, plunging into the abyss of significances, 'becomes the ceremonial guarantee of the miracle because it announces divine action itself.' In all his phases, Benjamin conceived the downfall of the subject and the salvation of man as inseparable. That defines the macrocosmic arc, the microcosmic figures of which drew his devoted concern.

Because what distinguishes his philosophy is its kind of concretion. Just as his thought sought again and again to free itself of all impulse to classify, the prime image of all hope for him is the name, of things and of men, and it is this that his reflection seeks to reconstruct. In this respect he seems to converge with the general intellectual current which protested against idealism and epistemology, demanding 'the things themselves' instead of their conceptual form, and which found an academically respectable expression in phenomenology and the ontological schools stemming from it. But the decisive differences between philosophers have always consisted in nuances; what is most bitterly irreconcilable is that which is similar but which thrives on different centres; and Benjamin's relation to today's accepted ideologies of the 'concrete' is no different. He saw through them as the mere mask of conceptual thinking at its wits end, just as he also rejected the existential-ontological concept of history as the mere distillate left after the substance of the historical dialectic had been boiled away. The later Nietzsche's critical insight that truth is not identical with a timeless *universal*, but rather that it is solely the historical which yields the figure of the absolute, became, perhaps without his knowing it, the canon of his practice. The programme is formulated in a note to his fragmentary main work, that 'in any case the eternal is more like lace trimmings on a dress than like an idea'. By this he in no way intended the innocuous illustration of concepts through colourful historical objects as Simmel did when he depicted his primitive metaphysics of form and life in the cup-handle, the actor, Venice. Rather, his desperate striving to break out of the prison of cultural conformism was directed at constellations of historical entities which do not remain simply interchangeable examples for ideas but which in their uniqueness constitute the ideas themselves as historical.

This brought him the reputation of an essayist. Until today his nimbus has remained that of the sophisticated 'literator', as he himself, with antiquarian coquetry, would have put it. In view of his wily aim in opposing the shopworn themes and jargon of philosophy—the latter he habitually termed 'procurer language'—it would be easy enough to dismiss the cliché of 'essayist' as a mere misunderstanding. But the recourse to 'misunderstandings' as a means of explaining the effect of intellectual phenomena does not lead very far. It presupposes that there is an intrinsic substance, often simply equated with the author's intention, which exists independently of its historical fate; such a substance is in principle hardly identifiable and this is all the more so with an author as complex and as fragmentary as Benjamin. Misunderstandings are the medium in which the noncommunicable is communicated. The provocative assertion that an essay on the Paris Arcades is of greater interest philosophically than are ponderous observations on the Being of beings is more attuned to the meaning of his work than the quest for that unchanging, self-identical conceptual skeleton which he relegated to the dustbin. Moreover, by not respecting the boundary between the man of letters and the philosopher, he turned empirical necessity into 'intelligible'—in the Kantian sense—virtue. To their disgrace the universities refused him, while the antiquarian in him felt itself drawn to academic life in much the same ironic manner as Kafka felt drawn to insurance companies. The perfidious reproach of being 'too intelligent' haunted him throughout his life; an Existentialist overlord had the effrontery to defame him as being 'touched by demons', as though the suffering of a person dominated and estranged by the mind should be considered his metaphysical death sentence, merely because it disturbs the all-too-lively I-Thou relationship. In fact, however, he shrank before every act of violence against words; ingenuity was fundamentally alien to him. The true reason that he aroused hatred was that, inevitably and without any polemical intention, his glance revealed the ordinary world in the eclipse which is its permanent light. At the same time, the incommensurable quality of his nature, undaunted by every tactic and incapable of indulging in the social games of the Republic of Intellects, permitted him to earn his living as an essayist, on his own and unprotected. That greatly developed the agility of his profound mind. He learned how to convict the prodigious and ponderous claims of the *prima philosophia* of their hollowness, with a silent chuckle. All of his utterances are equally near the centre. The articles scattered throughout the *Literarische Welt* and the *Frankfurter Zeitung* are hardly less indicative of his stubborn intention than are the books and longer studies in the *Zeitschrift für Sozial-*

forschung. The maxim in *One-Way Street* which asserts that today all decisive blows are struck left-handedly, was one he followed himself, yet without ever sacrificing the truth even in the slightest. Even his most precious literary *jeux* serve as studies for a genre, the masterwork, which he nevertheless thoroughly mistrusted.

The essay as form consists in the ability to regard historical moments, manifestations of the objective spirit, 'culture', as though they were natural. Benjamin could do this as no one else. The totality of his thought is characterized by what may be called 'natural history'. He was drawn to the petrified, frozen or obsolete elements of civilization, to everything in it devoid of domestic vitality no less irresistibly than is the collector to fossils or to the plant in the herbarium. Small glass balls containing a landscape upon which snow fell when shook were among his favourite objects. The French word for still-life, *nature morte*, could be written above the portals of his philosophical dungeons. The Hegelian concept of 'second nature', as the reification of self-estranged human relations, and also the Marxian category of 'commodity fetishism' occupy key positions in Benjamin's work. He is driven not merely to awaken congealed life in petrified objects—as in allegory—but also to scrutinize living things so that they present themselves as being ancient, 'ur-historical' and abruptly release their significance. Philosophy appropriates the fetishization of commodities for itself: everything must metamorphose into a thing in order to break the catastrophic spell of things. Benjamin's thought is so saturated with culture as its natural object that it swears loyalty to reification instead of flatly rejecting it. This is the origin of Benjamin's tendency to cede his intellectual power to objects diametrically opposed to it, the most extreme example of which was his study on 'The Work of Art in the Era of its Mechanical Reproduction'. The glance of his philosophy is Medusan. If the concept of myth, as the antipode to reconciliation, occupies a central position in it, especially during its openly theological phase, then everything, and especially the ephemeral, becomes in his own thought mythical. His critique of the domination of nature, programmatically stated in the last piece of *One-Way Street*, negates and transcends the ontological dualism of myth and reconciliation; reconciliation is that of myth itself. In the course of such criticism the concept of myth becomes secularized. Fate, which begins as the guilt of the living, becomes that of society: 'So long as one beggar remains, there is still myth.' Thus, Benjamin's philosophy, which once sought to conjure up 'essences' directly, as in his 'Critique of Force', moved ever more decisively towards dialectics. The latter did not intrude from without on a thought

233

which was inherently static, nor was it the product of mere development, but was rather anticipated in the *quid pro quo* between the most rigid and the most dynamic elements in his thought during all of its phases. His conception of 'dialectics at a standstill' emerged with increasing clarity.

The reconciliation of myth is the theme of Benjamin's philosophy. But, as in good musical variations, this theme rarely states itself openly; instead, it remains hidden and shifts the burden of its legitimation to Jewish mysticism, to which Benjamin was introduced in his youth by his friend, Gershom Scholem, the distinguished student of the *cabbala*. It is difficult to say to what extent he was influenced by the neo-platonic and antinomian-messianic tradition. There is much to indicate that Benjamin—who hardly ever showed his cards and who was motivated by a deeply seated opposition to thought of the shoot-from-the-hip variety, to 'free floating' intelligentsia—made use of the popular mystic technique of pseudo-epigraphy—never, to be sure, disclosing the texts, in order thus to outwit truth, which he suspected of being no longer accessible to autonomous reflection. In any case, his notion of the sacred text was derived from the cabbala. For him philosophy consisted essentially in commentary and criticism, and language as the crystallization of the 'name', took priority over its function as bearer of meaning and even of expression. The concern of philosophy with previously existent, codified doctrines is less foreign to its great tradition than Benjamin might have believed. Crucial writings or passages of Aristotle and Leibniz, Kant and Hegel, are 'critiques' not merely in the implicit sense of works which deal with problems already posed but rather as specific confrontations. It was only after they had banded together to form their own discipline and had begun to lose touch with their own thought that philosophers all deemed it necessary to cover themselves by beginning before the creation of the world, or, if at all possible, to incorporate it into the system. Benjamin maintained a determined Alexandrinism in the face of this trend and thereby provoked all fundamentalist furies. He transposed the idea of the sacred text into the sphere of enlightenment, into which, according to Scholem, Jewish mysticism itself tends to culminate dialectically. His 'essayism' consists in treating profane texts as though they were sacred. This does not mean that he clung to theological relics or, as the religious socialists, endowed the profane with transcendent significance. Rather, he looked to radical, defenceless profanation as the only chance for the theological heritage which squandered itself in profanity. The key to the picture puzzles is lost. They must, as a baroque poem about melancholy says, 'speak themselves'. The procedure resembles Thorstein Veblen's quip, that he studied foreign languages by staring at each word until he knew what it meant. The analogy with Kafka is unmistakable. But he distinguishes himself from the older Prague writer, who even at times of the most extreme negativity retains an element of the rural, epic tradition, through the far more pronounced moment of urbanity which serves as a contrast to the archaic, and through the resistance to demonic regression acquired by his thought through its affinity to enlightenment, a regression which often leaves Kakfa unable to distinguish between the *deus absconditus* and the devil. During his mature period, Benjamin was able to give himself over fully to socially critical insights without there being the slightest mental residue, and still without having to ban even one of his impulses. Exegetical power became the ability to see through the manifestations and utterances of bourgeois culture as hieroglyphs of its darkest secret—as ideologies. He spoke occasionally of the 'materialist toxins' that he had to add to his thought so that it might survive. Among the illusions that he renounced in order not to concede the necessity of renunciation, was that of the monadological, self-contained character of his own reflection, which he measured tirelessly and without flinching at the pain of objectification against the overwhelming trend of the collective. But he so utterly assimilated the foreign element to his own experience that the latter improved as a result.

Ascetic forces counterbalanced an imaginative power kindled ever anew by each object. This helped Benjamin to develop a philosophy directed against philosophy. It can well be described in terms of the categories which it does not use. A conception of them emerges if one examines his idiosyncratic distaste for words like 'personality'. From the very start his thought protested against the false claim that man and the human mind are self-constitutive and that an absolute originates in them. The incisiveness of this kind of reaction ought not to be confused with modern religious movements that attempt, in the sphere of philosophic reflection, to make of man the creature to which total social dependency has already degraded him independently of their efforts. His target is not an allegedly over-inflated subjectivism but rather the notion of a subjective dimension itself. Between myth and reconciliation, the poles of his philosophy, the subject evaporates. Before his Medusan glance, man turns into the stage on which an objective process unfolds. For this reason Benjamin's philosophy is no less a source of terror than a promise of happiness. Just as the domain of myth is ruled by multiplicity and ambiguity and not subjectivity, the un-equivocal character of reconciliation—conceived after the model of the 'name'—is the contrary of human autonomy. He reduces this autonomy to a moment of transition in a dialectical process, as with the tragic hero, and the reconciliation of men with the creation has as its condition the dissolution of all self-posited human existence. According to an oral statement, Benjamin accepted the 'self' solely as something mystical and not as metaphysical-epistemological, as 'substantiality'. Inwardness for him is not merely the seat of torpor and melancholic complacency; it is also the phantasma which dis-torts the potential image of man—he always contrasts it to the physical, external things. Thus, one will search his writings in vain for a concept like autonomy; yet others, such as totality, life, system, from the sphere of subjective metaphysics, are equally absent. What he praised in Karl Kraus, a writer as different from Benjamin in all other respects as possible, was one of his own traits—inhumanity against the deception of 'the universally human'; Kraus, it may be added, did not take kindly to this praise. The categories which Benjamin rejected, however, are those which compromise the essen-tial ideology of society. From time immemorial, the masters have used such categories to set themselves up as God. As a critic of force, Benjamin as it were revokes the unity of the subject to mythic turmoil in order to comprehend such unity as itself being only a natural condition; with his philosophy of language oriented on the cabbala, Benjamin saw subjective unity as scribbling of the Name. That links his materialistic period with his theological one. He viewed the modern world as archaic not in order to conserve the traces of a purportedly eternal truth but rather to escape the trance-like captivity of bourgeois immanence. He sees his task not in reconstructing the totality of bourgeois society but rather in examin-ing its blinded, nature-bound and diffuse elements under a micro-scope. His micrological and fragmentary method therefore never entirely integrated the idea of universal mediation, which in Hegel as in Marx produces the totality. He never wavered in his funda-mental conviction that the smallest cell of observed reality offsets the rest of the world. To interpret phenomena materialistically meant for him not so much to elucidate them as products of the social whole but rather to relate them directly, in their isolated singularity, to material tendencies and social struggles. Benjamin thus sought to avoid the danger of estrangement and reification, which threaten to transform all observation of capitalism as a system itself into a system. Motifs of the young Hegel, whom he hardly would have known, are prominent; in dialectical materialism, too, he sensed what Hegel called 'positivity', and opposed it in his way. In its close contact with material which was close at hand, in its affinity to that which is, his thought, despite all its strangeness and acumen, was always accompanied by a characteristic unconscious element, by a moment of naïveté. This naïveté enabled him at times to sympathize with groups in power-politics which, as he well knew, would have liquidated his own substance, unregimented intellectual experience. But also towards them he cunningly adopted the rôle of an exegete, as though one had only to interpret the objective spirit to satisfy its demands and to comprehend its horror in order to eliminate it. He preferred to supply heteronomy with speculative theories than to abandon speculation.

Politics and metaphysics, theology and materialism, myth and modernity, non-intentional matter and extravagant speculation—all the streets of Benjamin's city-tableau converge in the plan of the Paris book as in their Etoile. But he would never have agreed to use this project, destined for him *a priori*, as it were, to present a coherent exposition of his philosophy. Just as the conception arose out of a concrete occasion, it never in all the years that followed relinquished the form of a monograph. 'Dream Kitsch,' an article which appeared in the *Neue Rundschau*, was concerned with the shocklike flashes of obsolete elements from the nineteenth century in surrealism. The material point of departure was provided by a magazine article on the Paris arcades, which he and Franz Hessel planned to write. He clung to the title of the arcades article long after a plan had crystallized according to which extreme physiognomic traits of the nineteenth century were to be handled in a manner similar to that used in dealing with the Baroque in the book on the tragic drama. Out of these traits he intended to construe the idea of the epoch in terms of an ur-history of modernity. This 'history' was not designed to uncover archaic rudiments in the recent past, but rather to define the idea of newness, of the 'latest thing', as itself an archaic pattern. 'The form of the new means of production, which in the beginning was still dominated by the old form . . . has its correlative within the collective mind in images in which the new mingles with the old. These images embody desires, and in them the collective seeks both to transcend and to transfigure the unfinished character of the social product and the deficiencies in the order of social production. The images also display the emphatic effort to set oneself apart from the obsolete, which, however, means from the recent past. These tendencies guide the image-producing imagination, which received its initial impulse from the new, back to the ancient past. Dreams, in which every epoch sees the images of that which is to succeed it, now show the coming age mingled with elements of ur-history—that is to say, of a classless society. The experiences of this society, stored in the unconscious of the collective, join with the new to produce the utopia which has left its trace in a thousand configurations of life, from lasting buildings to the most fleeting fashions.' Such images, however, were for Benjamin much more important than Jung's archetypes of the collective unconscious; he thought of them as objective crystallizations of the historical dynamic and gave them the name of 'dialectical images'. A magnificently improvised theory of the gambler provided their model: they were to decipher historically-philosophically the phantasmagoria of the nineteenth century as the figure of hell. The original layer of the *Arcades* project, from about 1928, was then covered over by a second, materialist one, perhaps because the determination of the nineteenth century as hell became untenable with the rise of the Third Reich, perhaps because the thought of hell tended to lead in a political direction entirely different from that which Benjamin saw implied in the strategic rôle which Haussmann's boulevards were to play; but above all, probably because he happened to come across a forgotten work, written in prison by Auguste Blanqui, *L'éternité par les astres*, which, in accents of absolute despair, anticipates Nietzsche's theory of the eternal return. The second phase of the *Arcades* plan is documented in the memorandum, dating from 1935, entitled 'Paris, Capital of the Nineteenth Century'. This relates certain key figures of the epoch to categories of the world of images. Its subject-matter was supposed to consist of Fourier and Daguerre, of Grandville and Louis Philippe, of Baudelaire and Haussmann; instead it dealt with themes like fashions and *nouveauté*, fairs and cast-iron construction, the collector, the *flaneur*, prostitution. A passage on Grandville bears witness to the extreme excitement with which the interpretation was charged: 'World's Fairs erect a commodity universe. Grandville's phantasies endow the universe with commodity-character. They modernize it. Saturn's ring becomes a cast-iron balcony on which the inhabitants of Saturn take a breath of air in the evening. ... Fashion prescribes the ritual which determines how the fetish will be honoured, Grandville extends fashion's authority to the objects of everyday use as well as to the cosmos. By pursuing fashion to its extremes he reveals its nature. It stands in opposition to the organic. It couples the living body with the inorganic world. In the living it sees the prerogatives of the corpse. Fetishism, which succumbs to the sex appeal of the inorganic, is its vital nerve. The commodity cult puts it to good use.' Considerations of this sort led to the planned chapter on Baudelaire. Benjamin detached it from the larger project in order to make a shorter, three-part book; a large section of it appeared in the 1939–40 issue of the *Zeitschrift für Sozialforschung* as the article entitled, 'On Some Motifs of Baudelaire'. It is one of the few texts of the *Arcades* complex which he was able to complete. A second consists of the theses, 'On the Concept of History', which summarize, so to speak, the epistemological considerations which developed together with the *Arcades* project. Thousands of pages of this project have been preserved, studies of individual subjects which were hidden during the occupation of Paris. The whole, however, can hardly be reconstructed. Benjamin's intention was to eliminate all overt commentary and to have the meanings emerge solely through a shocking montage of the material. His aim was not merely for philosophy to catch up to surrealism, but for it to become surrealistic. In *One-Way Street* he wrote that citations from his works were like highwaymen, who suddenly descend on the reader to rob him of his convictions. He meant this literally. The culmination of his anti-subjectivism, his major work was to consist solely of citations. Only seldom are there interpretations noted which could not be integrated into the Baudelaire study or the theses 'On the Concept of History', and there is no canon to indicate how the audacious venture of a philosophy purified of argument might be carried out, or even how the citations might be meaningfully ordered. His philosophy of fragmentation remained itself fragmentary, the victim, perhaps, of a method, the feasibility of which in the medium of thought must remain an open question.

The method, however, cannot be separated from the content. Benjamin's ideal of knowledge did not stop at the reproduction of what already is. He mistrusted all limitations placed on the realm of possible knowledge, the pride of modern philosophy in its illusionless maturity, for in it he sensed a plot to sabotage the claim of happiness, the attempt to strengthen a situation which tolerates only what is more of the interminable same; he sensed the presence of myth itself. The utopian motif in him, however, is paired with his antiromanticism. He remained uncorrupted by all apparently similar attempts, such as Max Scheler's, to grasp transcendence through natural reason, as though the limiting process of the enlightenment could be revoked and one could simply reinstate the theologically grounded philosophies of the past. For this reason from its very inception his thought protected itself from the 'success' of unbroken cohesion by making the fragmentary its guiding principle. In order to achieve his aim he chose to remain completely outside of the manifest tradition of philosophy. Despite its great culture, the elements of that tradition enter his labyrinth scattered, submerged, obliquely. His incommensurability lies in the inordinate ability to give himself over to his object. By permitting thought to get, as it were, too close to its object, the object becomes as foreign as an everyday, familiar thing under a microscope. To interpret his lack of system and of a closed theoretical foundation as sufficient reason to align him with the representatives of 'intuition', eidetic or otherwise—and he was often misunderstood in this way, even by friends—is to overlook what is best in him. It is not his glance as such which lays claim to the unmediated possession of the absolute; rather his manner of seeing, the entire perspective is altered. The technique of enlargement brings the rigid in motion and the dynamic to rest. His preference in the *Arcades* for small or shabby objects like dust and plush is a complement of this technique, drawn as it is to everything that has slipped through the conventional conceptual net or to things which have been esteemed too trivial by the prevailing spirit for it to have left any traces other than those of hasty judgement. Benjamin, the dialectician of the imagination, which he defined as 'extrapolation at its most minute', sought, like Hegel, 'to observe the thing as it is, in and for itself'; that is, he refused to accept as ineluctable the threshold between consciousness and the thing-in-itself. But the distance of such observation has been shifted. Not because, as in Hegel, subject and object are ultimately developed as being identical, but rather because the subjective intention is seen to be extinguished in the object, Benjamin's thought is not content with intentions. The thoughts press close to its object, seek to touch it, smell it, taste it and so thereby transform itself. Through this secondary sensuousness, they hope to penetrate down to the veins of gold which no classificatory procedure can reach, and at the same time avoid succumbing to the contingency of blind intuition. The radical reduction of the distance of the object also establishes the relation to potential praxis which later guided Benjamin's thinking. What confronts experience in the *déjà vu* as opaque and without objectivity, what Proust hoped to gain for poetic reconstruction through involuntary memory, Benjamin sought to recapture and elevate to truth through the concept. He charged it with accomplishing what is otherwise reserved for nonconceptual experience. He strove to give thought the density of experience without having it therefore lose any of its stringency.

The utopia of knowledge, however, has utopia as its content. Benjamin called it 'the unreality of despair'. Philosophy condenses into experience so that it may have hope. But hope appears only in fragmented form. Benjamin overexposes the objects for the sake of the hidden contours which one day, in the state of reconciliation, will become evident, but in so doing he reveals the chasm separating that day and life as it is. The price of hope is life: 'Nature is messianic in its eternal and total transience', and happiness, according to a late fragment which risks everything, is its 'intrinsic rhythm'. Hence, the core of Benjamin's philosophy is the idea of the salvation of the dead as the restitution of distorted life through the consummation of its own reification down to the inorganic level. 'Only for the sake of the hopeless are we given hope', is the conclusion of the study of Goethe's *Elective Affinities*. In the paradox of the impossible possibility, mysticism and enlightenment are joined for the last time in him. He overcame the dream without betraying it and making himself an accomplice in that on which the philosophers have always agreed: that it shall not be. The character of the picture puzzle, as which he himself described the aphorisms in *One-Way Street* and which distinguished everything he ever wrote, originates in that paradox. It was nothing other than the explication and elucidation of this paradox, with the only means which philosophy has at its disposal, concepts, that drove Benjamin to immerse himself without reserve in the world of multiplicity.

NOTES ON KAFKA

For Gretel

Si Dieu le Père a créé les choses en les nommant, c'est en leur
ôtant leur nom, ou en leur donnant un autre que l'artiste les
recréé.

Marcel Proust

1

Kafka's popularity, that comfort in the uncomfortable which has made of him an information bureau of the human condition, be it eternal or modern, and which knowingly dispenses with the very scandal on which his work is built, leaves one reluctant to join the fray, even if it is to add a dissenting opinion. Yet it is just this false renown, fatal variant of the oblivion which Kafka so bitterly desired for himself, that compels one to dwell on the enigma. Of that which has been written on him, little counts; most is existentialism. He is assimilated into an established trend of thought while little attention is paid to those aspects of his work which resist such assimilation and which, precisely for this reason, require interpretation. As though Kafka's Sisyphean labours would have been necessary, as though the maelstrom force of his work could be explained, if all he had to say was that man had lost the possibility of salvation or that the way to the absolute is barred, that man's life is dark, confused, or, in currently fashionable terminology, 'suspended in nothingness', and that the only alternative left is for him to do his duty, humbly and without great aspirations, and to integrate himself into a collective which expects just this and which Kafka would not have had to affront had he been of one mind with it. To qualify such an interpretation by arguing that Kafka of course did not say this in so many words but rather worked as an artist with realistic symbolism is to admit a dissatisfaction with formulas but not much more. For an artistic representation is either realistic or symbolic; no matter how densely organized the symbols may be, their own degree of reality cannot detract from the symbolic character. Goethe's play, *Pandora*, is no less rich in sensuous depiction than a novel by Kafka, and yet there can be no doubt concerning the symbolism of Goethe's fragment, even though the power of the symbols—as with Elpore, who embodies hope—may exceed what was originally intended. If the notion of the symbol has any meaning whatsoever in aesthetics—and this is far from certain—then it con only be that the individual moments of the work of art point beyond themselves by virtue of their interrelations, that their totality coalesces into meaning. Nothing could be less true of Kafka. Even in a work such as Goethe's, which plays so profoundly with allegorical moments, these still relinquish their significance, by virtue of their context, to the thrust of the whole. In Kafka, however, everything is as hard, defined and distinct as possible; in this his works resemble the novel of adventure, as described by James Fenimore Cooper in his preface to *The Red Rover*: 'The true Augustan age of literature can never exist until works shall be as accurate in their typography as a "log-book", and as sententious in their matter as a "watch-bill".' Nowhere in Kafka does there glimmer the aura of the infinite idea; nowhere does the horizon open. Each sentence is literal and each signifies. The two moments are not merged, as the symbol would have it, but yawn apart and out of the abyss between them blinds the glaring ray of fascination. Here too, in its striving not for symbol but for allegory, Kafka's prose sides with the outcasts, the protest of his friend notwithstanding. Walter Benjamin rightly defined it as parable. It expresses itself not through expression but by its repudiation, by breaking off. It is a parabolic system the key to which has been stolen; yet any effort to make this fact itself the key is bound to go astray by confounding the abstract thesis of Kafka's work, the obscurity of the existent, with its substance. Each sentence says 'interpret me', and none will permit it. Each compels the reaction, 'that's the way it is', and with it the question, 'where have I seen that before?'; the *déjà vu* is declared permanent. Through the power with which Kafka commands interpretation, he collapses aesthetic distance. He demands a desperate effort of the allegedly 'disinterested' observer of an earlier time, overwhelms him, suggesting that far more than his intellectual equilibrium depends on whether he truly understands; life and death are at stake. Among Kafka's presuppositions, not the least is that the contemplative relation between text and reader is shaken to its very roots. His texts are designed not to sustain a constant distance between themselves and their victim but rather to agitate his feelings to a point where he fears that the narrative will shoot towards him like a locomotive in a three-dimensional film. Such aggressive physical proximity undermines the reader's habit of identifying himself with the figures in the novel. It is by reason of this principle that surrealism can rightfully claim him. He is Turandot set down in writing. Anyone who sees this and does not choose to run away must stick out his head, or rather try to batter down the wall with it at the risk of faring no better than his predecessors. As in fairy-tales, their fate serves not to deter but to entice. As long as the word has not been found, the reader must be held accountable.

2

Far more than for most other writers, it may be said of Kafka that not *verum* but *falsum* is *index sui*. He himself, however, contributed to the spread of the untruth. His two great novels, *The Castle* and *The Trial*, seem to bear the mark of philosophical theorems, if not in their details then in their general outlines, which despite all intellectual profundity, in no way belie the title given to a collection of Kafka's theoretical writings, 'Reflections on Sin, Pain, Hope and the True Way'. Still, the content of the title is not canonic for the literary work. The artist is not obliged to understand his own art, and there is particular reason to doubt whether Kafka was capable of such understanding. In any case, the aphorisms are hardly equal to his most enigmatic stories and episodes, such as 'Care of a Family Man' or 'The Bucket Rider'. Kafka's works protected themselves against the deadly aesthetic error of equating the philosophy that an author pumps into a work with its metaphysical substance. Were this so, the work of art would be stillborn; it would exhaust itself in what it says and would not unfold itself in time. To guard against this short-circuit, which jumps directly to the significance intended by the work, the first rule is: take everything literally; cover up nothing with concepts invoked from above. Kafka's authority is textual. Only fidelity to the letter, not oriented understanding, can be of help. In an art that is constantly obscuring and revoking itself, every determinate statement counterbalances the general proviso of indeterminateness. Kafka sought to sabotage this rule when he let it be announced at one point that messages from the castle must not be taken 'literally'. All the same, if one is not to lose all ground on which to stand, one must cling to the fact that at the beginning of *The Trial*, it is said that someone must have been spreading rumours about Josef K., 'for without having done anything wrong, he was arrested one fine morning'. Nor can one throw to the winds the fact that at the beginning of *The Castle*, K. asks 'what village is this that I have wandered into? Is there a castle here?' and hence, cannot possibly have been summoned there. He also knows nothing of Count Westwest, whose name is mentioned only once and who is thought of less and less until he is entirely forgotten, like the Prometheus of one of Kafka's fables, who merges with the rock to which he is chained and is then forgotten. Nevertheless, the principle of literalness, probably a reminiscence of the Torah exegesis of Jewish tradition, finds support in many of Kafka's texts. At times, words, metaphors in particular, detach themselves and achieve a certain autonomy. Josef K. dies 'like a dog', and Kafka reports the 'Investigations of A Dog'. Upon occasion the literalness is driven to the point of a pun. Thus, in the story of Barnabas' family, in *The Castle*, the official, Sortini, is described as having remained 'at the nozzle' during the Fire Department party. The colloquial German expression for devotion to duty is taken seriously, the respectable person stays at the nozzle of the fire-hose, and simultaneously an allusion is made, as in parapraxes, to the crude desire which drives the functionary to write the fateful letter to Amalia—Kafka, disparager of psychology, is abundantly rich in psychological insights, such as that into the relation between instinctual and obsessive personality. Without the principle of literalness as criterion, the ambiguities of Kafka would dissolve into indifferent equivalence. This principle, however, invalidates the most commonly held conception of the author, one which seeks to unite in him the claim to profundity with equivocation. Cocteau rightly pointed out that the introduction of anything startling in the form of a dream invariably removes its sting. It was to prevent such misuse that Kafka himself interrupted *The Trial* at a decisive point with a dream—he published the truly horrifying piece in *A Country Doctor*—and by contrast confirmed the reality of everything else, even if it should be that dream-reality suggested periodically in *The Castle* and *America* by passages so agonizingly drawn out that they leave the reader gasping for air. Among the moments of shock, not the least results from the fact that Kafka takes dreams *à la lettre*. Because everything that does not resemble the dream and its pre-logical logic is excluded, the dream itself is excluded. It is not the horrible which shocks, but its self-evidence. No sooner has the surveyor driven the bothersome assistants from his room in the inn than they climb back through the window without the novel stopping for one word more than required to communicate the event; the hero is too tired to drive them away again. The attitude that Kafka assumes towards dreams should be the reader's towards Kafka. He should dwell on the incommensurable, opaque details, the blind spots. The fact that Leni's fingers are connected by a web, or that the executioners resemble tenors, is more important than the Excursus on the law. It is true both of the mode of representation and of the language. Gestures often serve as counterpoints to words: the pre-linguistic that eludes all intention upsets the ambiguity, which, like a disease, has eaten into all signification in Kafka. ' "The letter," began K., "I have read it. Do you know the contents?" "No," said Barnabas, whose look seemed to imply more than his words. Perhaps K. was as mistaken in Barnabas' goodness as in the malice of the peasants, but his presence remained a comfort.' Or: ' "Well," she said extenuatingly, "there was a reason for laughing. You asked if I knew Klamm, and you see I"—here she involuntarily straightened up a little, and her triumphant glance, which had no connection whatever with what she was saying, swept over K.—"I am his mistress." ' Or in the scene of Frieda's parting from the surveyor: 'Frieda had let her head fall on K's shoulder; their arms round each other, they walked silently up and down. "If we had only," said Frieda after a while, slowly, quietly, almost serenely, as if she knew that only a very short respite of peace on K's shoulder was reserved for her and she wanted to enjoy it to the utmost, "If we had only gone away somewhere at once that night, we might be in peace now, always together, your hand always near enough for mine to grasp; oh, how much I need your companionship, how lost I have felt without it ever since I've known you! To have your company, believe me, is the only dream I've had, that and nothing else." ' Such gestures are the traces of experiences covered over by signification. The most recent state of a language that wells up in the mouths of those who speak it, the second Babylonian confusion, which Kafka's sober diction tirelessly opposes, compels him to invert the historical relation of concept and gesture. The gesture is the 'that's the way it is'; language, the configuration of which should be truth, is, as a broken one, untruth. ' "Also you should be far more reticent, nearly everything you have just said could have been implied in your behaviour with the help of a word here and there, and in any case does not redound particularly to your credit." ' The experiences sedimented in the gestures will eventually have to be followed by interpretation, one which recognizes in their mimesis a universal which has been repressed by sound common sense. In the scene of K's arrest at the beginning of *The Trial*, there is the following passage: 'Through the open window, he had another glimpse of the old woman who with genuine senile inquisitiveness had moved along to the window exactly opposite, in order to see all that could be seen.' Is there anyone who has lived in boarding houses and has not felt himself observed by the neighbours in precisely the same manner; together with the repulsive, the familiar, the unintelligible and the inevitable, such a person has seen the image of fate suddenly light up. The reader who succeeds in solving such rebuses will understand more of Kafka than all those who find in him ontology illustrated.

Here one may object that an interpretation can no more rely on this than on anything else in Kafka's deranged cosmos, that such experiences are nothing but contingent and private psychological projections. Anyone who believes that the neighbours are watching him from their windows or that the telephone speaks to him with its own singing voice—and Kafka's writing teems with such statements—is suffering from delusions of persecution and of relation, and anyone who seeks to make a kind of system out of such things has been infected by the paranoia; for such a person Kafka's works serve solely to rationalize his own psychological injuries. This objection can be answered only through reflection on the relation of Kafka's work itself to the zone of psychology. His words, 'for the last time, psychology', are well known as is his remark that everything of his could be interpreted psychoanalytically except that this interpretation would in turn require further interpretation *ad indefinitum*; yet neither such verdicts, nor the venerable haughtiness which is the most recent ideological defence of materialism, should tempt one to accept the thesis that Kafka has nothing to do with Freud. It would be a bad sign for his much praised profundity if one refused to acknowledge what exists in those depths. In their conception of hierarchy, Kafka and Freud are hardly to be distinguished. In *Totem and Taboo*, Freud writes: 'A king's taboo is too strong for his subject because the social difference between them is too great. But a minister may serve as a harmless intermediary between them. Transposed from the language of taboo into that of normal psychology this means the following: the subject, who fears the great temptation involved in contact with the king, can still tolerate dealings with an official whom he does not need to envy so much and whose position may even appear within his grasp. The minister, however, can temper his envy of the king by considering the power which he has been allotted. Thus smaller differences in the magical power leading to temptation are less to be feared than particularly great ones.' In *The Trial*, a high official says: 'Not even I can bear the sight of even the third door-keeper', and there are analagous moments in *The Castle*. This also sheds light on a decisive complex in Proust, snobbism as the will to sooth the dread of the taboo by winning acceptance among the initiates: 'For it was not just Klamm's proximity as such that was worth striving for but rather the fact that it was he, K., only he, no one else with his wish or with any other, who approached Klamm, not in order to rest with him but rather to pass beyond him, farther, into the castle.' The expression, *délire de toucher*, which Freud cites and which is equally germane to the sphere of the taboo, exactly describes the sexual magic that drives people together in Kafka, especially those of lower social station with those of a higher class. Even the 'temptation' suspected by Freud—that of murdering the father-figure—is alluded to in Kafka. At the conclusion of the chapter in *The Castle* in which the landlady explains to the surveyor that it is utterly impossible for him to speak with Herr Klamm in person, he has the last word: ' "Well, what are you afraid of? You're surely not afraid for Klamm, are you?" The landlady gazed silently after him as he ran down the stairs with the assistants following.' To come closest to understanding the relation between the explorer of the unconscious and the parabolist of impenetrability, one must remember that Freud conceived of an archetypal scene such as the murder of the primal father, a pre-historical narrative such as that of Moses, or the young child's observation of its parents having sexual relations, not as products of the imagination but in large measure as real events. In such eccentricities Kafka follows Freud with the devotion of a Till Eulenspiegel to the limits of absurdity. He snatches psychoanalysis from the grasp of psychology. Psychoanalysis itself is already in a certain sense opposed to the specifically psychological inasmuch as it derives the individual from amorphous and diffuse drives, the Ego from the Id. Personality is transformed from something substantial into a mere organizational principle of somatic impulses. In Freud as in Kafka the validity of the soul is excluded; Kafka, indeed, took virtually no notice of it from the very beginning. He distinguishes himself from the far older, scientifically inclined Freud, not through a more delicate spirituality but rather through a scepticism towards the Ego which, if anything, exceeds that of Freud. This is the function of Kafka's literalness. As though conducting an experiment, he studies what would happen if the results of psychoanalysis were to prove true not merely metaphorically but in the flesh. He accepts psychoanalysis in so far as it convicts civilization and bourgeois individuation of their illusoriness; he explodes it by taking it more exactly at its word than it does itself. According to Freud, psychoanalysis devotes its attention to the 'dregs of the world of appearances'. He is thinking of psychic phenomena, parapraxes, dreams and neurotic symptoms. Kafka sins against an ancient rule of the game by constructing art out of nothing but the refuse of reality. He does not directly outline the image of the society to come—for in his as in all great art, asceticism towards the future prevails—but rather depicts it as a montage composed of waste-products which the new order, in the process of forming itself, extracts from the perishing present. Instead of curing neurosis, he seeks in it itself the healing force, that of knowledge: the wounds with which society brands the individual are seen by the latter as ciphers of the social untruth, as the negative of truth. His power is one of demolition. He tears down the soothing façade to which a repressive reason increasingly conforms. In the process of demolition—never was the word more popular than in the year of Kafka's death—he does not stop at the subject as does psychology, but drives through to the bare material existence that emerges in the subjective sphere through the total collapse of a submissive consciousness, divest of all self-assertion. The flight through man and beyond into the non-human—that is Kafka's epic course. The decline of genius, the spasmodic lack of resistance which so completely converges with Kafka's morality, is paradoxically rewarded by the compelling authority of its expression. Such a posture, relaxed virtually to the breaking point, is heir to what was formerly metaphor, significance, mind, and it inherits it as though it were a physical reality of its own, as 'spiritual body'. It is as though the philosophical doctrine of the 'categorical intuition', which was becoming well known at the time that Kafka wrote, were to be honoured in hell. The windowless monad preserves itself as the magic lantern, mother of all images as in Proust and Joyce. That above which individuation lifts itself, what it conceals and what it drove from itself, is common to all but can only be grasped in solitude and undistracted concentration. To fully participate in the process that produces the abnormal experiences which in Kafka define the norm, one must have experienced an accident in a large city; uncounted witnesses come forward, proclaiming themselves acquaintances, as though the entire community had gathered to observe the moment when the powerful bus smashed into the flimsy taxicab. The permanent *déjà vu* is the *déjà vu* of all. This is the source of Kafka's success, which becomes betrayal only when the universal is distilled from his writings and the labours of deadly seclusion avoided. Perhaps the hidden aim of his art as a whole is the manageability, technification, collectivization of the *déjà vu*. The best, which is forgotten, is remembered and imprisoned in a bottle like the Cumaean sibyll. Except that in the process it changes into the worst: 'I want to die', and that is denied it. Made eternal, the transient is overtaken by a curse.

4

Eternalized gestures in Kafka are the momentaneous brought to a standstill. The shock is like a surrealistic arrangement of that which old photographs convey to the viewer. Such a snapshot, unclear, almost entirely faded, plays its rôle in *The Castle*. The landlady shows K. a photograph she has kept as a relic of her contact with Klamm and through him with the hierarchy. Only with difficulty can K. recognize anything on it. Yesterday's gaudy tableaux, drawn from the sphere of the circus—for which Kafka, with the avant-garde of his generation, felt an affinity—are frequently introduced into his work; perhaps everything was originally supposed to become a tableau and only an excess of intention prevented this, through long dialogues. Anything that balances on the pinnacle of the moment like a horse on its hindlegs is snapped, as though the pose ought to be preserved forever. The most gruesome example of this is probably to be found in *The Trial*: Josef K. opens the lumber-room, in which his warders had been beaten a day earlier, to find the scene faithfully repeated, including the appeal to himself. 'At once K. slammed the door shut and then beat on it with his fists, as if that would shut it still more securely.' This is the gesture of Kafka's own work, which—as Poe had already begun to do—turns away from the most extreme scenes as though no eye could survive the sight. In it what is perpetually the same and what is ephemeral merge. Over and over again, Titorelli paints that monotonous genre picture, the heath. The sameness or intriguing similarity of a variety of objects is one of Kafka's most persistent motifs; all possible demi-creatures step forward in pairs, often marked by the childish and the silly, oscillating between affability and cruelty like savages in children's books. Individuation has become such a burden for men and has remained so precarious, that they are mortally frightened whenever its veil is raised a little. Proust was familiar with the shiver of discomfort that comes over someone who has been made aware of his resemblance to an unknown relative. In Kafka, this becomes panic. The realm of the *déjà vu* is populated by doubles, *revenants*, buffoons, Hasidic dancers, boys who ape their teachers and then suddenly appear ancient, archaic; at one point, the surveyor wonders whether his assistants are fully alive. Yet there are also images of what is coming, men manufactured on the assembly-line, mechanically reproduced copies, Huxleyian Epsilons. The social origin of the individual ultimately reveals itself as the power to annihilate him. Kafka's work is an attempt to absorb this. There is nothing mad in his prose, unlike the writer from whom he learned decisively, Robert Walser; every sentence has been shaped by a mind in full control of itself; yet, at the same time, every sentence has been snatched from the zone of insanity into which all knowledge must venture if it is to become such in an age when sound common sense only reinforces universal blindness. The hermetic principle has, among others, the function of a protective measure: it keeps out the onrushing delusion, which would mean, however, its own collectivization. The work that shatters individuation will at no price want to be imitated; for this reason, surely, Kafka gave orders for it to be destroyed. No tourist trade was to blossom where it had gone; yet anyone who imitated its gestures without having been there would be guilty of pure effrontery in attempting to pocket the excitement and power of alienation without the risk. The result would be impotent affectation. Karl Kraus, and to a certain extent Schoenberg, reacted much like Kafka in this respect. Yet such inimitability also affects the situation of the critic. Confronted by Kafka his position is no more enviable than that of the disciple; it is, in advance, an apology for the world. Not that there is nothing to criticize in Kafka's work. Among the defects, which become obvious in the great novels, monotony is the most striking. The presentation of the ambiguous, uncertain, inaccessible, is repeated endlessly, often at the expense of the vividness that is always sought. The bad infinity of the matter represented spreads to the work of art. This fault may well reflect one in the content, a preponderance of the abstract idea, itself the myth that Kafka attacks. The portrayal seeks to make the uncertain still more uncertain but provokes the question, why the effort? If everything is questionable to begin with, then why not restrict oneself to the given minimum? Kafka would have replied that it was just this hopeless effort that he demanded, much as Kierkegaard sought to irritate the reader through his diffuseness and thus startle him out of aesthetic contemplation. Discussions concerning the virtues and deficiencies of such literary tactics are so fruitless because criticism can address itself only to that in a work wherein it seeks to be exemplary; where it says, 'as I am, so shall it be'. But precisely this claim is rejected by Kafka's disconsolate 'that's the way it is'. Nevertheless, at times the power of the images he conjures up cracks through their protective covering. Several subject the reader's selfawareness, to say nothing of the author, to a severe test: 'The Penal Colony' and 'The Metamorphosis', reports which had to await those of Bettelheim, Kogon and Rousset for their equals, much as the bird's eye photos of bombed out cities redeemed, as it were, Cubism, by realizing that through which the latter broke with reality. If there is hope in Kafka's work, it is in those extremes rather than in the milder phases: in the capacity to stand up to the worst by making it into language. Are these, then, the works which offer the key to an interpretation? There are grounds to think so. In 'The Metamorphosis', the path of the experience can be reconstructed from the literalness as an extension of the lines. 'These travelling salesmen are like bugs', is the German expression that Kafka must have picked up, speared up like an insect. Bugs—not *like* bugs. What becomes of a man who is a bug as big as a man? As big as adults must appear to the child, and as distorted, with gigantic, trampling legs and far-off, tiny heads, were one to catch and isolate the child's terrified vision; it could be photographed with an oblique camera. In Kafka, an entire lifetime is not enough to reach the next town, and the stoker's ship, the surveyor's inn, are of·dimensions so enormous that one would have to return to a long-forgotten past to find a time when man saw his own products similarly. Anyone who desires such vision must transform himself into a child and forget many things. He recognizes his father as the ogre he has always feared in infinitesimal omens; his revulsion against cheese rinds reveals itself as the ignominious, pre-human craving for them. The 'boarders' are visibly shrouded in the horror—their emanation—which hitherto clung almost imperceptibly to the word. Kafka's literary technique fastens on to words as Proust's involuntary recollection does to sensuous objects, only with the opposite result: instead of reflection on the human, the trial run of a model of dehumanization. Its pressure forces the subject into a regression which is, so to speak, biological and which prepares the ground for Kafka's animal parables. The crucial moment, however, towards which everything in Kafka is directed, is that in which men become aware that they are not themselves—that they themselves are things. The long and fatiguing imageless sections, beginning with the conversation with the father in 'The Judgement', serve the purpose of demonstrating to men what no image could, their unidentity, the complement of their copylike similarity. The lesser motives, conclusively demonstrated to the surveyor by the landlady and then also by Frieda, are alien to him—Kafka brilliantly anticipated the concept of the Ego-alien later developed by psychoanalysis. But the surveyor admits these motives. His individual and his social character are split as widely as in Chaplin's *Monsieur Verdoux*; Kafka's hermetic memoranda contain the social genesis of schizophrenia.

5

Kafka's world of images is sad and dilapidated, even where it sets its sights high, as in 'The Natural Theatre of Oklahoma'—as though he had foreseen the migration of workers from this state—or in the 'Care of a Family Man'; the fund of flash photographs is as chalky and mongoloid as a petty-bourgeois wedding by Henri Rousseau; the odour is that of unaired beds, the colour, the red of mattresses whose sheets have been lost; the dread Kafka evokes, that of vomiting. And yet most of his work is a reaction to unlimited power. To this power, that of the raging patriarch, Benjamin gave the name 'parasitic': it lives off the life it oppresses. But characteristically, the parasitic moment is displaced. Gregor Samsa, not his father, becomes the bug. It is not the powerful but the impotent who appear superfluous; none of them performs socially useful work. Even the fact that the accused bank clerk, Josef K., being preoccupied with his trial, cannot do his job properly, is recorded. They creep around among properties which have long since been amortized and which grant them their existence only as charity, since they have outlived themselves. The displacement is modelled on the ideological habit of glorifying the reproduction of life as an act of grace on behalf of those who dispose over the means of production, those who 'provide' work. It describes a social whole in which those whom society holds in its grip and through whom it maintains itself become superfluous. But the shabbiness in Kafka goes further. It is the cryptogram of capitalism's highly polished, glittering late phase, which he excludes in order to define it all the more precisely in its negative. Kafka scrutinizes the smudges left behind in the deluxe edition of the book of life by the fingers of power. No world could be more homogeneous than the stifling one which he compresses to a totality by means of petty-bourgeois dread; it is logically air-tight and empty of meaning like every system. Everything that he narrates belongs to the same order of reality. All of his stories take place in the same spaceless space, and all holes are so tightly plugged that one shudders whenever anything is mentioned that does not fit in, such as Spain and southern France at one point in *The Castle*; all of America, however, is incorporated into that space in the image of steerage. Mythologies are interconnected like Kafka's labyrinthian descriptions. The inferior, abstruse, deformed, however, is as essential to their continuum as are corruption and criminal asociality to totalitarian domination, and the love of excrement to the cult of hygiene. Intellectual and political systems desire nothing that does not resemble them. The more powerful they become, the more they seek to bring existing reality under a single heading, the more they oppress it, and the farther they remove themselves from it. Precisely for this reason, the slightest 'deviation' becomes a threat to their basic principle, as intolerable as are the strangers and solitaries to the powers-that-be in Kafka. Integration is disintegration, and in it the mythic spell converges with the rationality of domination. The so-called problem of contingency, which has been the cause of so much agony to philosophical systems, is their own creation. It is only because of their pure inexorability that whatever slips through their net becomes a mortal enemy, just as the mythical queen cannot rest while there is still someone, far beyond the mountains, the child of the fairy-tale, who is more beautiful than she. There is no system without its residue. From this Kafka prophesies. If it is true that everything that happens in his compulsive world combines the expression of utter necessity with that of the utter contingency peculiar to shabbiness, then it is no less true that he deciphers the notorious law in his mirror-writing. Consummate untruth is the contradiction of itself; it need not, therefore, be explicitly contradicted. Kafka unmasks monopolism by focusing on the waste-products of the liberal era that it liquidates. This historical moment, not anything allegedly metatemporal illuminating history from above, is the crystallization of his metaphysics; there is no eternity for him other than that of the endlessly repeated sacrifice, which culminates in the image of the last one. 'Only our notion of time permits us to speak of the Last Judgment; actually, it is a summary court in perpetual session.' The last sacrifice is always yesterday's. Precisely for this reason virtually every overt reference to anything historical —the 'Bucket Rider', drawn from the coal shortage, is a rare exception—is avoided in Kafka. His work assumes a hermetic stance towards history as well: a taboo hangs over this concept. To the eternity of the historical moment there corresponds an attitude which sees the way of the world as naturally fallen and invariant; the moment, the absolutely transient, is the likeness of the eternity of passing away, of damnation. The name of history may not be spoken since what would truly be history, the other, has not yet begun. 'To believe in progress is to believe that there has not yet been any.' In the midst of apparently static living conditions, those of peasants and artisans in a simple commodity economy, Kafka depicts everything historical as condemned, just as those conditions themselves are condemned. His scenery is always obsolete; the 'long, low building' that functions as a school is said to combine 'remarkably a look of great age with a provisional appearance'. Human beings are not very different. The obsolete is the stigma of the present; Kafka has taken an inventory of such marks. Yet for children, who have to do with the disintegration of the historical world, the obsolete is also the image of that in which history as such first appears; it is the 'child's image of modernity', the hope bequeathed them that history might yet come to be. 'The feeling of one who is in need and help comes, one who is happy not because he is saved—he is not saved—but rather because new, young people come, confident, ready to take up the struggle, ignorant, of course, of what stands before them, yet in an ignorance which does not cause the observer to lose hope but rather fills him with awe, with joy, with tears. Hatred of him against whom the struggle is waged is also present.' For this struggle there is a call to arms: 'In our house, this enormous suburban house, a rented barracks overgrown with indestructible medieval ruins, there was proclaimed today, on a misty, icy winter morning, the following call to arms: "Fellow Tenants, I possess five toy guns. They are hanging in my closet, one on each hook. The first is mine, the rest are for anyone who wants them. Should there be more than four, the others will have to bring their own weapons and deposit them in my closet. For there will have to be unity; without unity we will not move forward. Incidentally, I only have guns which are entirely useless for any other purpose, the mechanism is ruined, the wads are torn off, only the hammers still snap. Therefore, it will not be very difficult to procure more such weapons should they be needed. But fundamentally, I will be just as happy, in the beginning, with people who have no guns. Those of us who do, will, at the crucial moment, take the unarmed into our midst. This is a strategy which proved itself with the first American farmers against the Indians; why shouldn't it prove itself here as well, since the conditions are, after all, similar. We can even forget about guns, then, for the duration, and even the five guns are not absolutely necessary, and they will be used simply because they are already here. If the other four do not want to carry them, then they can forget about them. I alone will carry one, as the leader. But we shouldn't have a leader, and so I, too, will destroy my gun or lay it aside." That was the first call to arms. In our house no one has the time or desire to read such calls, much less consider them. Soon the little papers were swimming along in the stream of dirt which originates in the attic, is nourished by all the corridors and spills down the stairs to struggle there with the opposing stream that swells upwards from below. But a week later came a second call: "Fellow Tenants! So far no one has reported to me. I was, in so far as the necessity of earning my living allowed, constantly at home, and during the time of my absence, when the door to my room was always left open, a sheet of paper lay on my table on which anyone who so desired could enrol. No one has done so." ' This is the figure of the revolution in Kafka's narratives.

6

Klaus Mann insisted that there was a similarity between Kafka's world and that of the Third Reich. And while it is true that any direct political allusion would have violated the spirit of a work whose 'hatred of him against whom the struggle is waged' was far too implacable to have sanctioned any kind of aesthetic realism, any acceptance of the façade of reality at face-value—nevertheless, it is National Socialism far more than the hidden dominion of God that his work cites. Dialectical theology fails in its attempt to appropriate him not merely because of the mythical character of the powers at work, an aspect which Benjamin rightly emphasized, but also because in Kafka, unlike *Fear and Trembling*, ambiguity and obscurity are attributed not exclusively to the Other as such but to human beings and to the conditions in which they live. Precisely that 'infinite qualitative distinction' taught by Kierkegaard and Barth is levelled off; there is no real distinction, Kafka writes, between town and castle. Kafka's method was verified when the obsolete liberal traits that he surveyed, stemming from the anarchy of commodity production, changed into the forms of fascist organization. And it was not only Kafka's prophecy of terror and torture that was fulfilled. 'State and Party'—they meet in attics, live in taverns, like Hitler and Goebbels in the *Kaiserhof*, a band of conspirators installed as the police. Their usurpation reveals that inherent in the myth of power. In *The Castle* the officials wear a special uniform, as the SS did—one which any pariah can make himself if need be. In fascism, too, the elites are self-appointed. Arrest is assault, judgment violence. The Party always allowed its potential victims a dubious, corrupt chance to bargain and negotiate, as do Kafka's inaccessible functionaries; he could have invented the expression, 'protective custody', had it not already become current during the First World War. Gisa, the blonde schoolmistress, cruel and fond of animals—probably the only pretty girl depicted by Kafka who is free from mutilation, as though her hardness scorned the Kafkaesque maelstrom—stems from the pre-adamite race of Hitler *Jungfrauen* who hated the Jews long before there were any. Acts of unbridled violence are performed by figures in subordinate positions, types such as non-commissioned officers, prisoners-of-war and concierges. They are all *déclassés*, caught up in the collapse of the organized collective and permitted to survive, like Gregor Samsa's father. As in the era of defective capitalism, the burden of guilt is shifted from the sphere of production to the agents of circulation or to those who provide services, travelling salesmen, bank employees, waiters. The unemployed—in *The Castle*—and emigrants—in *America*—are dressed and preserved like fossils of the process of *déclassement*. The economic tendencies whose relics they represent almost before those tendencies had prevailed, were by no means as foreign to Kafka as his hermetic procedure might suggest. A glimpse of this is to be found in a remarkable empirical passage from *America*, the first of his novels: 'It was some kind of wholesale ordering and transporting business, which, to the best of Karl's memory, was unlike anything in Europe. The business consisted in serving as a middleman; not, however, between producers and consumers, or perhaps the sellers, but rather in distributing all goods and basic products among the large factory cartels.' It was this very monopolistic apparatus of distribution, 'of gigantic dimensions', that destroyed trade and traffic, the hippocratic face of which Kafka immortalized. The historical verdict is the product of disguised domination, and thus becomes integrated into the myth, that of blind force endlessly reproducing itself. In the latest phase of this force, that of bureaucratic control, he recognizes the earliest stage; its waste-products become pre-historical. The rents and deformations of the modern age are in his eyes traces of the stone age; the chalk figures on yesterday's school blackboard, left unerased, become the true cave drawings. The daring foreshortening in which such regressions appear, however, also reveals the trend of society. With his transposition into archetypes, the bourgeois comes to an end. The loss of his individual features, the disclosure of the horror teeming under the stone of culture marks the disintegration of individuality itself. The horror, however, consists in the fact that the bourgeois was unable to find a successor; 'no one has done so'. Perhaps this is what is meant by the tale of Gracchus, the once wild hunter, a man of force who was unable to die. Just as the bourgeoisie failed to die. History becomes Hell in Kafka because the chance which might have saved was missed. This hell was inaugurated by the late bourgeoisie itself. In the concentration camps, the boundary between life and death was eradicated. A middleground was created, inhabited by living skeletons and putrefying bodies, victims unable to take their own lives, Satan's laughter at the hope of abolishing death. As in Kafka's twisted epics, what perished there was that which had provided the criterion of experience—life lived out to its end. Gracchus is the consummate refutation of the possibility banished from the world: to die after a long and full life.

260

7

The hermetic character of Kafka's writings offers the temptation not merely to set the idea of his work in abstract opposition to history—as he himself frequently does—but in addition to refine the work itself out of history with ready profundity. Yet it is precisely this hermetic quality that links it to the literary movement of the decade surrounding the First World War; one of the focal points of this movement was Prague and its milieu was Kafka's. One must have read Kurt Wolff's black soft-bound editions of 'The Last Judgment', 'The Judgment', 'Metamorphosis', and the 'Stoker' chapter to have experienced Kafka in his authentic horizon, that of expressionism. His epic temperament sought to avoid its characteristic linguistic gesture, although lines like: 'Pepi, proud, head tossed back, smile never changing, irrefutably aware of her dignity, twirling her braid at every turn, hurried back and forth'; or: 'K. stepped out on to the stoop in the wildly swirling wind and peered into the darkness', display his consummate mastery of the style. Proper names, especially in the shorter prose pieces, stripped of first names, like Wese and Schmar, recall the list of characters in expressionist plays. It is no rarity for Kafka's language to disavow its content as audaciously as in that ecstatic description of the little barmaid—its verve sweeps the narrative up out of the desolate stagnancy of the story. In his liquidation of the dream through its ubiquity, Kafka, the epic writer, follows the expressionist impulse farther than any but the most radical of the poets. His work has the tone of the ultra-left; to level it down to the 'universally human' is to falsify it conformistically. Debatable formulations such as the 'trilogy of solitude', retain their value because they emphasize a precondition inherent in every line of Kafka. The hermetic principle is that of completely estranged subjectivity. It is no accident that Kafka resisted all social involvement in the controversies of which Brod reports; only for the sake of such resistance did this involvement become thematic in *The Castle*. He is Kierkegaard's pupil solely with regard to 'objectless inwardness'. This inwardness explains extreme traits. What is enclosed in Kafka's glass ball is even more monotonous, more coherent and hence more horrible than the system outside, because in absolute subjective space and in absolute subjective time there is no room for anything that might disturb their intrinsic principle, that of inexorable estrangement. Again and again, the space-time continuum of 'empirical realism' is exploded through small acts of sabotage, like perspective in contemporary painting; as, for instance, when the land-surveyor, wandering about, is surprised by nightfall which comes much too soon. The undifferentiated character of autarchic subjectivity strengthens the feeling of uncertainty and the monotony of compulsive repetition. Inwardness, revolving in itself and devoid of all resistance, is denied all those things which might put a stop to its interminable movement and which thus take on an aura of mystery. A spell hangs over Kafka's space; imprisoned in itself, the subject holds its breath, as though it were not permitted to touch anything unlike itself. Under this spell pure subjectivity turns into mythology, and spiritualism, carried to its logical extreme, turns into the cult of nature. Kafka's eccentric interest in nudism and nature-cures, his tolerance, however qualified, of Rudolf Steiner's wild superstitions, are not rudiments of intellectual insecurity but rather conform to a principle, which, in implacably denying itself all basis of differentiation, itself loses the power to differentiate and threatens to succumb to the very regression which Kafka uses with such mastery as a literary technique—to the equivocal, amorphous, nameless. 'The mind sets itself in opposition to nature as a free and autonomous entity because it sees nature as demonic, both in external reality and in itself. In that the autonomous mind appears as something physical, however, nature takes possession of it at the point when it emerges in its most historical form—the objectless interior ... The natural element of the mere, inherently "historical" mind may be called mythical.' Absolute subjectivity is also subjectless. The self lives solely through transformation into otherness; as the secure residue of the subject which cuts itself off from everything alien it becomes the blind residue of the world. The more the I of expressionism is thrown back upon itself, the more like the excluded world of things it becomes. By virtue of this similarity Kafka forces expressionism—the chimerical aspect of which he, more than any of his friends, must have sensed, and to which he nevertheless remained faithful—into the form of a torturous epic; pure subjectivity, being of necessity estranged from itself as well and having become a thing, assumes the dimensions of objectivity which expresses itself through its own estrangement. The boundary between what is human and the world of things becomes blurred. This forms the basis of the frequently noted affinity with Klee. Kafka called his writing 'scribbling'. The thinglike becomes a graphic sign; his spellbound figures do not determine their actions but rather behave as if each had fallen into a magnetic field.[1] It is

[1] This dooms all dramatizations. Drama is possible only in so far as freedom—even in its painful birth-pangs—is visible; all other action is futile. Kafka's figures are struck by a fly-swatter even before they can

precisely this as it were external determination of persons existing inwardly which gives Kafka's prose the inscrutable semblance of sober objectivity. The zone in which it is impossible to die is also the no-man's-land between man and thing: within it meet Odradek, which Benjamin viewed as an angel in Klee's style, and Gracchus, the humble descendant of Nimrod. The understanding of these most advanced, incommensurable productions, and of several others that similarly evade current conceptions of Kafka, may one day provide the key to the whole. His entire work, however, is permeated by the theme of depersonalization in sex. Just as, according to the rite of the Third Reich, girls were not permitted to refuse medal-of-honour winners, Kafka's spell, the great taboo, extinguishes all the lesser taboos which pertain to the sphere of the individual. The textbook example of this is the punishing of Amalia and her family —by tribal rite—because she refuses to submit to Sortini. In the ruling powers, the family triumphs as an archaic collective over its later, individualized form. Helpless, driven together like animals, men and women are coupled. Kafka fashioned his own neurotic guilt feelings, his infantile sexuality as well as his obsession with 'purity', into an instrument with which to etch away the approved notions of eroticism. The absence of choice and of memory which characterizes the life of white collar workers in the huge cities of the twentieth century becomes, as later in Eliot's 'Waste Land', the image of an archaic past. It is anything but hetaeric. In the suspension of its rules, patriarchal society reveals its true secret, that of direct, barbaric oppression. Women are reified as mere means to an end: as sexual objects and as connections. But in the gloom Kafka gropes for an image of happiness. It emerges out of the hermetically secluded subject's incredulity at the paradox that it can be loved all the same. As incomprehensible as is the inclination displayed by all women for the prisoner in *The Trial*, is all hope; Kafka's disenchanted eros is also ecstatic masculine gratitude. When poor Frieda calls herself Klamm's beloved, the word's aura is brighter than at the most sublime moments in Balzac or Baudelaire; when, while denying the presence of the surveyor hidden under the table to the searching innkeeper, 'she places her little foot on his chest', and then bends down and 'quickly kisses' him, she finds the

---

make a move; to drag them on to the tragic stage as heroes is to make a mockery of them. André Gide would have remained the author of 'Paludes', had he not made the mistake of attempting to do *The Trial*; amid the rising tide of illiteracy, he, at least, ought not to have forgotten that for works of art which deserve the name, the medium is not a matter of indifference. Adaptations should be reserved for the culture industry.

gesture for which one can wait an entire lifetime in vain; and the hours which the two spend lying together 'in little puddles of beer and other garbage which covered the floor', are those of fulfilment in a world so foreign that 'even the air did not have a particle of the air at home'. This dimension was made accessible to lyric poetry by Brecht. In both writers, however, the language of ecstasy is far removed from that of expressionism. Confronted by the task of squaring the circle, of finding words for the space of objectless inwardness, in spite of the fact that the scope of every word transcends the absolute immediacy of that which it is supposed to evoke —the contradiction on which all expressionist literature founders —Kafka mastered it ingeniously through the visual element. As the medium of gestures, it asserts its priority. Only the visible can be narrated, yet in the process it becomes completely alien, a picture. In the most literal sense. Kafka saves the idea of expressionism not by listening in vain for 'primal sounds', but by transferring the practices of expressionist painting to literature. His attitude towards expressionist painting is similar to that of Utrillo to the picture postcards which are supposed to have served as the models for his frosty streets. In the eyes of the panic-stricken person who has withdrawn all affective cathexis from objects, they petrify into a third thing, neither dream, which can only be falsified, nor the aping of reality, but rather its enigmatic image composed of its scattered fragments. Many decisive parts in Kafka read as though they had been written in imitation of expressionist paintings which should have been painted but never were. At the end of *The Trial*, Josef K.'s eye falls 'on the top storey of the house bordering on the quarry. As a light sprung on, the shutters flew open, a man, weak and thin in the distance and height, leaned suddenly far out and stretched his arms out even farther. Who was it? A friend? a good man?' This kind of transfer is at the heart of Kafka's picture-world. This world is built on the strict exclusion of everything musical, in the sense of being like music, on the refusal to reject myth through antithesis; according to Brod, Kafka was unmusical, judged by usual criteria. His mute battlecry against myth is: not to resist. And this asceticism endows him with the most profound relation to music in passages such as the song of the telephone in *The Castle*, the musicology in the 'Investigations of a Dog', and in one of the last completed stories, 'Josephine'. By avoiding all musical effects, his brittle prose functions like music. It breaks off its meaning like broken pillars of life in nineteenth-century cemeteries, and the lines which describe the break are its hieroglyphics.

8

An expressionist epic is a paradox. It tells of something about which nothing can be told, of the totally self-contained subject, which is unfree and which, in fact, can hardly be said to exist. Dissociated into the compulsive moments of its own restrictive and confined existence, stripped of identity with itself, its life has no continuity; objectless inwardness is space in the precise sense that everything it produces obeys the law of timeless repetition. This law is not unrelated to the ahistorical aspect of Kafka's work. Form which is constituted through time as the unity of inner meaning is not possible for him; the verdict condemning the large epic which he carries out was observed by Lukács in authors as early as Flaubert and Jacobsen. The fragmentary quality of the three large novels, works which, moreover, are hardly covered any more by the concept of the novel, is determined by their inner form. They do not permit themselves to be brought to an end as the totality of a rounded temporal experience. The dialectic of expressionism in Kafka forces the novel-form ever closer to the serialized adventure story. Kafka loved such novels. By adopting their technique he at the same time dissociated himself from the established literary mores. To the list of his known literary models should be added, in addition to Walser, surely the beginning of Poe's 'Arthur Gordon Pym' and several chapters of Kürnberger's *Amerikamüde*, such as the description of a New York apartment. Above all, however, Kafka allied himself with apocryphal literary genres. Universal suspicion, a trait etched deeply into the physiognomy of the present age, he learned from the detective novel. In detective novels, the world of things has gained mastery over the abstract subject and Kafka uses this aspect to refashion things into ever-present emblems. The large works are rather like detective novels in which the criminal fails to be exposed. Even more instructive is his relationship to Sade, regardless of whether or not Kafka knew him. Like the innocents in Sade—not to mention those in American grotesque films and the 'funnies'—Kafka's subject, especially the emigrant Karl Rossmann, passes from one desperate and hopeless situation to the next; the stations of the epic adventure become those of a modern passion. The closed complex of immanence becomes concrete in the form of a flight from prisons. In the absence of contrast, the monstrous becomes the entire world, as in Sade, the norm, whereas the unreflective adventure novel, by concentrating on extraordinary events thus confirms the rule of the ordinary. In Sade and Kafka, however, reason is at work; by making madness the stylistic principle, the objective insanity is allowed to emerge. Both authors are in the tradition of enlightenment, although they represent different stages. In Kafka its disenchanting touch is his 'that's the way it is'. He reports what actually happens, though without any illusion concerning the subject, which, possessing the greatest degree of self-awareness—of its nullity—throws itself on the junkpile, no different from what the death-machine does to its victims. He wrote the consummate Robinson Crusoe story, that of the phase in which each man has become his own Robinson, adrift with his accumulated things on a rudderless raft. The connection between the Robinson Crusoe legend and allegory, originating in Defoe himself, is not alien to the great tradition of the enlightenment. It is part of the early-bourgeois struggle against religious authority. In the Eighth Part of the *Axiomata* directed against the orthodox chief pastor Goeze, by an author Kafka esteemed highly, Lessing, there is the story of a 'discharged Lutheran preacher from the Pfalz' and his family, 'which consisted of foundlings of both sexes'. Their ship is wrecked and the family saves itself and a catechism on a small, uninhabited group of islands in the Bermudas. Generations later a Hessian minister finds their descendants on the island. They speak a German 'in which he thought he heard nothing but phrases and expressions from Luther's catechism'. They are orthodox, 'with the exception of a few trivia. The catechism had naturally been used up during the 150 years and they had nothing remaining except the boards of the cover. This cover, they said, contains everything we know. "It used to contain it, my dear friends," said the chaplain. "It still does, it still contains it!" they said. "We ourselves cannot read, of course, and we hardly even know what reading is. But our fathers heard their fathers read from it. And our forefathers knew the man who engraved the cover. The man's name was Luther, and he lived soon after Christ." ' Perhaps even closer to Kafka's style is Lessing's 'Parable', which shares with the later writer a moment, unintentional certainly, of obscurity. The man to whom it was addressed, Goeze, misunderstood it completely. The parable form as such, however, is hardly to be separated from a rationalistic intention. By embedding human meaning and theories in natural materials—is not Aesop's ass a descendant of Ocnos'?—the mind recognizes itself in them. It thus breaks the spell of myth by staring it in the eye without giving ground. Several passages from Lessing's parable, which he intended to reissue under the title, 'The Palace on Fire', exemplify this all the more for the fact that they are far removed from that awareness of being caught in myth which dawns in analogous passages in Kafka. 'A wise, resourceful king of a great, great realm had in his capital city a palace of immeasurable size and extraordinary architecture. The size was immeasurable because he had gathered within it all the people whom he needed as assistants or agents for his government. The architecture was extraordinary because it violated all the accepted rules. . . . After many, many years, the entire palace was still as pure and as perfect as when it had left the hands of its builders—from the outside somewhat puzzling, from within light and harmony everywhere. Anyone who claimed to know something about architecture was particularly offended by the exterior, which was broken up by a few scattered windows, large and small, round and rectangular, but which therefore had all the more doors and gates of different shapes and sizes. . . . It was difficult to understand why so many varied entrances were necessary, since one large portal on each side would have been more decorous and no less efficient. For few people were willing to concede that for each person who was summoned to the palace, the shortest and easiest way to where he was needed was through one of the many small entrances. And thus all kinds of disputes arose among the supposed experts, of whom the most contentious were generally those who had had the least opportunity to see the interior of the palace. Moreover, there was something that one would have thought would simplify and end the dispute but which instead complicated it still more and provided the richest fuel for its stubborn survival. Namely, there were certain old plans which were believed to stem from the original architects of the palace, and these plans were marked up with words and signs, for which the language and character were as good as lost. . . . Once, when the dispute over the plans was not so much settled as dormant—once at midnight the watchman's voice suddenly rang out: "Fire! fire in the palace! ". . . Everyone leaped from his bed and, acting as though the fire were not in the palace but in his own house, ran for what he considered his most precious possession—his plan. If we can only save that, everyone thought. Even if the palace burns down there, its authenticity is safe here! . . . With all this zealous quibbling the palace might indeed have burned to the ground, if it had burned. But the startled watchman had mistaken the northern lights for a conflagration.' It would require only the slightest shift in accent for this story, a link connecting Pascal and Kierkegaard's *Diapsalms to Myself*, to become one by Kafka. Had Lessing merely placed stronger emphasis on the bizarre and monstrous lines of the edifice at the expense of its utility; had he only used the statement that even if the palace burns down there, its authenticity is preserved in the plans, as a favourite answer of all those ministries whose sole legal principle is 'quod non est in actis non est in mundo', and the apology for religion against its pedantic exegesis would have become the denunciation of the noumenal power itself through the medium of its own exegesis. The increased obscurity and ambiguity of the parabolic intention are consequences of the enlightenment. The more its rationalism reduces objective matters to human dimensions, the more barren and unintelligible become the outlines of the merely existing world which man can never entirely dissolve into subjectivity and from which he has already drained everything familiar. Kafka reacts in the spirit of the enlightenment to its reversion to mythology. He has often been compared to the cabbala. Whether justifiably or not can be decided only by those who know that text. If, however, it is true that, in its late phase, Jewish mysticism vanishes and becomes rational, then this fact affords insight into the affinity of Kafka, a product of the late enlightenment, with antinomian mysticism.

9

Kafka's theology, if one can speak of such at all, is antinomian with respect to the very same God which Lessing defended against the orthodoxy, the God of the enlightenment. This God, however, is a *deus absconditus*. Kafka thus becomes not a proponent of dialectical theology, as is often asserted, but its accuser. Its 'absolute difference' converges with the mythic powers. Totally abstract, and indeterminate, purged of all anthropomorphic and mythological qualities, God becomes the ominously ambiguous and threatening deity who evokes nothing but dread and terror. His 'purity'— patterned after the mind—which expressionist inwardness sets up as absolute, recreates the archaic terror of nature-bound man in. the horror of that which is radically unknown. Kafka's work preserves the moment in which the purified faith was revealed to be impure, in which demythologizing appeared as demonology. He remains a rationalist, however, in his attempt to rectify the myth which thus emerges, to reopen the trial against it, as though before an appellate court. The variations of myths which were found in his unpublished writings bears witness to his efforts in search of such a corrective. The *Trial* novel is itself the trial of the trial. Kafka used motifs from Kierkegaard's *Fear and Trembling* not as heir but as critic. In Kafka's statement to whoever it may concern, he describes the court which sits in judgment over men in order to convict law itself. Concerning the latter's mythic character he left no doubt. At one point in the *Trial*, the goddesses of justice, war and the hunt are treated as one. Kierkegaard's theory of objective despair affects absolute inwardness itself. Absolute estrangement, abandoned to the existence from which it has withdrawn, is examined and revealed as the hell which it inherently was already in Kierkegaard, although unconsciously. As hell seen from the perspective of salvation. Kafka's artistic alienation, the means by which objective estrangement is made visible, receives its legitimation from the work's inner substance. His writing feigns a standpoint from which the creation appears as lacerated and mutilated as it itself conceives helf to be. In the middle ages, Jews were tortured and executed 'perversely'—i.e. inversely; as early as Tacitus, their religion was branded as perverse in a famous passage. Offenders were hung head down. Kafka, the land-surveyor, photographs the earth's surface just as it must have appeared to these victims during the endless hours of their dying. It is for nothing less than such unmitigated torture that the perspective of redemption presents itself to him. To include him among the pessimists, the existentialists of despair, is as misguided as to make him a prophet of salvation. He honoured Nietzsche's verdict on the words optimism and pessimism. The light-source which shows the world's crevices to be infernal is the optimal one. But what for dialectical theology is light and shadow is reversed. The absolute does not turn its absurd side to the finite creature—a doctrine which already in Kierkegaard leads to things much more vexing than mere paradox and which in Kafka would have amounted to the enthroning of madness. Rather, the world is revealed to be as absurd as it would be for the *intellectus archetypus*. The middle realm of the finite and the contingent becomes infernal to the eye of the artificial angel.

This is the point to which Kafka stretches expressionism. The subject objectifies itself in renouncing the last vestiges of complicity. Of course, this is apparently contradicted by the theory that can be read out of Kafka, as well as by the stories of the Byzantine respect which he not without scurrility, personally paid to strange powers. But the often noted irony of these traits is itself part of the didactic content. It was not humility that Kafka preached, but rather the most tried and tested mode of behaviour against myth—cunning. The only chance, in Kafka's eyes, however feeble and minute, of preventing the world from being all-triumphant, was to concede it the victory from the beginning. Like the youngest boy in the fairy tale, one must make oneself completely unobtrusive, small, a defenceless victim, instead of insisting on one's rights according to the mores of the world, that of exchange, which unremittingly reproduced injustice. Kafka's humor hopes to reconcile myth through a kind of mimicry. In this as well he follows that tradition of enlightenment which reaches from the Homeric myth to Hegel and Marx, in whom the spontaneous deed, the act of freedom, coincides with the culmination of the objective trend. Since then, however, the crushing burden of human existence has exceeded all bounds in relation to the subject and with this development the untruth of the abstract utopia has also increased. As was done thousands of years ago, Kafka seeks salvation in the incorporation of the powers of the adversary. The subject seeks to break the spell of reification by reifying itself. It prepares to complete the fate which befell it. 'For the last time, psychology'—Kafka's figures are instructed to leave their psyches at the door, at a moment of the social struggle in which the sole chance of the bourgeois individual lies in the negation of his own composition, as well as of the class situation which has condemned him to be what he is. Like his countryman, Gustav Mahler, Kafka sides with the deserters. Instead of human dignity, the supreme bourgeois concept, there emerges in him the salutary recollection of the similarity between man and animal, an idea upon which a whole group of his narratives thrives. Immersion in the inner space of individuation, which culminates in such self-contemplation, stumbles upon the principle of individuation, the postulation of the self by the self, officially sanctioned by philosophy, the mythic defiance. The subject seeks to make amends by abandoning this defiance. Kafka does not glorify the world through subordination; he resists it through nonviolence. Faced by the latter, power must acknowledge itself as that which it is, and it is on this fact alone that he counts. Myth is to succumb to its own reflected image. The heroes of the *Trial* and the *Castle* become guilty not through their guilt—they have none—but because they try to get justice on their side. 'The original sin, the ancient injustice committed by man, consists in his protest—one which he never ceases to make—that he has suffered injustice, that the original sin was done against him.' It is for this reason that their clever speeches, especially those of the land-surveyor, have something of the inane, doltish, naïve about them—their sound reasoning strengthens the delusion against which it protests. Through reification of the subject, demanded by the world in any event, Kafka seeks to beat the world at its own game—the moribund become harbinger of Sabbath rest. This is the other side of Kafka's theory of the unsuccessful death—the fact that the mutilated creation cannot die any more is the sole promise of immortality which the rationalist Kafka permits to survive the ban on images. It is tied to the salvation of things, of those which are no longer enmeshed in the network of guilt, those which are non-exchangeable, useless. This is what is meant in his work by the phenomenon of obsolescence, in its innermost layer of meaning. His world of ideas —as in the 'Natural Theatre of Oklahoma'—resembles a world of shopkeepers; no theologoumenon could describe it more accurately than the title of an America film comedy, 'Shopworn Angel'. Whereas the interiors, where men live, are the homes of the catastrophe, the hide-outs of childhood, forsaken spots like the bottom of the stairs, are the places of hope. The resurrection of the dead would have to take place in the auto graveyards. The innocence of what is useless provides the counterpoint to the parasitical: 'Idleness is the beginning of all vice, the crown of all virtue.' According to the testimony brought by Kafka's work, in a world caught in its own toils, everything positive, every contribution, even the very work which reproduces life, helps increase that entanglement. 'Our task is to do the negative—the positive has already been given us.' The only cure for the half-uselessness of a life which does not live would be its entire inutility. Kafka thus allies himself with death. The creation gains priority over the living. The self, innermost fortress of myth, is smashed, repudiated as the illusion of mere nature. 'The artist waited until K. had calmed himself, and then, finding no other way out, decided to continue writing. The first small stroke that he made was a deliverance for K., although the artist appeared to accomplish it only in overcoming the greatest resistance; the writing, moreover, was no longer as beautiful, above all there seemed to be lack of gold; pale and uncertain the line progressed, the letter grew very large. It was a J and was almost finished when the artist stamped furiously with his foot into the mound on the grave, causing the earth to fly up into the air. At last K. understood him; there was no longer any time left to plead with him. With all his fingers he clawed at the dirt, which offered scarcely any resistance. Everything seemed prepared. A thin surface crust seemed to have been put there only for the sake of appearance; directly beneath it yawned a large hole with steep walls, into which K., turned over on his back by a soft breeze, sank. While below, his head still straining upwards, he was already being absorbed into the impenetrable depths, above his name, lavishly embellished, flashed across the stone. Enchanted by this sight he awoke.' The name alone, revealed through a natural death, not the living soul, vouches for that in man which is immortal.

ACKNOWLEDGEMENTS

It is not often that a translator has the good fortune of being able to consult with the author he is translating, and it is an even rarer advantage when the author has an intimate knowledge of the language into which his work is being translated. If a text as difficult as *Prisms* can now be presented in English, a decisive factor has been the assistance and encouragement afforded us so generously, despite an exceedingly demanding schedule, by both Professor Adorno and his wife, Dr. Gretel Adorno. Dr. Erwin Haeberle of Yale University and Professor Herbert Marcuse, of the University of California at La Jolla, provided valuable assistance as did Irving Wohlfarth and Jeremy J. Shapiro. Finally, a particular debt of gratitude is due Roberto Schwarz, of the University of Sao Paolo, who introduced us to the work of Adorno and the Frankfurt School. Needless to say—and yet never to be omitted—we alone are responsible for any inaccuracies and insufficiencies.

NOTE

The inadequacy of existing translations compelled us to retranslate all quotations from the German, although, as in the case of Kafka, we consulted them with profit.

272